Interpreting
Television

Interpreting
Television

Karen Lury

Hodder Arnold

A MEMBER OF THE HODDER HEADLINE GROUP

First published in Great Britain in 2005 by
Hodder Education, a member of the Hodder Headline Group,
338 Euston Road, London NW1 3BH

www.hoddereducation.co.uk

Distributed in the United States of America by
Oxford University Press Inc.
198 Madison Avenue, New York, NY10016

British Library Cataloguing in Publication Data
A catalogue record for this book is available from the British Library

Library of Congress Cataloging-in-Publication Data
A catalog record for this book is available from the Library of Congress

ISBN-10 0 340 806 13 3
ISBN-13 978 0 340 806 13 5

1 2 3 4 5 6 7 8 9 10

Typeset in 10/13 Adobe Garamond by Servis Filmsetting Ltd, Manchester.
Printed and bound in Malta by Gutenberg Press.

What do you think about this book? Or any other Hodder Education title? Please send your comments
to the feedback section on www.hoddereducation.co.uk.

Contents

Acknowledgements

This book could not have been completed without a tremendous amount of support and the various contributions of numerous friends and colleagues. In particular, I would like to thank Simon Frith and Christine Geraghty, who read drafts of chapters and who, in different ways, ensured my arguments were clearer and stronger. Of my colleagues at Glasgow, I would like to acknowledge specifically the contributions of Ian Garwood and Ian Goode, who supplied me with examples, observations and corrections just when I needed them most. I would also like to extend particular thanks to Michael McCann, who obligingly provided me with copies of endless different programmes, however outlandish they might have seemed, and who also provided valuable insight into the workings of Sky Sports Interactive. There are numerous other colleagues here and elsewhere who read parts of the book as it was being completed or who – perhaps unknowingly – provided me with inspiration. So I also thank Jeanette Berrie, Caroline Beven, Karen Boyle, John Corner, Minty Donald, Dimitris Eleftheriotis, Richard Haynes, Stephanie Marriott, Nick Millar, Elke Weissman, Evie and the staff at Offshore. In addition I would like to thank my sister, Celia Lury, and my brothers, Giles and Adam Lury. I also acknowledge the patience and professionalism of the different editors I have worked with at Arnold. Work for the book was also completed via the AHRB's extended research leave scheme.

The book would not have been completed without the insight and support offered by my husband, Tim Niel, whose willingness to engage in half-baked arguments at practically any time of the day meant that, finally, I felt I had something to say. I dedicate the book to him and to our three daughters, Delilah, Alice and Edith, who have changed the way I see television and, of course, the world.

Illustrations list

Introduction

This is a book about television. More specifically, it is a book about television form – the way in which television produces and constructs sounds and images and how it organizes space and time. This makes my approach narrower than many other introductory books, since I leave to one side, or only implicitly refer to, important aspects that more often make up the study of television. For instance, I do not directly refer to audiences, institutions, genre, the 'everyday', modernity or postmodernity; these aspects have been written about extensively elsewhere in relation to television. I offer a series of analyses which integrate information concerning the technological make-up of television images and sounds with a careful description of the style and formal operations of different television programmes. In this sense, my work is probably closest to existing studies by John T. Caldwell (1995) and Jeremy Butler (2002). However, unlike Butler or Caldwell, my viewing context is British and my approach less specifically technical and, possibly, more idiosyncratic.

While my analyses are informed by my reading of other writers, some of whom are referred to directly, I do not adopt one theoretical framework. For better or worse, my approach mirrors the activity of television, since it is, in some sense, parasitic on other disciplines, drawing on aspects of film studies, sociology, aesthetics and communication studies. While the focus and title of each chapter – Image, Sound, Time and Space – might suggest a certain level of abstraction, each chapter is grounded entirely in a series of concrete examples. I have tried, as far as possible, to cover all types of television programming, although some – news, children's programmes, dramatic fiction and light entertainment – probably feature more than others. Each chapter concludes with a more extensive case study in which I demonstrate that an exclusive focus on one formal aspect of a programme (sound, image, space or time) can promote a rich understanding of how the programme's central concerns can often be detected even within a deliberately limited formal investigation.

Although each chapter is quite extensive, I fully expect the reader to feel that there are programmes or instances of television that I should or could have included. Equally, readers may well be able to identify some programmes with which to refute certain observations I have made. Indeed, I hope the general response to some aspects of each chapter will be, 'Yes, but . . .', where the reader can supply evidence from their own viewing. This is important, for while I do discuss specific programmes and draw on my own viewing habits and experiences, the reader should feel that other programmes might be substituted or used to test my observations.

In the end, this is a much more personal book than I had intended originally. I have drawn palpably on my own viewing experience and memories. As the book progressed, I realized that what I had to offer, alongside careful and detailed description, was an indication of how the interpretation of television is informed by the distinctive ways in which people view television. The kind of television you are familiar with is informed by biography, by where you live, who you live with, your personal tastes and, often, by how old you are. This is not simply a question of *what* you watch, but also *how* you watch and how your memories of television have accumulated. As one of my tutors once remarked, I have watched a lot of television (and I continue to do so). I like television, and television viewing plays a large part in memories of my family life as a child and, now, in daily life with my own children. This is not to say that I am uncritical of specific television programmes or that I like everything I see on television (including those programmes I discuss in this book). Indeed, I hope the model of analysis I provide will support readers who wish actively to challenge or change the television programmes they see or may one day go on to make.

Each chapter follows a similar trajectory. After a brief introduction which serves to identify particular points of interest, I introduce the key terms of my argument. These terms are then worked through in relation to specific programme examples; while certain linking arguments are developed throughout the chapter, each section could be read or consulted in isolation. Each chapter concludes with a case study which demonstrates how a focus on formal aspects can be used to 'open up' a specific text to interpretation. In most instances, I have deliberately chosen programmes that I believe to be well known or widely available. The one exception is the case study for the chapter on time, which is a live broadcast – the millennium night on 31 December 1999. While some readers may not remember this specific broadcast, it acts as a model for the analysis of similar 'live' broadcasts. This might include the regular New Year's Eve celebrations, charity telethons, the Olympic Games or other public events.

Image

In this chapter I investigate the technological basis and formal qualities of the television image. This involves a discussion of the technological make-up of both the analogue and digital image and their differing levels of complexity and resolution. This leads on to a discussion of two broad categories, within which I examine the *function* of different images on television, which I identify as images which *dramatize* and images which *demonstrate*. This is followed by a discussion which concentrates on the different *qualities* of the television image. In this section I explore features such as the aspect ratio and the composition and employment of different shots (the long shot, medium shot and close-up). Graphic effects such as chroma key and digital compositing are also discussed. Next, I look in detail at the effects of different kinds of colour (black and white, the 'bleach bypass effect' and saturated colour), as well as the way in which lighting informs the mood and impact of particular images. Finally, I discuss the texture of different television images, suggesting that in certain kinds of animation there is an almost perceptible tactile quality to the images presented.

The case study for this chapter is *CSI: Crime Scene Investigation*, an American prime-time drama. My argument is that *CSI* employs images which emphasize the potential of television images to *dramatize* as the series is noted for its rich *mise-en-scène* and heightened use of colour. However, the narrative drive of the series – which is to solve crimes through a process of forensic investigation – is also interesting, since it enables the programme to refer directly to the way in which images on television are used to *demonstrate*.

Sound

I begin this chapter by exploring, briefly, the way in which the 'sound' of television may be related to the mediation of sound by other technologies, such as CD players, the radio and the telephone. I then go on to discuss, in some detail, four broad categories which can be used to define the use of sound on television: sound as voice, sound as music, sound as sound and sound as silence.

In the section on sound as voice, I discuss the way in which the sound of the human voice is heard and mediated on television, looking at aspects such as the voice-over (continuity announcers, sports commentators), and the 'qualities' of the voice, in terms of accent, pitch and pace. This is followed by an exploration of the talking head on television. The section concludes by looking at the way in which television generally privileges dialogue over other sounds, and I demonstrate how 'ventriloquism' can be used to understand the different ways in which the voice and image are related on television. This then leads to a brief discussion of the distinctive effects of choosing whether to subtitle or overdub a programme's dialogue.

In the next section, on sound as music, I look first at the use of music as soundtrack and, particularly, the use of popular music on television. I then go on to discuss the way in which music can be heard as 'score' on television, paying particular attention to its use in theme tunes, programme interludes and station idents.

In the section on sound as sound, I concentrate on the way in which 'concrete sound' is employed in different television programmes. I briefly point to the ways in which the sound effect is used in different kinds of programming – sports broadcasts, wildlife programmes and light-entertainment shows. Here, I pay some attention to the 'sound of the crowd', looking at the laughter track and also the way in which the sound of the studio audience generates atmosphere and affects the progress of the game show, specifically in *Who Wants to be a Millionaire?*

In the last section, I examine the rare occasions in which television features sound as silence, discussing the absence of sound as audible 'blinks' between programmes and referring to instances when it has been used to mark incidents of historic consequence or in relation to catastrophic events.

The case study for this chapter focuses on the use of sound in the pre-school children's programme, *Teletubbies*. I demonstrate that the immersive 'sound world' orchestrated by the directors and producers – in terms of voice, sound effects, music and silence – all operate to support the broad pedagogical aims of the programme.

Time

This chapter is concerned with the organization and operation of time on television. First, I present three different ways in which time is expressed on television: as *recorded time*, via the *relaying of time* and as *liveness* (which incorporates aspects of recorded time and the relaying of time). The following sections investigate the different ways in which time is organized by television: through *scheduling* practices, via different *technologies*, through *narrative* and, finally, how time as a commodity is expressed within an *economy*.

In relation to scheduling, I address changes to the nature of the broadcast day instigated by the massive expansion of television channels and suggest how these changes have had an effect on how programmes are marketed, commissioned and produced. Ultimately, I conclude that there is a perceptible shift towards programme-led, rather than channel-directed, viewing.

In the next section, the different technologies I discuss include the remote control, the analogue VCR and the recent emergence of the digital personal video recorder. At the end of this section, I direct my attention to a significant technological development within television production itself, the process of satellite news gathering (SNG). My discussion of narrative limits itself to three different practices: repetition, 'chasing time' and 'counting down'. First, I look at the way in which repetition is used in a variety of different genres: in sports, news and some fiction programmes. Second, chasing time is identified as a narrative 'pressure' in certain types of programme, particularly 'reality' shows such as *Big Brother*, but also in other mainstream game shows. I use the notion of counting down to examine how time is organized in a series of different programmes, including chart shows (for popular music, or in other 'list' programmes), as well as programmes such as *Restoration* and *Britain's Best . . .*, which use the energy generated by the countdown narrative to encourage the audience to participate in the creation of different 'canons'.

The case study for this chapter is the millennium night broadcast from the BBC on 31 December 1999. I provide a brief chronology of events leading up to the British 'midnight' and use it to explore questions of liveness, the different narrative organizations of time and, in particular, to draw out the implications of the interaction between 'real time' and 'broadcast time'. My argument is that this relationship is so often characterized by narrative slips and the problems of contingency that this has implications for television's ability to 'tell time' coherently. By this I mean not just that television is often unable to fulfil the promise of an endlessly interesting 'now', but also that it creates problems in relation to the expression of history and public memory. While television's attempt to 'produce history' is apparently explicit within the programme, the actual experience of time, history and memory is quite contradictory.

Space

In the final chapter of the book, I begin by arguing that there is a necessary distinction between the appearance of 'space' and the construction of 'place' on television. I suggest that the operation of space can be seen on television in instances which emphasize certain characteristics, such as abstraction (via scientific models or written text) and the sense of being 'anywhere-at-once' (which generally relates to television's potential as a broadcast medium). In terms of place, I identify how television effectively constructs illusory but seemingly tangible 'places' on screen with which the viewer becomes familiar and understands in an intuitive way. Having made this distinction, I then go on to clarify how space and place are organized on television, suggesting that space is more often expressed through images which are explicitly two-dimensional, such as diagrams, text and still photographs, whereas place is more often created through images which use movement and editing to create depth, such as film, video and animation. In the following sections, I demonstrate how certain programmes emphasize their spatial qualities or, alternatively, concentrate on the production of an illusory 'place'.

First, I relate space to some news, shopping and 'dating' channels and discuss how text, graphs and still photographs organize space so that the viewer is encouraged to look 'over' the image rather than 'into' the screen. Second, in relation to place, I identify the sitcom as a genre that is concerned to create a fixed and familiar place in which to situate its characters. In particular, I examine the *mise-en-scène*, camera style, editing, performance and writing in *The Royle Family* to demonstrate quite how sensually abundant this kind of 'place' can be. In the third section, I suggest that one of the most distinctive aspects of television is the way in which it routinely integrates space and place within one programme-context. Here, I discuss in detail the ITV newsroom and specific news reports to illustrate how the interaction of space and place has implications for the presentation and reception of news. The final two sections investigate the relations of space and place in a slightly different way. In my discussion of interactivity, I point out that this is not a new process on television. However, I go on to explore how one successful development – Sky Sports Interactive – has implications for the way in which sports programming, in particular, football, is organized by television. Then, in a discussion of split-screen in dramatic fiction, I contrast its use in two different programmes – the American series *24* and the British series *Trial and Retribution* – to demonstrate how this technique can create certain effects and encourage different viewing relationships.

My final case study is of a British light-entertainment show, *Ant and Dec's Saturday Night Takeaway*. Part of my discussion illustrates how space and place operate within this particular programme, but I also use the analysis to further develop arguments first made by Richard Dyer (1992) in relation to utopia and entertainment. While, obviously, his use of utopia relates directly to my discussions of space and place, it is Dyer's insistence on the significance of 'non-representational forms' that I suggest is important, not only to the immediate concerns of the chapter, but also to the book as a whole.

Like Dyer, my concern in this book is to demonstrate that non-representational forms – quantities and qualities such as sound, music, light, colour and pace, as well as the illusion of space and place – are meaningful in themselves and, thus, not only for the ways in which they support or direct the 'meaning' or narrative ambitions of particular programmes. My contention is that these non-representational, formal aspects of television do more than this; that, in some sense, they direct or generate emotions, feeling and energy, in ways that can exceed their apparent function or intended aim. This is most obvious, perhaps, in a genre such as light entertainment, a genre that seeks only to 'entertain', but, potentially, does more: transports its audience, takes it elsewhere, creating a transient sense of community, a shared present. In relation to light entertainment this transcendent effect may be felt to be appropriate, spectacular and even entrancing. In other genres the effect of non-representational forms may be felt to be distracting and potentially disturbing. My hope, however, is that this book will demonstrate how important it is to pay attention to the formal aspects of television, not just for the way in which they can illustrate how programmes 'make meaning', but how they are, *in themselves*, 'meaningful'.

chapter one

Image

Introduction

In this chapter I will be looking at the technological basis and formal qualities of the television image. Fundamentally I will be looking at the television image as you would any other image from film, photography or painting, and I will address the organization of space, colour and texture within a frame. In doing so I will discuss issues such as the use by television of different kinds of moving image media (film, video, computer-generated images) and the changing dimensions of the television image itself. I will discuss certain attributes of different television programmes' *mise-en-scène*, looking at set design, lighting and the framing of characters. To begin this exploration I want to foreground certain key characteristics of the television image, both in terms of its technological determination and as it is experienced by viewers.

The television image is a *moving* image. As such, television is the same as film, in that film also presents images which appear to be moving or which represent movement. In film, this effect is produced by static images, which are moved frame by frame. However, television is distinct from film since the image itself is also always in movement; each framed image is always moving. In film, the illusion of movement is achieved when a series of still images (film frames) are projected at a speed fast enough for the human brain to be persuaded that what is being seen is one moving image rather than a sequence of static images (the standard speed is usually 24 frames per second). In contrast, when we are watching analogue television, the *image* is itself constantly moving as the screen is lit up, point by point, line by line, in response to an electronic signal that is scanned across the television screen. One of the easiest ways to understand this is to think about the fact that while it is possible to imagine (and even handle) a film 'still' (that is, one frame from a film), taking an image from the television is more often termed a video 'grab'. The implications of this terminology ('smash and grab') suggest that such an activity is inappropriate for television. In looking at the television image, then, it is important to remember that it has a temporal as well as a spatial dimension. There are aspects of the image, such as live broadcasting, which will therefore be addressed more fully in the chapter on time.

The television image is the poor relation of the cinematic image. Before the widespread application of digital technology, the television image, compared to the film image, offered lower resolution (blurry outlines) and a reduced colour palette (less density, a narrower range of hues). These factors, aligned with the fact that the television screen is much smaller than the cinema screen, meant that, aesthetically, the television image was less dense, less complex, less interesting in comparison to film. Even today, the television image in certain contexts seems rather 'flat' when contrasted with the literal and experiential 'fullness' or complexity of the film image. Unsurprisingly, therefore, it is still rare for either popular or academic critics to value or examine the formal properties of the television image. One notable exception is John T. Caldwell's book, *Televisuality*, which addressed the changes to the look and qualities of the image in American network television in the light of both heightened commercial pressure and the increasing employment of electronic video and computer-imaging techniques (Caldwell 1995).

The television image is 'everywhere', but it is also ephemeral. As a series of images which are constantly in motion and transmitted 24 hours a day, the visual aspect of television is both pervasive and relentless. When we go to 'see a film' we know it is a visual experience that will have a beginning and an end, and going to the cinema appears to be something that we control and choose to do. In relation to television, we ask (usually desultorily) whether there is anything 'on television'. Of course, the answer is that there is always something to see (under normal conditions the image is always there if we turn on the television), but there is not necessarily anything we want to watch, and television continues to transmit images whether we want to see them or not; specific programmes do begin and end, but the availability of the television image nearly always remains constant. Television's images therefore appear less controllable, unending, even overwhelming.

Yet there is also a curiously ephemeral, transitive quality to the television image; in terms of its technological make-up, the image is half gone and fading before it is even completed (although we rarely see this, of course). In addition, as a signal being transmitted continuously the image is still subject to possible interference or 'noise' relating to bad weather or the relative location of transmitters and receivers (from electric pylons to the television set). With the increasing use of cable and satellite technology this kind of noise is now no longer an issue for many people, but it can still prove a problem for particular viewers in certain locations. When I was confined to a hospital room over Christmas one year, one of my recurrent problems was searching for the best place to put the television aerial to combat the fuzziness and doubling of the image. Despite the fact that poor reception is perhaps becoming less common, the problem of television reception was and remains a popular theme for television comedy; for example, one *Mr. Bean* episode is devoted entirely to his attempt to create a better picture, and the cover of this book is also a reference to the sometimes tortuous process individuals can suffer to establish better picture quality. As we will see later in this chapter, the varying quality of the television image is a continuing concern for cinematographers working in television, particularly in the American context, where the poor and often variable transmission of colour and contrast has long been associated with the NTSC system used for television in the United States and South America.

In the rest of the chapter I will discuss three key features of the television image: its *technological basis*, its different *functions* and, finally, its *aesthetic qualities* (composition, colour and texture). I will then illustrate how an examination of these different qualities of the image will be important in the textual analysis of the American crime series *CSI: Crime Scene Investigation*.

Technological basis

As I have already suggested, the technological make-up of the television image is significant in that it establishes a distinction between film and television as visual media. As will become clear, the technological basis of the television image might also be seen to be important because it seems to emphasize certain functions that are inherently appropriate to television, although part of my intention in this chapter is to try to avoid a too easy technological determining of the television image. Certainly, with the introduction of digital image-making to television it is no longer possible to assume a seamless connection between the technological aspects of television and the function and value of its images. First, however, I will describe briefly how the television image is constructed and viewed, examining both analogue and digital images.

The analogue image

Two incompatible analogue television systems currently dominate the production of the television image. Both were developed after the Second World War, in response to the development of colour television. In both North and South America, the NTSC system (National Television System Committee) was adopted, while in Europe the PAL system (Phase Alternate Line) dominated, with another system, SECAM (Système Electronique Couleur Avec Memoire), employed in France and Eastern Europe. For my purposes here, all these systems can be understood to work by following the same basic principles. In the first instance, the television camera scans the scene (objects, landscape, people) in front of its lens. It picks up the information (the variations of light and shadow) as an electronic signal, which is recorded as a sequence of pulses that scan horizontally across a screen inside the camera, from left to right, resulting in a series of lines which proceed down the screen to build up the television image. Importantly, in all analogue systems, the lines are traced by the camera in an alternate fashion: first the odd lines are scanned (first, third, fifth, and so on) and, once this is completed, the even lines are scanned (second, fourth, sixth). This process is called 'interlaced' scanning and the final picture is effectively 'weaved'. The resulting image is then transmitted as a signal to the television set in the home, where an electron gun replicates the process initiated by the television camera, firing electrons sequentially at the back of the television screen and reproducing the series of horizontal lines that are scanned in an interlaced fashion down the screen. The screen of the television set is layered with phosphor, which transmits light in relation to the intensity of the signal received. In a black and white screen there is one kind of phosphor that glows white when struck by the electron beam. In a colour television there are three electron beams (red, green and blue) hitting the screen-coating, which has red, green or blue phosphors arranged in dots or stripes. A key distinction between black and white and colour television is that the colour television screen has a thin metal screen – a 'shadow mask' – which is perforated with small holes, aligned with the dots or stripes on the colour television screen.

In a sense, the television signal acts almost as if it were an electronic tracing finger, and the television screen reveals the image, point by point, line by line. The key distinction between NTSC and PAL is that the number of scanned lines is different (425 in NTSC and 625 in PAL). Each time a set of (even or odd) lines is scanned, this produces one 'field' (or a half frame) and in the PAL system this process takes $1/50^{th}$ of a second (NTSC scans at $1/60^{th}$). Thus an entire frame (two fields, both the odd and even lines together) is completed every $1/25^{th}$ of a second, which is fast enough for the human brain to perceive the image both as complete (whole) and to register represented movement (without it appearing too 'jerky'). The image is, therefore, as in film, intimately connected to the human eye–brain phenomenon, the 'persistence of vision'. In television the effect is also enhanced by the fact that the individual phosphor flares caused by the variations of the electronic signal take some time to fade. This is partly why interlaced scanning is implemented in the analogue system, as it ensures that the top half of each individual image (or frame) is revisited before the initial set of scanned lines (the first field) begins to fade.

It is because the television image is constituted via a continual signal that it is so vulnerable to 'noise', that is, interference from external factors such as location and the weather. The problems of noise, poor resolution or simply erratic transmission may be half-accepted, even expected for some live transmissions – in a rather tautologous manner, a poor image is understood in some way as a guarantee that the pictures are 'real'. However, even for fictional programmes that have been produced with a great deal of skill and expertise, the organization of transmission and reception will have an effect on the quality of the image for each home viewer. As Tom del Ruth, a director of photography (DP) with an extensive body of work in American television (including *The X-Files, ER* and *The West Wing*), has observed (Goldman 2002):

> 'Most DP's [directors of photography] get 98% of what they want into the final TV master, but once that master is sent to the network, it's uplinked and sent by satellite to downlinks all over the country, which distribute those images to cable companies, who dominate most American TV sets right now' he says. 'Each of those downloaded images can still be adjusted electronically at the download site – they can control brightness, remove colours, and so on, and they can do it automatically. But they can't possibly know what was in the mind of the people shooting the material originally. So, sometimes, what the viewing public sees has little relationship to what was originally done in the telecine room. I'm actually a little shocked that our industry is not more careful with its representative imagery.'

The careful and deliberate lighting organized by the DP as a drama is filmed, and the equally careful attention paid to the colour and contrast of images as they are transferred from film to tape in American drama, are sometimes misread and 'adjusted' after the master tape has been finished. As del Ruth notes, this may even occur 'automatically' during transmission. Presumably, or potentially, such images may even be adjusted again, at the point of reception, with the different facilities that are increasingly available on individual television sets. The way in which the television image has to negotiate the limits of transmission and reception is also addressed in an article in *American Cinematographer* (Probst 1995) on the work of John Bartley. Bartley, another American director of photography who is noted for his work on creating the distinctive lighting for *The X-Files*, suggests that he implicitly uses the expected limitations of NTSC transmission to tease the audience:

> Having won the Golden Globe Award for Best Dramatic Series, *The X-Files* seems to be about testing limits. And with a photographic style ranging from an abyss of blackness to blinding white light, Bartley is also skirting the boundaries of NTSC's transmission capabilities. 'You don't want to show the audience too much. You just want to feel that there's something there. It's hard to keep that dark look.'

This makes a virtue out of the limitations of television reception (since poor visibility adds to the suspense), but it also usefully illustrates how the television image, despite both its pervasiveness and proliferation, is in some senses more fragile and mutable, in terms of its final resolution, than we might initially expect. Ironically, aspects of the image highlighted here – its 'everywhere' capability, its continual presence and its vulnerability – are all connected to the fact that it is an image that is an electronic signal; this suggests that television is, in some ways, more akin to radar than to film.

So what can the technological basis of the television image suggest about what might seem to be the most effective, powerful or 'appropriate' images for television? As I have suggested, the two most significant features are, first, that the image is produced via scanning – that the television image is a constant stream of light; and, second (and linked to the process of scanning), that the television image can be understood to be tactile, since there seems to be an intimate, seamless connection between what is 'picked up' by the camera and what is reproduced by the television set. The image produced is lifted from the real, an 'electronic trace'. This suggests that the most appropriate purpose for the television image would be to produce images that are both live (so that transmission and reception are truly seamless) and 'actual' (that is, taken directly from the real world, both revealing and informative). Television, as is well known, means 'seeing at a distance'. It is not surprising, perhaps, that in the UK, a Channel 4 programme devoted to television's '100 Greatest Moments' revealed that the most effective 'moment' selected by the audience was the television images (and sounds) of the American moon landing in 1969. Although such a poll is clearly not definitive (it was, of course, subject to the particular demographics of the Channel 4 audience and to its time of production in 1997), the choice of this moment remains significant. It is indicative, I think, of the analogue era of television, where the ability to see 'things' from far away, 'up close', appears as the most important and appropriate activity for the television image. While the images transmitted of the moon landing itself were of poor quality and necessarily empty (after all, there was not much to 'see' on the moon), they were a direct connection to events taking place 'there and then', and presented a visceral, intimate link to the 'here and now' of every viewer. The absurd level of scrutiny many of the images have since experienced, in the countless conspiracy theories questioning whether or not the moon landing actually took place, reveal how precisely these images express the television image's problematic composition and reception. As images, the live pictures of the astronauts walking on the moon serve to guarantee real events and express technological feats (both the landing itself and the transmission of live pictures), which, in this instance, directly allude to the success and power of the United States government and, indirectly, to television itself. Yet because the television image is easily and frequently manipulated or interfered with (both at the point of transmission and reception), these pictures remain open to suspicion. Unsurprisingly, the concern around the manipulation of the television image has only intensified as it is increasingly constructed via digital rather than analogue methods. This is despite the fact that other problems – such as poor resolution, a limited range of colour and the small squarish frame of the television image – are being overcome. As I will outline in the next section (following arguments developed by John T. Caldwell), this may mean that the apparently 'appropriate' use of the television image, which relied upon its veracity and its connection to the real, is potentially, and conveniently, being displaced by situations which celebrate the potential richness, complexity and diversity of the digital television image.

The digital image

In the UK, while over 50 per cent of homes now receive digital television, the majority do so via a set-top 'decoder', which translates digital images for the analogue set. In the future, technologies such as high-definition television and other forms of digital television can and will store and transmit digital images directly, and act in ways that are not dissimilar to a computer. In this context, I will describe the present status of the television image and concentrate on the use and appearance of the digital image as it is currently employed and, for the most part, received. I will then suggest what the changing technological basis for the television image may imply about how we use and experience television.

Digital video cameras, like ordinary video cameras, scan the scene and people before them using an electric beam to pick up a signal, registering the variations of light and shade. Unlike the ordinary video camera, a digital camera translates this information into a binary code (0s and 1s), which is the computer's primary 'language'. This binary code may then be represented as a sequential series of pixels (the small building blocks of light which make up the digital image). These pixels are then arranged across the monitor or display screen in a series of horizontal lines, which, as in the analogue image, also proceed down the screen vertically (in this instance, the arrangement of lines is progressive, so that the first line is followed directly by the second, and so on). The number of horizontal lines which can be stored and displayed by digital systems is far greater than in analogue models – up to 1,080 lines can be used, as opposed to the 625 lines in the PAL analogue image. The digital image can also offer far greater density within individual lines. While the analogue system displays perhaps the equivalent of 704 'points of light' across each line, the digital image can make use of up to 1,920 pixels (equivalent to points of light) for each individual line. Unsurprisingly, then, the digital image offers much greater resolution, in terms of both its horizontal (across the screen) and vertical (down the screen) dimensions. In addition, the number of frames per second is also much higher – up to 60 frames per second, over twice the speed of analogue systems.

There are two key distinctions between the digital television image and that produced via analogue systems. First, digital images are based upon a conversion of 'real-world' information (the transmission of light) into the language of computers (binary code and, ultimately, pixels). While this means that the digital television image is still a temporal image (it is always in movement), it is a mapped image, a recreation. The second distinction relates to the memory of the system. In the digital image, each pixel can be remembered and revisited at will. This makes it dissimilar to the analogue image, since in this system the pulses of phosphor can be 'refired', but are never exactly the same. In the digital system, the television image is no longer the sketchy trace of an electronic finger, but ordered electronic data.

Since the digital television image offers a series of pixel building blocks, which offer greater resolution and flexibility, the development of digital television has mostly been to explore the potential flexibility and complexity of the image. John T. Caldwell (1995: 134–60) usefully outlines many techniques employed by the American networks when digital technology was used to produce a variety of spectacular graphic effects for title sequences and advertisements. Increasingly, as the potential of the digital image can be accessed by viewers at home as well as by producers, the television image has been employed in the construction of the television screen as an 'information space', a substitute for the multi-layered, flexible computer screen. In the UK, the BBC has pioneered this development, to some extent, most notably through its extensions to natural history programming. In its *Walking with Dinosaurs* series, the CGI (computer-generated image) effects central to the programmes' appeal – recreating dinosaurs 'as if' they could be seen in their natural habitat today – were supplemented by a wide array of interactive features made available to digital viewers.

Although such developments might seem inevitable as television seemingly moves towards convergence with the computer, there are two interesting ironies here, which demonstrate that the shift towards digital images and digital television itself is not as obvious or as easy as it might appear at first. First, in the *Walking with Dinosaurs* series, while the CGI used did seem to change the perception of how good 'special effects' could be on television (better than before), in fact, according to the producers, the effects were achievable (and affordable) because the television image remains less dense and less complex than the cinematic image. Mike Milne (2005), the director of computer animation at Frame Store, the company responsible for the CGI effects, commented:

> TV only needs a third of the picture resolution that film does, so you don't need such powerful computers to create the images. Also, this is a documentary and in a documentary you're just watching the dinosaurs' everyday life. So if you can animate one animal for a minute just acting naturally, then you can animate a crowd of them. And if your animation is really good, you can use it in several different ways.

This admission bears a close resemblance to the way in which the film standards of cartoon animation – notably the 'full' cel animation developed for feature films by Disney – were adapted for television in the late 1950s and early 1960s. The system of 'reduced' animation developed by Hanna-Barbera also relied on limited movement and the creation of a reduced series of animated cycles for their characters. Like the animation methods described by Mike Milne, Hanna-Barbera developed a working method and, ultimately, a style for television animation, primarily for reasons of economy. Yet, again, like the CGI effects described above, reduced cel animation was successful arguably for reasons that were not just about economics, but also connected to the aesthetic qualities of the television medium itself. The smaller frame of the television screen both allowed for, and perhaps even benefited from, a less dense *mise-en-scène*, while the dominance of the voice and dialogue in the cartoons made for television was also in accord with the storytelling methods of other popular television genres, such as the sitcom and the soap opera. Indeed, the reduced form of television animation is still proving popular today, as shown by the continuing success of original Hanna-Barbera series, such as *Scooby Doo*, or more recent Japanese series, such as *Pokemon*. More traditional forms of animation even played their part in *Walking with Dinosaurs*, as many of the most spectacular effects were not achieved through digital images, but through the more standard practices of filming scale models and puppets – including, in this instance, animatronic models.

The second irony relates to the experience of the digital home viewer, for whom the options available could be said to have *extended* rather than *deepened* the viewing experience. The producers of the series claimed that the digital viewer could access four potential programmes at once. In practice, this meant that the image would be broken up into a series of related and competing information spaces, some with text, others with moving images. This 'busyness', of course, potentially distracts the viewer from a considered appreciation of the spectacular effects that the publicity and indeed the programme itself suggests are the main pleasure or selling point of the series. A key problem for all producers of this kind of service is that the majority of television sets are still currently viewed at a distance, across the living room, so that the television screen is as much as five to seven feet away from the viewer. The computer screen, in contrast, is usually viewed at a much shorter distance, across a desk, so that here, the shift from written text to different kinds of images in different locations is perhaps more easily managed and comprehended by the viewer/user. It is difficult to know whether the development of larger and flatter television screens will make this mixed visual environment more or less comprehensible and pleasurable for the digital television viewer. At the present time, despite the fact that the full implications and possible practices of the digital image have yet to emerge, there are clear indications that the conventions of visual narrative – and narrative space – on television are shifting, perhaps most noticeably in relation to news programming. I shall return to these changes and developments in the final chapter on space.

Functions of the image

The content of television's images is overwhelmingly diverse; like film, television can and does visualize stories, through live action and animation, that address practically any and all subject matter. Unlike most feature films, however, television also routinely uses images in ways that are similar to print media such as books and magazines and, in doing so, frequently reproduces extended sequences of images that are neither animated nor live action.

Photographs, graphs, computer models, paintings, icons and typography are all employed by television in a variety of different contexts. Like books and magazines, television therefore uses images as illustration. Yet the function of the television image is less passive than this description implies. On television, images that appear to illustrate are really being used as visual evidence and their appearance implicitly and explicitly asks the television audience to observe, to witness and to make judgements from a wide variety of visual material. The range and content of television images is so vast it would be pointless to describe them all here. Instead, I want to try and identify two particular functions of the image on television. I will not describe what the images are (at least not in detail), but will focus instead on what they do and what purpose they serve, for both producers and audience.

Images which dramatize

Television fictions – genres such as drama, soap opera and sitcom – are made visible by images which serve to make up the different scenes or 'world' of the programme. The images that make up these programmes, images of actors, sets and 'real-world' locations, are designed to produce a visible *mise-en-scène* that the audience knows is not real. Nonetheless, the audience is willing to suspend disbelief as it invests in the different places and spaces these images create. As in film, of course, the 'real-world' locations they present may actually be a literal visual substitution of one place, which then appears to be another. The London seen in an adaptation of *Martin Chuzzlewit* is a juxtaposition of carefully dressed sets and a contemporary city street filled with the appropriate props and extras. The location in this and other period dramas may not even be London itself, as both Manchester and Glasgow often 'stand in' for nineteenth-century London, as filming in these smaller cities is cheaper and easier to organize and the architecture similar and appropriate to the period. Even in a series that uses contemporary locations, such as *The X-Files*, it is Vancouver and locations in Canada that substitute for Washington, DC and rural parts of the United States. The power of dramatized television images may even encourage, in certain contexts, the substitution of the 'fake' visualization of the television place over the real location. The British pre-school children's show, *Balamory*, uses for its exterior scenes many aspects of the small town, Tobermory, on the Isle of Mull. Not surprisingly, due to the success of the show, tourism to the Isle of Mull increased by 40 per cent in 2003–04. The impact of 'toddler tourism', which treats the town as if it *were* Balamory, has apparently provoked a mixed response from residents. Less is known about the young visitors' own experiences; particularly as the real location of Tobermory and the 'dramatized' Balamory are not really the same at all. Although clearly based in Tobermory, certain key pieces of architecture that feature regularly and prominently in the show (such as the pink castle of the inventor/aristocrat, Archie) are actually elsewhere.

On television, images which dramatize tend to be less complex and less rich in detail than those produced for high-budget feature films, but their duration and status as images seen again and again can mean that the television viewer's relationship with visually quite impoverished scenes may be intense. While the visual complexity of the sets (and hence the visual images) for a soap opera such as *EastEnders* is limited – and it is undeniable that key sets, such as the Queen Vic pub or the cramped interiors of the houses, are not exactly visually exciting – the long duration of the show means that even the most ordinary and mundane of places can, for the long-term viewer, become imbued with a series of visually inspired memories of different characters and plot lines. A location such as the small square within the 'Square' of *EastEnders* has been used repeatedly for a variety of different encounters and incidents: different characters have watched tearfully from bedroom windows as their partners have walked away, and it continually serves as a place for secret and chance meetings.

My own most vivid memory of the garden is of the now-deceased character, Cindy Beale, who, one Christmas Eve, was heavily pregnant with twins and about to go into labour. She was sitting in the small square, on a bench, by the Square's Christmas tree, crying – a fairly unusual activity for her otherwise generally hard-nosed, bitchy character. I do not recall the precise narrative reasons for her crying, although it was an accepted part of her character and situation that she never really loved her husband, the father of the twins. The significance here is that the memory is visually inspired, and it is the composition of the scene which resonates; shot from an unusually high angle, Cindy was sitting on a bench, crying in the dark, lit by the lights of the Christmas tree set up in the square, an image which is recalled for me when the Christmas tree returns, every year. The Christmas tree in the Square is, of course, a relatively simplistic and clichéd visual motif, and it has been used in a variety of different ways and often serves as a location for different characters' self-reflection. However, for the regular viewer, each time it is used the tree represents not just a key part of the *mise-en-scène* within the current narrative context, but is also overlaid with memories of the programme and characters.

In the same way that knowledge of each character's biography becomes important to the narrative richness of a soap opera like *EastEnders*, the repetition of key images and the revisiting of particular locations is also important to the development of sentiment and empathy by the viewer of the series. Therefore, despite the relative visual poverty of the sets, images and design of some television series, the viewer may be compensated by the 'time-rich' quality of these images, which are revisited frequently and on a long-term basis. While film images can be seen again, as the film is reviewed in the cinema or repeated on tape, television's fictional images routinely recreate the same places for weeks or even years on end. Throughout this extended period of viewing, the series has to allow for both incremental and radical changes. Incremental, 'natural' changes may inspire nostalgia on the part of the viewer since they bear witness, almost imperceptibly at times, to the way in which we, along with the characters and the settings, have changed. Radical changes, involving major plot and character upheavals, are often associated with more disturbing and visually spectacular events, both for the viewer and for the characters. In long-running series, such changes are often visually signposted through catastrophic events: helicopters collide with the tops of hospitals, planes crash on villages, nightclubs burn down.

The importance of the time spent viewing in relation to the visual dimension of television also occurs in non-fiction genres. Game shows, music programmes, news and current affairs are also seen regularly and over long periods of time by the television audience. Light entertainment, current affairs and news programmes borrow and develop their sets from quite a limited repertoire of designs, lighting and other visual effects, but their resonance and significance are still important to the viewing audience. For example, the set and lighting for

Fig 1.1 *Who Wants to be a Millionaire?* Rex Features

the hugely successful game show, *Who Wants to be a Millionaire?*, is quite openly based on the relatively sparse set design of the earlier, 'highbrow', long-running BBC quiz show, *Mastermind*. One of the central visual motifs in *Who Wants to be a Millionaire?* is the way in which the contestant, during questioning, is isolated both by framing and by the lighting in the studio. This, as one of the show's original producers commented, allows for a close focus on the 'drama of the human face'. The concentrated, anxious expression of the contestant, who appears to be totally isolated, perched on a chair in a darkened auditorium, is undoubtedly very effective, and it is also directly reminiscent of the setting for *Mastermind*. The position and lighting of the contestant sitting in the 'Mastermind' chair was the most familiar, effective and, thus, most frequently parodied visual motif of the series. Ironically, the 'drama of the human face' first organized by *Mastermind* probably evolved in response to the fact that the set had to be easy to move, as one of the features of the series was that it was usually located in a different university hall each week. Although it was severely limited as a visual spectacle (one chair and a spotlight), the *Mastermind* chair, partly as a result of its longevity, accrued a certain notoriety and cult status. More recently, the different 'diary room' chairs used in the several series of *Big Brother* have also acquired a cult value and demonstrate how the visual iconography of television does not actually have to be particularly complex or unique to be effective.

Increasingly, in television, sets and locations, and the dramatized images which create them, are computer generated. As I will go on to explore in the chapter on space, the digitally-generated visual dimensions of several contemporary newsrooms produce flexible, virtual places, which celebrate privileged aspects of modern media, such as speed, technology and interactivity. While it is well known that newsrooms are now increasingly virtual, the use of CGI has also increased in fictional series. In certain US series, entire environments may be digitally produced. For example, in the series *CSI: Crime Scene Investigation*, 'difficult' locations – such as casinos – may be entirely computer generated. As Sam Nicholson of Stargate Digital, the company responsible for such images, comments (Feeny 2003):

> For instance, for the new 'Las Vegas' show, we had to ask ourselves some questions. How difficult is it to shoot in a casino? Or to shoot in an airport? It is almost impossible. So we came up with a 360 degree virtual environment, which is a texture mapped, photo-real casino that looks like a twenty million dollar set.

'Difficult' locations are those which are expensive and hard to control in terms of lighting and sound. However, as Nicholson explains, CGI is now routinely used in some series not simply for spectacular environments, but almost solely as a cheaper alternative (in terms of time, budget and casting) to location shooting (Feeny 2003):

> We have been using a similar technique for the past two years with *ER*, so that the actors don't have to fly to Chicago. When they walk to the waterfront or they are on top of the hospital and the helicopters come in, we are actually in a parking lot at Warner Bros. The helicopters are virtual, everything is artificial – there is very little reality.

It is still evident that, as John T. Caldwell has described, television often uses CGI to create spectacular images. Increasingly, however, it seems that television now also uses CGI to substitute for real places and objects for reasons more to do with convenience; in fact, CGI is beginning to substitute for the filming of ordinary locations and its presence may be unknown to the general audience. I do not want to suggest that this is necessarily a cause for concern. For my purposes, whether they are produced via a photographed and 'dressed' reality or entirely digitally generated, television images which present an illusion of the 'real world', or which build fantasy places, such as the game show studio or the small town of Balamory, are images whose function is to *dramatize*. Whether digitally created or not, when television uses images to dramatize, 'everything' as Nicholson put it, 'is artificial'.

Images which demonstrate

Television also employs images whose work seems to be the opposite of artifice; instead, images are used as evidence, as demonstration. Images in documentaries, news and current affairs programmes are often images that are being used directly as visual evidence. Frequently, these images seem to express a particular kind of claim to reality and are presented as if the 'truth' of the events can be read or directly interpreted from the images themselves. Actuality footage (film produced within a documentary context, whether this is observational material or staged interviews), archive (old newsreels, previous documentary programmes), photographs and surveillance material from CCTV (closed-circuit television) may all be juxtaposed in programmes designed to inform and educate the audience. The interpretation of this visual evidence is often directed (but not fully determined) by the argument constructed via a voice-over, or as developed by an on-screen presenter. The function of these images is to encourage the audience to observe, witness and, perhaps, make judgements about the people, places and situations being *described*.

Not all demonstrative images have such a close relationship to the 'real'. Other kinds of image – paintings, drawings, maps, graphs and computer models – are more akin to illustrations as they are used to make a variety of different kinds of information more interesting or accessible. One regular use of images that demonstrate occurs in weather reports, which use a variety of maps and visual indicators, which the on-screen weather forecaster directs to predict future weather conditions. Although there is some diversity as to the colour and design of the maps and figures in the different channels' weather reports, one aspect tends to remain uniform – the presenter stands in front of the map, shot from about the knees up, so that he or she and the map are seen 'face on' by the viewer, thus closely imitating the conventional position of a teacher at the blackboard. Interestingly, on Scottish television, one local weather report, produced by STV, radically alters both the presentation and perspective, so that the presenter is not seen and, instead, the viewer is guided via a voice-over on an eye-level tour of a three-dimensional map of Scotland. The weather report in this instance imitates a flight simulation computer game rather than a lecture. Both ways of presenting the weather make sense, but it is surprising, on first viewing, how unnatural this 'flight simulation' weather report feels, even though, ultimately, it does produce a more immediate and intimate sense of the geography. In its fuller exploration of the actual geography of Scotland (down the coastline and then across the central belt of Scotland, from Glasgow to Edinburgh), it reveals the significant differences between 'national' representations of British weather and the specifics of local climate. Notoriously, for instance, Glasgow, as a city on the west coast of Scotland, often has more rain than the east coast capital city of Edinburgh. On the more conventionally presented national weather report, both cities are often categorized verbally as 'central belt', or simply as 'Scotland', while graphically the distance between them is also represented as (relatively) insignificant. Thus, 'rain' in Scotland may actually means it rains in Glasgow but not in Edinburgh. Of course, with two minutes of airtime and a desire to address the weather for the whole of the United Kingdom, some 'shorthand', both verbal and visual, is needed (hence, in part, the use of a map and icons in the first place). Nonetheless, the 'flight simulation' model of weather forecasting does reveal the way in which weather maps, along with the icons which illustrate cities, storms, wind speeds and temperature, are constructed images that do more than simply 'illustrate' the weather in an apparently neutral or objective fashion. If this is a problem in a relatively small country such as the UK, it will be even more extreme in other countries, where national broadcasters may have to negotiate far greater expanses of country; after all, the land mass of the entire island of Great Britain is approximately one-eighth the size of the state of California in the United States.

Another regular but less frequent use of maps, graphs and simulations is in the reporting of political elections. In the UK, a regular feature of the General Election coverage on the BBC has been Peter Snow's enthusiastic presentation of incoming results using a varying display of different computer models. In these reports, Snow directs the viewer to witness seats in a virtual House of Parliament turning red or blue, and to watch as a map of Britain similarly shifts in colour in response to past, predicted and actual poll results. Such is television's apparent obsession with 'visualizing' information in this way that it has been an object of successful parody in numerous television shows, from *The Two Ronnies* to *Brass Eye*. I will present a more detailed exploration of these kinds of images in the final chapter on space.

It is true that in some instances such visualization seems excessive and redundant. However, what is clear in this context is that in this mode of presentation, television is using images for more than 'illustration'. For example, we could think about the way in which television reproduces a visual model such as the computer simulation of the DNA helix – a relatively frequent occurrence in a range of different contexts, from science documentaries to news programmes. On the one hand, the image is simply an illustration of a complex mathematical and scientific process that ultimately determined the shape and nature of the molecular structure of the human gene sequence. On the other hand, it is also more than an illustration, since the three-dimensional nature of the helix and, therefore, its 'visualization' is actually integral and essential to the understanding of the structure and function of DNA. The structure of DNA only makes sense if it is understood in relation to its visualization as a helix; the relationship between genes can only be understood if they are envisaged in this particular structure. While television can and does use this kind of demonstrative image innocently (reproducing images that have emerged via a carefully proven and tested scientific process), it also constantly fabricates such images, as I have suggested in my brief discussion of weather reports.

Another familiar example of the same process would be a graphic image sequence often employed in a variety of different shampoo advertisements. Shampoo advertisements frequently begin with celebrities or models flicking their hair attractively and acting out or discussing the relative merits of the product in question. This sequence will be a piece of dramatized footage set almost anywhere, from an airy studio apartment, to a hairdresser's salon, to a jungle stream. The advertisement then cuts to a graphic animated display, where hair follicles are apparently magnified and revealed (initially) to be frayed, rough or dry. Once this has been established, the viewer then sees how, 'scientifically', the shampoo product moisturizes individual hairs – animated 'molecules' of the specified vitamins, proteins or 'organic essences' bombard the hair follicles so that they become smooth, sleek and shiny. I do not believe that the audience is really fooled into believing the 'truth claims' of these advertisements. Yet these image sequences are successful and this must be, in part, because the audience has learned – from television, but also within other educational contexts – to think or to know about the world in visual terms. Although the visualization of how the shampoo supposedly works may actually be nonsensical, it does imitate successfully a visual mode of understanding used in other, more authoritative contexts, such as medical textbooks. Images that demonstrate on television are not simply about representing statistical or scientific information so that it is easier to understand. While they may do this, it is also the case that this kind of image sequence appears to embody, rather than simply illustrate, knowledge and information. By so doing, television is able to imbue these sequences with a particular kind of authority. In a shampoo advertisement this allusion may be patently absurd (even to the advertisers themselves – Jennifer Aniston's advice to viewers in her advertisements for L'Oréal shampoos included the coy aside to the audience that they should 'Concentrate – this is the science bit'), but the potential of this kind of visual display to convince and teach audiences means that these images are regularly reproduced in many different contexts, both with and without qualification.

Qualities of the image

Composition

Framing the image (1) – the aspect ratio

The composition of the television image, like many other images – in painting, photography and film – is defined, in part, through its relationship to its frame. The frame separates the image from the world which surrounds it. The size and shape of the frame will also determine how subjects, objects, scenes and events are composed. Previously, the television set (and now, increasingly, the television screen, as television monitors have become flatter and bigger) was the exterior frame or 'mould' which separated the television image from the world around it. The size, dimensions and appearance of the television set, along with its location, are extremely diverse and have changed quite significantly over the years. Since the aim of my discussion here is to examine, almost exclusively, the formal aspects of the television image, I don't intend to explore the significance of the television 'set' much further, but direct the reader to two key texts which do so in fascinating detail. Lynn Spigel's *Make Room for TV* explores the personal, social and aesthetic negotiation involved as different television models were integrated into the family home in 1950s America (Spigel 1992). Anna McCarthy's *Ambient Television* describes a parallel history for the television set as she describes the different locations and uses for television in a variety of sites outside the home, in bars, airports and shopping malls (McCarthy 2001). Both books illustrate how the situation or, literally, the 'setting' of the television image can impact on how its images are employed and interpreted by viewers.

In the context of this chapter, I will concentrate on how the television image is framed at the point of production and transmission and refer only briefly to its appearance at the point of reception. It is, in some senses, then, the 'interior' frame of the image that interests me here. In television, as in film, this framing of the image is referred to as the 'aspect ratio'. This ratio is a mathematical formula which describes the relationship between the height and width of the image that is transmitted and/or projected. Previously, the standard aspect ratio in television replicated the aspect ratio that had been used most commonly in Hollywood film-making until the introduction of widescreen technology in the 1950s. This was 4:3 (or 1.33:1), that is, four units horizontally to every three vertically, known as the 'academy' ratio after the Hollywood Academy of Motion Picture Arts and Sciences. From the late 1950s, however, Hollywood film-making developed and moved increasingly to employ a widescreen aspect ratio for the majority of its films, using an aspect ratio closer to 16:9 (or 1.77:1).

Today, for most films screened in the cinema, the average aspect ratio is 1.85:1 and it may be wider still. This widescreen ratio, for obvious reasons, is often termed a landscape orientation.

Widescreen filming has been seen as a direct response to the competition for audiences between Hollywood and the emerging television industry during the 1950s. By emphasizing the size of the cinematic image as fundamentally different to television, widescreen technology was, arguably, a way of distinguishing and celebrating the film image as offering 'more' – more spectacle, a better view – than the television image. Even fairly recently, an advertisement played in cinemas and designed to encourage audiences to visit the cinema highlighted this distinction. The advertisement began with some magnificent, highly colourful and densely populated image sequences from Bertolucci's epic film, *The Last Emperor* (1987). As the advertisement progresses, the film's epic scenes are gradually painted out by a small figure who appears in the foreground, until we are left with only a small boxed fragment of the initial image, being played out in a facsimile of a television screen. The message of the advertisement is clear: cinema offers *more* than television ever could. The simple fact of its size means that it offers a bigger spectacle and thus the potential for more intense visual excitement.

Evidently, the film image is not easily reduced to the dimensions of the television frame and it remains the case that when television does transmit films made for widescreen projection, the original image has to be shrunk, squeezed or 'panned and scanned'. Panning and scanning used to be the most common way in which films were screened on television. This process involved the entire film being reshot before transmission; within each scene the most important elements are selected, and the pan-and-scan frame moves (or scans) across the film image to incorporate different elements of the image in terms of their varying narrative significance. This process produces two significant problems. First, the decision as to which elements are the most important is always arguable; second, the movement of the pan-and-scan frame creates a moving camera shot and this may be directly contradictory to the aesthetic intent of the original version of the film, which may have been designed to emphasize the relationship between the characters or objects in a carefully crafted static image. A third problem which can arise from panning and scanning is the need for additional edits. As examples, we might imagine a conversation, a musical number or a western shoot-out that takes place between two characters, who, in the original versions of the films, are framed in a wide shot and placed at different sides of the screen. In the adaptation of these scenes for television transmission, a decision may be made simply to cut out the distance between the two characters and instead produce sequences where, instead of one image, the television audience sees a series of cropped shots of each character individually framed, as they talk, sing or shoot at each other, thus creating a series of edits that were not present in the original film.

It is not surprising, therefore, that this process is far less common than it used to be, at least on British television. Films and other programmes originally shot in wider formats are now more likely to be 'shrunk' to fit the transmission aspect ratio. This procedure involves a straightforward reduction of the image and, while this has the benefit of retaining most of the visual information and the original composition of the image, it results in a 'letter-box' effect for the television viewer. The letter-box effect refers to the way in which the reduced image leaves certain parts of the television image blank – these margins, usually at the top and bottom of the image, are generally 'blacked out' when they appear on the television screen, thereby framing the image as if it were being seen through a letter box. It used to be accepted that television viewers and producers were made anxious or distracted by the letter-box effect; it now seems, perhaps due to the huge increase in the number of films that are screened on television (via specialist channels, but more specifically through the massive home video market), that this is no longer the case.

Currently, the whole issue of the aspect ratio is in flux in the UK and the USA. The development and increasing take-up of both digital production and transmission and the development of widescreen (or at least wider screens) for television sets means that most television programmes are now shot in wider formats than the original ratio of 4:3 (1.33:1). The standard ratio for shooting is now more often 16:9 (1.77:1), and this means that television directors shoot in a format that is once more close to (but still not quite as wide as) the dimensions of the film image. However, at the present time, in the UK, most people are still watching on television sets that are set up to receive images in a ratio of 4:3. For these viewers, if a programme shot in 16:9 was 'shrunk' for transmission to a screen set up to view in 4:3, the letter-box margins at the top and bottom of the screen would necessarily take up quite a significant amount of screen space. A short-term measure aimed at reducing this problem, adopted in the UK by the BBC, instructs that programmes (intentionally) shot in 16:9 must 'protect' their image so that it can be seen in 14:9. This means that although they are shooting in a wider format, the most 'significant' elements (particularly, for instance, when characters or objects come in or out of shot) must make sense within the 14:9 ratio. Then, when the programmes are screened on a standard television set, the letter-box effect is still evident, but the margins take up less screen space.

In the United States, while there are plans to move production and transmission entirely to high-definition television (and thus, at the same time, to wider aspect ratios), this has not yet occurred. Therefore, television companies and television directors with an eye on future transmission now often shoot their programmes 'as if' they were for 16:9 transmission, but 'protect' the image so that it can be seen successfully via the current aspect ratio of 4:3. So, once again, while a wider composition is possible and encouraged, the important visual information in each scene – such as the composition and activity of the characters – is still arranged to fit the smaller frame. Unsurprisingly, this can be frustrating for many directors of photography. Michael Bonavillain, who is director of photography on the prime-time American suspense/spy drama, *Alias*, explains (Oppenheimer 2002: 88):

> We don't just protect for high-def broadcast, we shoot for it . . . but we also make sure it looks good in standard definition. The hard thing about going for two formats is trying to surprise the viewer. For example, if you have an actor come into frame unexpectedly, do you have him react when he comes into the 16x9 frame, or when he comes into the 4x3 frame? There's a split second timing that can make an actor look either slow or prescient depending on how you choose to go. We try to split the difference, but it's frustrating.

Bonavillain makes clear the kinds of problems that this shift from one format to another involves for producers; what is also implicit is that a wider frame may well have an effect on *how*, as well as *where*, things can happen in the television image. While the impact of a change in the aspect ratio cannot really be predicted, it seems likely that changes in the frame, allowed and encouraged by the changing technology of television, may directly impact on established conventions associated with the television image, particularly as it applies to the image in drama. Tom del Ruth, for example, speculates how a wider aspect ratio could both affect the economics of how a television scene is filmed and, ultimately, establish a different way of shooting and composing images in prime-time television drama. In a discussion concerning widescreen aspect ratios (Oppenheimer 2000: 83), in relation to his work on the US drama series, *The West Wing*, del Ruth observes:

> Switching to 1.77:1 [16:9] would save us set-up time and coverage. We could stack two or three actors in one shot without having to go to individual singles, which is what we have to do in 1.33:1 [4:3]. As it stands now, we only get one-and-a-half or maybe two people in a raking shot, the shots get so wide perspective-wise, that the image of the [third] person's head gets too small, and we lose the strength that's needed to tell a story on TV.

Potentially, therefore, the wider aspect ratio may save money, as single set-ups and shots incorporating several actors at a time effectively substitute for the current practice of labour- and time-intensive 'single shots' (head shots of individual characters which are intercut to produce sequences of dialogue involving several characters in one scene). Previously, as del Ruth indicates, using singles and intercutting between them seemed to be the only way in which the visual interest and dramatic intensity of scenes involving several characters at once could be managed on the small screen. The need to see – in detail – the individual character's response, expression and performance is the 'strength' that del Ruth is implying gets 'lost' when characters' heads become 'too small' and therefore less easily seen by the viewing audience. Presumably, the wider frame of a larger aspect ratio encourages a more populated image as there is simply more space available. What this indicates is that a distinctive feature of television's visual regime – the use of close-up shots of individual characters – when compared with cinema, may, at least in some dramatic contexts, be about to change.

If the intent is to produce a dramatic programme that is as close as possible to a feature film, then the wider aspect ratio does seem to offer a potentially exciting and, perhaps, appropriate development. Yet, as I have already indicated, the function of the television image is not just dramatic. If we think about the range of images which *demonstrate*, it might be reasonable to wonder what kind of effect a widescreen aspect ratio would have on the way in which they are presented, and how such images make meaning for the television viewer. Does a wider aspect ratio make the weather report better, more effective or more aesthetically pleasing? In a programme about DIY, does a wider aspect ratio really make any difference at all to the way in which the viewer responds to the image?

Surprisingly, however, it may be that the wider aspect ratio does have an effect on some of these images. For example, it does seem (as I will explore in more detail in the chapter on space) that the presentation of television news has already begun to adapt to this new 'frame', largely by reducing the amount of time that the image is filled solely by news anchor's head and shoulders (thereby eliminating the previous emphasis on talking head). There also appears to be an associated increase in the application of different kinds of text and image, which serve to 'fill up' the image. Everyday news presentation has become much busier in terms of its visual information, and now includes rolling subtitles, several video screens (or one large video 'wall') and additional graphic sequences. Perhaps other genres which previously relied on the talking head – including programmes such as talk and chat shows and some game shows – will build their images differently, incorporating more action, or employ other kinds of visual information to fill the frame. For instance, while *Who Wants to be a Millionaire?* does copy closely the original framing of contestants initiated by *Mastermind*, during questioning in *Who Wants to be a Millionaire?* the questions and possible answers are made visible at the bottom of the screen to the viewer at home. This is designed to encourage viewers to play along, but it also helpfully fills the screen with additional visual information, providing – coincidentally – a frame within the frame for the previously mentioned 'drama of the human face'.

In addition, other categories of the television image could be produced for a wider aspect ratio. It is difficult to predict whether the wider frame will encourage a different kind of animation, for instance, or make earlier animated programmes less appealing. For just as films and television programmes shot for wider screen formats currently have to adapt to today's narrower frame, existing visual material – archive footage (on 8 mm, 16 mm or early video) as well as contemporary amateur film and video (shot on a range of different formats) – will all have to adapt to this new wider framing. Ironically, this means that the letter-box effect may be turned on its head. This is because material originally shot in the 4:3 format, if presented without alteration, will need to be transmitted on wider screens, with black margins framing the image vertically at either side. Alternatively, the image will have to be cropped (to make it flatter) and enlarged to fit the new wider ratio. While this might seem to be the obvious way forward, if a close-up shot of a face (which television currently relies on extensively) is cropped and then blown up, it would be possible for the head to fill a screen that could be as large as 48 inches across. And if – as is common on television – this head appears to be directly talking at you, in the privacy of your own living room, television viewing potentially becomes a rather alarming encounter.

Evidently, therefore, since television images are *promiscuous* images – in that they are rarely destined to appear in just one context, for just one time – and because so many television images actually originate from sources other than television itself, no one aspect ratio will ever be appropriate for every image shown on television. While it seems likely that the new, wider ratio will come to dominate production, many television images will remain, or become, compromised images – shrunk, blown up and cut about – both at the point of transmission and, increasingly, at the point of reception, as viewers at home use their remote controls to manipulate the images they see.

Framing the image (2) – choosing the shots

As in film, television directors and/or directors of photography can choose a variety of different framings for each 'shot' they take. Broadly speaking, these shots relate to how close the camera is to the objects, people or scene being filmed (and this distance may be related either to the actual location of the camera or to how the scene is filmed via the use of different lenses). In what follows I will provide a very brief summary of the most common kinds of framing on television: the establishing shot, the long shot, the medium shot and the close-up. My intention is not to replicate the technical and rigorous description of shots that are described much more effectively in a variety of different production manuals. Instead, I want to indicate how certain shots function within specific television contexts. Paradoxically, however, I will also demonstrate that on television, just as with film, it is all but impossible to establish conventions or to claim that a specific composition always 'means' the same thing, whatever its context.

Establishing shot

This is usually a wide shot of a building, landscape or cityscape. In television drama, such shots are often used in a less spectacular but generally similar way to film. In film, it is often (though not always) the case that a wide establishing shot will be followed by a move, pan or edit to a close shot of the action, people or objects that make up a tiny fraction of the original image. The establishing shot therefore initiates, or motivates, the relationships between the images that tell the story. A famous example of this would the arrival of John Wayne's character, Ethan, as he approaches his brother's homestead at the beginning of John Ford's classic western, *The Searchers* (1956). After a brief prologue featuring various members of the family around the house, the camera turns away from this domestic activity and presents the viewer with an establishing shot of the iconic American landscape in which the house is set. Almost imperceptibly at first, in the distance we see that there is a tiny figure on a horse that moves closer and closer to the camera. Is that Uncle Ethan? Yes it is, and so the movie begins.

In television, where the screen is less likely to be static, an establishing shot will often begin with a part of a building (a window, a spire) and then pan down and across the building to pick up the action involving the characters. It is almost as if television directors believe that the audience is unlikely to 'wait around' for the action to emerge and, while wishing to comment visually on the beauty and/or the specific nature of the setting, the intent is to guide the viewer into the action as quickly as possible. For example, in the classic television series, *Inspector Morse* (which involves a series of murder cases solved by a police detective in the picturesque university city of Oxford), many establishing shots begin by picking out key aspects of the city's famous architecture. In a scene set in a college quadrangle, for example, the camera will begin by picking out the top of the characteristically ancient rooftops of the college buildings, but will then sweep down to ground level to catch up with Morse and his assistant, Lewis, as they stride through the grounds of the quadrangle itself. In many ways, these establishing shots act as they would in film, as they set the scene by giving (or reminding) the audience information about location and time of day. In addition, such shots give the programme an added aesthetic appeal; the 'dreaming spires' of Oxford are perhaps as iconic as the barren vistas of the American West. Yet on television, in many instances, establishing shots ask the audience explicitly to 'catch up' with what is happening, and viewers rarely have the luxury (or the potential tedium) of *waiting* to see what will happen.

Television also uses one kind of establishing shot in a way that it is almost never used in film. Between scenes, or before and after commercial breaks, many television programmes use a repeated visual motif (the outside of a building, a bar, a cityscape) before cutting directly to the interior for the next scene. This is particularly common in sitcoms (*Roseanne*, for example, used static shots of the Connors' house), but can involve more elaborate sequences, as when *CSI: Crime Scene Investigation* sweeps across the fantastic and distinctive neon-lit cityscape of Las Vegas. These sequences act as temporal markers and, although their spatial qualities are significant, they rarely contain any specific narrative information pertinent to the scenes that they begin or end. This is deliberate because many of the shots, or shot sequences, are used again and again as visual bridges between one scene and the next (and, as I go on to explore in the chapter on sound, they are often accompanied by a repeated phrase of music or mixed ambient sound). Therefore, while the establishing shot used in this way on television is reminding the viewer that they are 'there' – whether this is with CSI in Las Vegas, at Roseanne's house or in Teletubbyland – it is also providing a visualized temporal structure and pace for the programme, informing the viewer that the previous sequence has finished or that the commercial break is over.

Long shot

Long shots, where characters can be seen from head to foot, are not that common on television. Potentially, this is quite surprising, as many television genres involve people standing around – in sports, game shows, music programmes, variety shows, award ceremonies and, increasingly, news programmes. The long shot on television is usually determined by the theatrical origin of the programme or by the activity of the individual who is being filmed. The long shot situates the viewing audience away from the performer/character/individual, as if they were on a stage. Most music performers, stand-up comics, newscasters, game show or chat show hosts are literally situated on stage – whether this is at a theatre or music venue or fabricated in the television studio. Attendance at an actual theatrical presentation, however, offers the audience an experience television cannot reproduce. However far away you are from the stage, as part of a theatrical audience you will probably feel both physically and emotionally close to the performer and, undeniably, there will be an intimate charge from this proximity. Even if the television transmission is live, it cannot offer this kind of emotional excitement; instead, it frequently substitutes a mediated proximity (an abundance of different perspectives, many of them close-up shots) for actual proximity (being there). Of course, the situation may not be as straightforward as this – 'being there' at Glastonbury or the Superbowl does not necessarily mean that you are actually that close to the performers – in fact, your view might well be better if you were at home watching television. At the same time, however, being there offers a range of sensations that have nothing to do with *seeing* the event – the smell of popcorn or cannabis, the noise of the crowd (which may include you singing along or chanting), the warmth and touch of other bodies, known and unknown, that press around you in the crowd, the coldness of the day or the stickiness of the mud when it rains – all of which are absent from television.

The long shot therefore presents events as if they were a theatrical encounter, but since it does so necessarily by picturing them as if they were far away, this kind of framing does very little to encourage a sense of participation by the viewer. There is a clear impetus for the television image, then, to offer more visual excitement – and close-up shots allow the viewer to seem (visually) closer. There is therefore a tendency on television to use the long shot only for a brief instance, when performers either enter or leave the 'stage'. Unless the performer's entire body is important to the impact of their act (and this might apply to performers like the stand-up comic Lee Evans, or even Elvis Presley), long shots do not feature prominently in contemporary television, although in earlier years of television the framing of the television image was more explicitly dictated by a presumed familiarity with the proscenium arch of the theatrical stage. Fewer edits, long shots and less movement were also determined by the fact that television cameras were heavy and less mobile and because a great deal of television was recorded live.

In contemporary television drama, however, the long shot is avoided. Instead it seems evident that directors compose their shots to emphasize the intimacy of the small screen. As Pierre Sorlin (1998: 121) has observed that in a great deal of television drama (particularly in soap opera), it would seem that 'for most of the time we watch people talk'. Television, in its use of the close-up in preference to the long shot, is an economic medium. For if we are interested mainly in watching people talk, we will be concerned primarily with their lips, eyes and faces and it is simply unnecessary, or excessive, to spend time looking at their feet.

Yet, as perhaps for every aspect of the television image I have discussed so far, conventions apparently exist only to be broken. Here, for example, Alan Caso, the director of photography for the HBO drama, *Six Feet Under*, indicates that a decision to provide wide (and thus also long) shots is, in fact, a key part of the show's aesthetic, something which deliberately distinguishes it from other prime-time American dramas (Magid 2002: 72):

> 'Producers have this desperate need to constantly move the camera,' says Caso, who adds that this trend is not always appropriate. 'I think that shows like *CSI*, *NYPD Blue* and *ER* really need [movement], but this show absolutely does not. We actually took our approach to the other extreme. We said, "Let's just format this like we're shooting for 1.85:1 and it's going to be on the big screen. Let's not be afraid of the wide shot – let's go *really* wide. Let's provide these proscenia for the actors to play in and make bold statements about the emptiness of someone's life by isolating him, creating a conflict with the composition of the frame, or show his misery by making him look small and insignificant in the frame."'

The producers' intent here, then, is overtly theatrical (hence the mention of 'proscenia'), but also 'painterly'. Alan Ball, the series creator, makes this explicit (Magid 2002: 74) when he states:

> Our show is not so much about cutting back and forth between close-ups; it's about actually composing a picture within a frame, and I wanted those compositions to have some subtext. I think Alan [Caso] loves the wide shots because that's when he really gets to paint with the light.

Therefore, the series is constructed deliberately to subvert the conventions of television drama; it expects and encourages the viewer to read the image as if it were a painting, to admire composition and to interpret each character's emotions and situation from their composition in the frame. Long shots are part of a deliberate strategy to encourage the audience to admire the qualities rather than just the content of the television image.

In contrast to the highbrow aesthetic of this American drama, another programme that also employs a greater number of long shots than many other television programmes is the BBC's pre-school children's show, *Teletubbies*. There are many sequences in the programme where an entire Teletubby character (or, indeed, all four Teletubbies) can be seen from head to foot. There are perhaps two particular reasons for this: first, as a show which encourages its audience to 'join in', to run around or dance like the Tubbies, the viewer will need to see every part of the body moving at the same time; second, the amount of extra information or interest – in terms of expression – that you get if you provide a close-up of a Tubby's hands or face is actually very limited. Tubbies, who are played by actors dressed in large coloured suits, do not have fingers or a very wide range of facial expressions. In addition, the producers have an expressed motivation to offer their young audience a wider horizon, an intention that is arguably a deliberate move away from the established, 'cosy' intimacy of many studio-set children's programmes. Chris Watts, the lighting director for the series, states (Calhoun 1999):

> Anne Wood and Andy Davenport [the series' creator and producer] wanted to break away, I think, from the false-looking sets that have plagued children's television, and they wanted to get away from animation. They want to give children who live in a tower block, who can't see a piece of green grass, their own playing field for half an hour. They felt they couldn't do that in a studio set, because it would never, ever have the feeling of open air and countryside, no matter how you try to light it.

Once more, it seems there are no fixed criteria for the way in which particular shots are used on television; the immense variety of contexts, the diversity of the producers' intentions, as well as the way in which a long shot can be used and viewed by different audiences, means that even a composition that seems to be clearly theatrical, and in direct opposition to the intimacy associated with television's mode of reception, is actually employed – very successfully – in entirely different visual contexts and encourages equally disparate modes of engagement from its audience.

The medium shot

This framing presents events, actors and presenters almost as if they were face-to-face with us: generally, the lower part of the body is cut out of the frame and the individual's head and shoulders therefore dominate the image. The frequency of this kind of composition, which features in practically every kind of television programme, rather obviously illustrates something about the content of television's images; they are nearly always of *people*. Even television programmes that are not strictly about people and which do not need to feature people on screen at all – such as wildlife programmes or programmes about architecture –

often include a presenter (framed frequently in a medium shot). Why do we need to *see* as well as hear people on television? On news programmes, of course, the reporter's authority is partly underwritten by their apparent proximity to the events taking place. In arts documentaries and wildlife programmes, the mid-shot of the human presenter often acts as a pivot for extended sequences of otherwise uninhabited visual spectacle (uninhabited, that is, by humans), but the presenter is repeatedly returned to, placed in a variety of different contexts. On television, therefore, directors seem overwhelmingly preoccupied by the need to present the human form and thus rarely allow other species, or abstract forms, to dominate. As a gallery of images, television is more akin to the family album than an art museum. The medium shot is symptomatic of a visual medium that is about picturing people and is more interested in looking at them than looking at the image as an image for 'art's sake'. Nobody expects family snaps to be beautiful – in fact, if they are too beautiful, too composed or too clever, this might seem a little peculiar or, at least, pretentious.

The close-up

As I have already noted, one of the most frequently used shots in television is the close-up, generally of the human face. In drama, game shows, sports programmes, music video and documentary, there is constant return to the human face, often not simply in the form of a head-and-shoulders shot, but in an even more intimate framing in which the face fills the screen. The recurrence and persistence of the close-up has been explained through reference to the smallness of the screen and, therefore, the television viewer's need to be as close as possible, so as to recognize individuals and see what is 'going on'. However, I think the prevalence of the close-up suggests that there is more to it than this. The frequent proximity of the face and the emotions displayed means that the close-up on television is both sensational and, oddly perhaps, mundane. Our intimate proximity to the face would seem almost hysterical (alarming and/or funny) in another medium, such as cinema. On television, however, although the impact may be excessively emotional at times, this is not always the case, and, even in these more extreme instances, it rarely seems peculiar or threatening. In fact, television's proximity to the people, objects and events it represents is entirely conventional. It is almost as if television presents a world where things can be known simply by being close by. In one of the earliest studies on outside television broadcasting, an analysis of General McArthur visiting Chicago in 1951, the authors, Lang and Lang (reprinted 1993: 193), report how the televisation of a public event used close-ups to create a particular effect. This was seen to produce a response from the television audience that was personal and emotional rather than rational or intellectual.

> Moreover, in view of the selectivity of the coverage with its emphasis on close-ups, it was possible for each viewer to see himself in a *personal* relationship to the General. As the announcer shouted out: 'Look at that chin! Look at those eyes!' – each viewer, regardless of what might have been meant by it, could seek a personal interpretation which best expressed, for him, the real feeling underlying the exterior which appeared on the television screen.

In their article, Lang and Lang concentrate on the disparity between the experience of the actual event and the same event represented by television. What I am interested in here is the appearance of the close-up and the accompanying voice-over – 'that chin! . . . those eyes!' As is now entirely conventional in similar public events, the announcer is all too obviously, and apparently redundantly, describing what can be seen on-screen. What Lang and Lang's observation makes explicit is that it is television's emphasis on appearance and our proximity to it which produces a 'feeling' in and for the viewer.

A similar and equally common practice in a vast diversity of different documentaries is the way in which photographs of people, events and objects are filmed. The frequent use of the rostrum camera mobilizes the still photographic image so that the point of view moves around the image, 'seeking out' something, though what this is, exactly, may not be entirely clear. In many instances, the camera zooms in to the eyes and mouth of the person photographed or lingers significantly on an article of clothing or jewellery. It is common for the same photograph to be used several times in the course of one documentary, and the gradual revelations about the events or individual are matched by the close-up scrutiny of one increasingly familiar image. Of course, mobilizing a static photograph is perhaps necessitated by the need to present a 'moving image' to keep viewers interested, but I think it also relates to the tactile, sensual approach television has to such material. The use of the rostrum camera allows the image to be 'pored over', pulled closer to view, and repetition and proximity allow viewers to trace and follow the features of faces, places and objects. And while the audience's understanding may be directed by what is heard in the voice-over, this cannot and does not anchor its meaning entirely.

The director's intent may be to shift the meaning of one photograph so that it represents, at different times, 'a doctor', 'her husband' and 'the killer'. Nonetheless, despite the fact that the audience is being set up to read the image differently each time, there will always be a gap between what is seen and felt and what is heard and understood. This is because the image does not really explain the voice-over and the argument being made, and the voice-over cannot explain the image entirely or completely. By both fragmenting and moving in to the image, the audience is pulled in different directions. On the one hand, getting closer indicates that we should indulge in greater scrutiny, look for details that we had not noticed before, and asks that we perform an active and penetrating gaze. On the other hand, we may find that we are not seeing more, but less, as the image blurs at close quarters; or that, confronted with a fragment, we see only the unremarkable – a beard, eyes and glasses. Thus what we 'feel' we know from these isolated elements may not be the same as what we are being 'told' by the voice-over. Of course, we may indeed feel that we are 'looking into the eyes of the killer', yet at the same time we also know that this is ridiculous, a performance on our part. For, equally, we may also be 'seeing' a resemblance between this face and that of a relative whom we had forgotten until now.

Fragmentation and extreme close-up may also reduce what was originally photographic (particular, realistic) to a graphic representation, as the movement flattens and distorts our initial view of the image. As the features of the face take on graphic qualities, we may become distracted by details, whether these are flecks of silver in the beard or a reflection in the lenses of the spectacles. The meaningfulness, or our understanding, of the image may be reduced to an awareness of texture, of light and shade, the abstract rather than the concrete. The use of the rostrum camera is one way in which the photograph takes part in the 'performance' of the documentary. This shift between the realistic 'representation' of the photograph and the abstract, graphic qualities of texture and light relate closely to what John Corner (2003) has argued to be the way in which the television image in documentary can be 'looked through' and 'looked at'. I would argue, however, that it is in fact common to other kinds of television programming. The use of the close-up in a soap opera such as *EastEnders*, a US drama such as *CSI: Crime Scene Investigation* or numerous advertisements and news programmes also promotes what Corner has identified as the 'kinetic' properties of the image.

We may see this at work again in the use of the close-up in medical and natural history documentaries. In the BBC's successful series, *The Human Body*, there are many instances in which the camera appears literally to go inside the body, into the lungs or the valves of the heart. We are therefore very close – perhaps too close for comfort – crowded into the most intimate and delicate places of the body. Blood or air, at times, seemingly rushes towards the camera lens and the effect of being inside and up close is further supported by sound effects of air rushing past or the warm, watery sounds of blood being pumped round the body. In one sense, the images and sounds are justified by the voice-over, which explains, for example, how many litres of air can be expelled at any one time or how many heartbeats occur per day. Clearly, however, more than this is going on. The images and sounds are literally sensational, unexplainable, even revolting. This seems to be an obvious attempt by the programme-makers to stimulate a physical, sensual response. The audience's understanding of how air passes through the lungs or blood travels round the body is not, in any intellectual sense, necessarily enhanced by such images and sounds. Indeed, they may even be distracting. But these sequences inspire a fascination, an experience that is tactile, sticky and alarming. The effect is indeed kinetic, a simulated roller-coaster ride; the point of view is chaotic and orientation is all but impossible as the landscape is so unfamiliar. What is being learnt here cannot fully be articulated and it is not necessarily useful, but television is full of equally spectacular and apparently redundant experiences. The close-up seems to offer the possibility of an intimate understanding through vision, where we are encouraged to 'read off' emotions, facts or character through a detailed examination of different subjects and objects seen 'up close', although at the same time the presentation of the close-up itself may serve to distract from this process.

Graphic effects

The application of digital technology has increased the number and variety of visual effects available to the television programme-maker. I do not intend to list all the possible effects here, but will focus on the few which appear frequently on contemporary television.

Electronic effects – keying

The most common electronic effect on television is the technique of 'keying'. This practice involves the removal of a portion of the video image, creating a 'hole' that can then be filled by another image from elsewhere – a kind of virtual patch. Practically all television news presentation has, at some time, used keying to place an image, title or headline to one side of the newscaster's head. While this effect is now so familiar to most viewers that it seems relatively banal, it has quite a surprising effect on the construction of space within the frame. It can also allow for some quite bizarre images. It produces a very obviously 'faked' image, since it combines both a representation of 'real' space (the news anchor) and flat or 'graphic' space (a photograph, a headline or drawing). Perhaps because it is used in programmes that are understood to have a position of authority (such as newscasts and weather and sports reports), it is frequently the technique most often parodied or ridiculed elsewhere on television. Programmes which feature numerous out-takes of blunders, or 'bloopers', in which something has inadvertently gone awry, often include those moments where keying falters or 'drops out', leaving presenters stranded, with their virtual clothes removed.

Electronic effects – colour separation overlay

Colour separation overlay (or chroma key – an automatic self-matting process) is essentially similar to keying; it is a technique where a specific colour can be picked out automatically from a scene and removed. Most often this is the colour blue (although it can be yellow or green), but blue is most often used as blue hues are not generally found in human skin colour. One frequent use for this technique is in news interviews, for instance when an interviewee is speaking from an Edinburgh television studio but addressing a news anchor in London. In this situation the interviewee will be seated in front of a blue screen in the Edinburgh studio, with direct audio and (perhaps) visual links to the studio in London. When the interviewee's image is transmitted, however, the blue of the screen behind them will be removed and a familiar 'postcard' view of their general rather than specific location will be laid in – very often, for Edinburgh, this is a view of the famous castle. This background view, or 'wallpaper', can be a still or moving image, but it is usually both anonymous (people seen in the view are generally too far away to be recognizable) and, in a very general sense, a direct symbolic representation of the place the person is speaking from. What is significant here is that it is the place, rather than the individual's expertise or person, that is being established by the wallpaper. In the instance I have referred to, for example, Edinburgh Castle is designed to represent Edinburgh rather than the character of the person, their occupation or status.

In fictional television, colour separation overlay is frequently employed to enable characters to fly. Unfortunately, the effect can seem rather clumsy or cheap and is one of the notorious instances where the kinds of special effects achieved in cinema are obviously superior to those routinely found in television. The clumsiness of the resulting image arises for a number of reasons: first, it can be difficult to align the shadows and brightness of the 'floating image' with the background image; in addition, it is both time-consuming and expensive to provide details such as shadows; it is also very difficult to make sure that the perspective of the two images is the same – if it is not, the integration between the two will seem 'not quite right', even to the non-expert viewer. This means that the mismatch in origin (the difference between the matted image and the background) and the absence of visual cues that relate to depth and volume (shadows and perspective) result in image sequences that, while working as literal representations (the audience understands that the characters are meant to be flying), actually look rather flat and unrealistic. For instance, while seen as ground-breaking at the time, the 'flying' effects in the BBC's 1988 production of *The Lion, the Witch and the Wardrobe* seem to suffer from this: the characters seem to 'hover' rather than truly fly and there is a sense that you can somehow 'see the join' between the two sets of images.

Digital compositing

More recently, the integration of digital techniques into television production has allowed for the same effects to be achieved, but at a far higher quality than before. In *The Human Body*, for example, there are numerous sequences which use a range of different visual techniques and their presence was explicitly part of the programme's appeal. In fact, as is the case in many such landmark documentary series, a special episode, 'The Making of *The Human Body*', was produced to celebrate the achievements of the producer, director, art director and various specialist camera operators.

This episode pays particular attention to one memorable sequence in the third programme in the series, 'First Steps'. In this sequence we see the presenter of the series, Robert Winston, standing in what appears to be a large pool, or perhaps the ocean. The camera is static and presents Winston face-on, in mid-shot and close-up, entirely submerged and dressed in a diving suit and glass 'bubble' helmet. From this appropriate visual context, he describes a unique ability of very young babies, the 'diving reflex'. This reflex, only recently discovered, seemingly allows very young babies to effectively hold their breath and even briefly swim underwater without any apparent distress on their part. As he explains how fantastic this ability is, the audience suddenly sees a naked baby rising up from the bottom of the screen in front of Winston. The baby swims gracefully and calmly up towards the surface of the pool. As the sequence continues, other babies glide gently in and out of shot, passing in front of Winston, who reaches out gently to touch and occasionally guide them upwards.

It is undoubtedly a beautiful and, as Winston claims, perhaps a rather 'magical' sequence. It is achieved in part through a visual effect that works in a similar way to keying. What the process allows is for any background or clothed figures in blue to be removed. In the sequence described, the original blue of the water surrounding the babies as well as the blue suited figures of their mothers and helpers have been wiped automatically by a computer, so that the art director is able to lift the image of the baby. This 'silhouette' image is then placed onto another background image, made up of two further images: a 'clean water' background created by the art director and the shots of Winston in his diving suit in the original pool. The resulting image sequence, therefore, is a mixture of Winston in the pool, speaking to the camera, with a series of different babies 'matted' in to a screen that is actually a composite of several images. The smooth integration of the three different image layers is remarkable, and it does indeed appear as if Winston is in a large pool, with a small group of unattended 'water babies'. The 'magic' ability of the babies, therefore, is related implicitly to the 'magic' abilities of computers.

Unsurprisingly, special effects are frequently used in this way in science and nature documentaries – it is seen as somehow appropriate that specialist technology employed for such effects is used to demonstrate information that is often presented as awesome or magical. The wonder of the natural world or the complexity of scientific findings are matched and envisioned by the wonderful abilities of the camera operators, art directors and their visual technologies.

Increasingly, computer-generated composites are used to create entire environments (as I have already noted, they are used in US prime-time dramas such as *CSI* and *ER*). They are also common in music videos, music programmes and, as I have suggested, news presentation. Since the computer can deal effectively with a greater amount of fine detail and attend to the integration of lighting and perspective in a relatively cost-effective way, the 'amateur' look of electronic matting may be increasingly effaced. However, as we will see in my discussion of news presentation in the chapter on space, the effects may be more coherent and integrated, but may need time to become comprehensible and thus useful to the viewer. Currently, it seems to me that such effects can also initiate a rather disturbingly 'elastic' representation of space.

Split-screen

Another visual effect which has direct implications for the understanding of the 'space' of the television screen is the use of a split-screen. This technique refers to the division of the image into two or more individual 'screens', which allows for different image sequences to be played out within the same television frame. Until recently this was a technique that had been limited primarily to news, sport and some documentary presentation. However, with the success of the US drama serial, *24*, and, to a lesser extent, the British drama series, *Trial and Retribution*, split-screen is now used explicitly as an aesthetic device. However, as the effect of split-screen is particularly significant in relation to the organization and comprehension of space on television, I will return to this discussion in the final chapter on space.

Colour

The broadcast of colour transmission began earlier in the United States than in the United Kingdom. While a first attempt had been made by the network CBS to introduce colour television in 1951, the technological process used and the initiative itself were abandoned in the same year, and it was not until 1954 that NBC became the colourful 'peacock' network, transmitting colour programmes. The colour system used in the USA was named after the National Television Standards Committee (NTSC), made up of manufacturers of television sets (excluding CBS) and led by the Radio Corporation of America (RCA), the company which controlled NBC. Partly because colour involved the purchase of new sets and partly because other networks took time transferring to colour, 'colour television' was not really established in the USA until at least 1966, when CBS finally began broadcasting in colour. As Jeremy Butler (2002: 205–7) notes, there is an undoubted, but perhaps unsurprising, irony here, in that CBS was initially the pioneer of colour television, but became the last network to commit to colour broadcasting. The NTSC system has been notorious for the vagaries of its system, leading some commentators to cite it as 'Never Twice the Same Colour', and, as I have indicated, even today, many industry professionals see it as potentially damaging to the aesthetic quality and impact of their work.

In the UK, which uses a different system (PAL), there have been fewer problems, but the take-up of colour television was later and, perhaps, even slower. The first transmission of colour programming occurred on BBC Two on 1 July 1967 and went on to feature both home-grown 'spectaculars' such as the Wimbledon tennis tournament, and the transmission of coloured American imports such as *Star Trek*. However, since the move from black and white to colour in the UK was designed to coincide with a shift in the electronic frequency used to transmit the television signal (from VHF to UHF), so as to allow for more channels, it was some time before the transformation to colour could be completed. By 1972, only 17 per cent of households had colour television sets and it was not until the early 1980s that the last of the VHF transmitters was turned off, indicating that the take-up of colour television had at last been established. There are two important points here. First, of course, television was not always in colour. Second, the length of time that colour television took to become established could suggest that the take-up of newer technological innovations – such as digital television – may take longer than expected.

While I think it important to establish some historical background to the fact of colour television, my intent in this context is really to suggest why thinking about colour on television is important, referring not only to some specific instances of how colour is used, but also more generally to how certain categories of programmes have, at different times, developed colour palettes which the audience learns to recognize and associate with particular moods and atmospheres. Ultimately, the discussion of colour will lead into a discussion of lighting practices and how they affect the qualities and the colour of the image seen on television.

Black and white

Obviously, most early programmes made for television were made in black and white. As a child growing up in the 1970s, I predominantly watched black and white television; like many middle-class families, I imagine, when the original black and white television was superseded by a colour set in the living room, the black and white set was relegated for the 'children's use'. Yet, even for me, black and white television images have now become associated with a range of associations that they did not initially have.

First, black and white suggests that the images are 'old' or, in a different way, that they represent the 'past'. Black and white images may literally be old and represent the past, of course, because they are in fact archive images – old newsreel, photographs, old fiction films or television programmes. The incorporation of black and white images into contemporary programmes, therefore, calls on both their actual status (as real images of the past) and the way in which they can be used to *refer* to the past. For example, 'old' black and white images are commonly seen in documentaries about earlier periods of history, such as the two world wars, generally because these images were originally in black and white. At the same time, however, their black and white quality also incidentally confirms their status as historical documents. They are both *from* the past and also *refer* to the past stylistically. Inevitably, therefore, in order to suggest or refer to the 'past', black and white images are used in several ways. A familiar visual cliché in contemporary television programmes is to use black and white images to suggest that something that happened in the past is being remembered by an individual (as a subjective flashback or reconstruction). Alternatively, black and white images may also be produced in homage to a previous visual style, specifically in reference to genres associated with earlier eras of fiction film, such as film noir. The use of black and white in these instances is primarily driven by aesthetic considerations.

Since black and white images are associated with the perceived glamour of early Hollywood stars and genres, it is sometimes used by stars wishing to create an iconic status for themselves. Unsurprisingly, for instance, Madonna has used black and white images in several of her music videos (including 'Vogue', 'Cherish' and 'Justify my love') and she also, rather notoriously, insisted that she be filmed exclusively in black and white for a programme dedicated to her in the BBC's arts series, *Omnibus*. Since black and white images are now exceptional (in that they are no longer the way in which the television image is generally received), their distinctiveness has been used in a variety of contexts, in documentaries, advertisements and music videos, each of which use their lack of colour and other visual techniques to call up a variety of associations, ranging from documentary authenticity, such as the newsreel or surveillance video, to Hollywood glamour and 'fine art' photography, such as the glamour photography of the studio era or the landscape photography of Ansel Adams.

Making colour look like 'black and white'

One distinctive process that calls upon the 'authenticity' associated with black and white images, yet remains in colour, is a procedure operated in digital post-production but akin to a film-processing technique known as 'bleach bypass' or 'skip bleach'. In this process, the 'bleach bath' step in the processing of the film is left out, so that, in effect, a black and white image is superimposed over the colour image. This has a twofold effect: it increases the contrast (darkening shadows and, in some instances, the grainy effect of the film), while at the same time greying or reducing the saturation (intensity) of the colour. Famous recent examples of this process in feature film have been *Seven* and *21 Grams*. In television, the process has been achieved not through the manipulation of a film print but in a digital suite, most notably on the drama series, *CSI: Crime Scene Investigation*. Roy H. Wagner, the original director of photography on the first series, explains: 'We'd go into the timing bay, or digital darkroom, and really play with the negative. We were hypercrushing, overly saturating, going into the base of the film, pulling the grain back up and doing all the things you'd do in bleach-bypass without actually doing bleach-bypass' (Bankston 2001: 62).

Since the programme focuses on the often rather gruesome activities of a forensic science laboratory, the grainy, documentary effect was clearly tied to a desire to create a mood of seriousness or lend a sense of edginess to the series. A similar effect was also reproduced in the Second World War drama serial, *Band of Brothers*, most notably in the episode which involves the army unit liberating a concentration camp. In this instance, the hint of black and white that lurks in the image wishes to call on its historical associations, but it is also present, as in *CSI*, for stylistic reasons. As Wagner notes, in the case of *CSI*, the producer, Jerry Bruckheimer (known for producing many glossy Hollywood films, such as *Top Gun*), seemed, initially, at least, to want to make the series as distinctive and stylized as possible, to catch the audience's attention: 'Bruckheimer had demanded a show so stylistically different that a channel-surfing audience would be forced to stop and view the unusual looking images' (Bankston 2001: 64). Sadly, in Wagner's opinion, this desire for novelty did not last, and, once the series had become an established success, he claims: 'In time, pressure was exerted to create a more "beautiful light" approach to the photography' (Bankston 2001: 65). It is evident that later series of *CSI* do seem less harsh and that the light is generally softer and 'kinder', to the female actors in particular.

Beautiful light

'Beautiful light' can be loosely attributed to two qualities of the television image and its colour. The first of these, as implied by Roy Wagner, above, is that beautiful light makes the images look 'pretty'. Second, and obviously, it also refers to the practice of making the actors look 'beautiful'. Beautiful light is not necessarily 'naturalistic' lighting; in fact, colours may be enhanced artificially to give warmth and depth to the scene. Perhaps surprisingly, in the BBC's successful series of related stories set in a textiles factory, *Clocking Off II*, the producers explicitly wanted the series to look 'beautiful' and not 'grimy and industrial', as might be expected. The cinematographer, Peter Greenhalgh, explains how colour was a key part of the aesthetic for the show. Discussing the brief from the executive producer of the programme, Nicola Schindler, Greenhalgh (2001) claims:

> She was looking for a lot of colours, tight shots and moving images. This time I think we've gone a little further in trying to achieve an enhanced look. I've gone for a lot of out of focus colours. I would often just put a fluorescent tube with a colour on it, well in the back of the shot, just to give the depth.

Although the stories varied from week to week and incorporated both passionate and bleak accounts of life, love and death, the 'warmth' of the lighting and the surprising depth and complexity of the colour palette imbued the images with a quality and richness not normally associated with a contemporary ordinary setting on British television, thereby establishing a distinctive look for the series, which marked it as different from the less overtly stylized look and colour of the more familiar everyday pictured in popular British soap operas, such as *EastEnders* and *Coronation Street*. These programmes involve similar storylines (and employ some of the same actors), but present their images with less concern to create depth and (generally) with a less intense range of colour.

One series that mixes beautiful light with harsher atmospheric lighting is the teenage gothic/comedy drama, *Buffy the Vampire Slayer*. In this series, the producer and cinematographers have to negotiate the need to present the attractive, glamorous heroine, Buffy (Sarah Michelle Geller), in a beautiful light, with the need for lighting appropriate to the grotesque, evil vampires, monsters and other villains with whom the vampire slayer and monster killer commonly shares the frame. In an article in *American Cinematographer*, Michael Gershman, the cinematographer for the series, comments on the practicalities of lighting for this kind of dynamic (Oppenheimer 1999: 93):

> Standing on the catwalk, Buffy and another student were illuminated from below. 'This is where she finds out he's a bad guy,' says Gershman of the scene. 'I played the light pattern on him because he's a bad guy, but I didn't use it so much on her. I kept her pretty pure and clean.'

As with film lighting, in television drama there is often a conventional link between 'clean' lighting – lighting which throws little or no shadow on to the face, so that features seem less harsh and the face more beatific – and the implicit 'pureness' of the character and apparent prettiness of the actor. As most lighting production manuals suggest, many female and, often, leading male actors in television drama are photographed in a way that avoids hard, ageing shadows on the face. This may be achieved through the use of lights to 'fill' the shadows and by so-called 'sissy' boards, which can be used to bounce or reflect light attractively on to the face. Although the techniques used may be different, it is undeniable that lighting and colour can be used on television to make even unconventionally attractive actors seem beautiful. One actor who seems to me to have benefited from this kind of practice is David Caruso (initially in *NYPD Blue* and later in *CSI: Miami*). Caruso has a snub nose, frown lines and red hair and is therefore not conventionally attractive, let alone handsome; nonetheless, with good lighting he can be romantically appealing to women on- and off-screen.

High-key lighting and saturated colour

High-key lighting is strongly associated with television. This kind of lighting is produced when the main light sources are fixed at a set distance from the subjects and scene, with the main concern being visibility and legibility rather than 'atmosphere'. In interviews, some game shows, chat shows and other studio-based programmes, a fixed key light and a range of established fill lights often work to provide self-effacing lighting, which is deliberately non-atmospheric and apparently neutral. This kind of lighting, where colours are generally bright and saturated and subjects evenly lit, is associated strongly with 'daytime' television and conventional sitcoms, which are shot in a television studio. This kind of lighting is not naturalistic; it does not simulate the kind of light that would actually be provided by natural light sources, such as windows or table lamps, which may be part of the set. Instead, the purpose may be more akin to certain kinds of window or shop display, where every object and detail is made visible and attractive to the viewer; this kind of lighting has strong associations with consumption, and is therefore particularly obvious on home shopping channels, where objects are not simply on display but presented as commodities to be bought.

On these channels and on sitcoms, daytime magazine programmes and game shows, the use of high-key lighting may be driven by the need to keep production costs down. In terms of economics, having a fixed, and therefore reusable, lighting set-up makes this kind of practice cost-effective. Equally, in terms of aesthetics, the fixed and repetitive routines of actors/presenters from show to show, the limited movement of the cameras in a studio-bound set, as well as the small size of the television image and the relative lack of complexity and detail in the sets themselves, all allow for a pragmatic rather than adventurous approach to lighting. The look of high-key lighting was closely associated with television in general and not just the few genres in which it now commonly appears. Despite the fact that it is no longer universally applied within television (not even within specific genres such as the game show) the high-key look still seems to imply 'television'. For instance, in Peter Weir's film, *The Truman Show*, the saturated colour and the 'television look' of the lighting within Truman's everyday world is important, since at the beginning it makes clear to the movie audience that the everyday which Truman (Jim Carrey) inhabits is actually a totally fabricated television set – for his world is simply too perfect, too 'well lit', artificial, since it looks like 'television'.

The saturated colour and full illumination of this 'television look' is closely associated with, but actually pushed to its extreme by, American prime-time television dramas from the 1980s, such as *Dallas* and *Dynasty*. More recently, as John T. Caldwell suggests, from the late 1980s and the early 1990s (with series such as *Beauty and the Beast*, *Twin Peaks*, *ER* and *The X-Files*), atmospheric lighting and video-enhancing techniques became increasingly common and American television dramas directly imitated cinematic effects in their use of lighting and colour. Thus, what had previously seemed luxurious and expensive – the 'saturated', glossy look of earlier television dramas – actually began to seem 'cheap'. It was 'cheap' both because it was seen to be vulgar and because it was presumed to be related to the need to keep down costs. This cheapness is also supported by the fact that, as a look, it is now associated with daytime chat shows and magazine programmes, repeats of dramas from the 1970s and 1980s and contemporary, but deliberately kitsch, light-entertainment shows. When this kind of look does appear in contemporary drama it is usually as parody. In these instances, the saturated cartoon-like colours and flat lighting, which emphasize detail over depth, are a deliberate aesthetic choice. For instance, in *Married . . . with Children*, the sitcom's aesthetic is made to look deliberately cheap, vulgar and studio-bound; colours are over-saturated and the lighting is clearly artificial and flat – appropriately so, as the family is meant to be vulgar and the show an implicit parody of earlier sitcoms. More recently, the overblown antics of the characters in the British drama series, *Footballers' Wives*, are supported by the glossy, super-glamorized, almost cartoon look produced via the lighting, colour, setting and costumes employed by the programme. Again, this is entirely appropriate, as the show is both a homage to and a parody of the spectacular dramas of the 1980s and is making a direct visual connection to the glossy and trashy celebrity culture engineered via the equally brightly coloured, shiny and cheap print magazines, such as *Hello!* and *Heat*.

The high-key look on television can be seen to function on a continuum, from less extreme situations, such as *This Morning*, a daytime magazine show in which the colours are bright and the lighting rather flat, to the deliberately juicy, intensely saturated colour orchestrated for a children's drama such as *My Parents Are Aliens*. Children's television is perhaps one of the few areas on contemporary television where saturated colour and flat lighting still predominate, without the associations with cheapness and without ironic intent. One reason for this, perhaps, is that live-action programmes are competing with animation for the child's attention. Children's animation offers a fantastic array of bright, saturated colours. In shows such as *Powerpuff Girls*, *Teenage Mutant Ninja Turtles* and even *The*

Simpsons, the colour palette is so sticky and seductive, it is, perhaps, not ridiculous to see it as a televisual equivalent to the display of sweets in the pic 'n' mix at Woolworth's.

Texture

It might seem perverse to discuss texture in relation to the television image, as it is a quality associated with handcrafted artworks exhibiting tangible, tactile qualities, such as oil paintings or textiles. Like cinema, television can only really allude to texture through effects of lighting and movement. And like film, television directors may use filters, gauzes and other techniques, either to soften the image or to make it seem rougher, edgier, 'harsh', thereby creating the illusion of texture for the viewer. I have already discussed one way – the all but bleach bypass process, which uses a video technique to produce a grainy, textured image. It is in animation, however, that an interest in the texture of the television image is most evident.

Earlier animated series produced by Hanna-Barbera, such as *Scooby-Doo* and *The Hair Bear Bunch*, did not pay a great deal of attention to texture; the colours are evenly saturated, without shading, and the characters drawn with simple black lines outlining their figures and features. In the backgrounds, however, there is a definite attempt to create perspective and texture; ironically, this creates a slight sense of distortion, for it can seem as if the characters, who are clearly two-dimensional, are not fully integrated into the three-dimensional scene. In more recent series, such as *Dexter's Laboratory*, black outlines and two-dimensional characters are used in a much more stylized, integrated and knowing fashion. In this series, the characters and settings are caricatures, and their smooth outlines and flat saturated colours present a coherent comic-book aesthetic, but one which is articulated via a cinematic styling, where the fast-paced action is organized via a far more frenetic use of cuts, zooms and pans than would be expected in 'classic' Hanna-Barbera programmes. The illusion of texture here is smooth.

Other animated programmes subvert the smoothness of the majority of television animation: *Roobarb and Custard*, a short children's animation first produced for the BBC in the 1970s, has been celebrated for its unique texture, characterized by a shaky line and the way in which the colours of the characters seem to 'boil'. The wobbly effect occurred because fewer drawings per second were produced than was standard for animation (making the image jerk and lines apparently shift from moment to moment). In addition, the colour was hand-inked by the animator, with large colour marker pens. This made the colours of the characters – Roobarb the dog was a vivid green, Custard the cat a shocking pink – swirl and vibrate. This kind of animated look is now termed the 'Roobarb and Custard' effect; it occurred partly as a consequence of the limited budget and the small number of animators involved, and partly through deliberate design.

British television animation might be said to have a small but significant tradition of producing handcrafted animation that often lends the television image a unique, tangible texture. In particular, the work of Smallfilms, which produced a range of short animated programmes for children in the 1970s, seems to me to evoke a tangible texture in their work. Smallfilms was responsible for *Ivor the Engine*, *Bagpuss* and *The Clangers*, all of which were very popular on their initial screening and some of which – most notably *Bagpuss* – continue to be successful in the UK today, with merchandise such as soft toys and videos being produced and sold nearly 30 years after the initial transmission by the BBC. The handmade, tactile feel to the films was achieved partly because the films were made on very small budgets and therefore necessary economies were made with the filming process. But these were also aesthetic choices to do with the material used to make the sets and the puppets themselves. The 'Clangers', a charming race of aliens who lived on their own planet, were hand-knitted, even slightly shabby looking. As they were filmed in a rather stuttering stop-motion movement, the Clangers' appearance and style of movement inadvertently made the process of filming explicit. As in most stop-motion animation, the movement was achieved by the animator physically manipulating the models/puppets between each frame, so that once the film is screened at a normal speed, the models appear to move of their own accord. In *The Clangers*, the simple, slightly amateur look of the film means that this process is almost perceptible. What then becomes implicit or is evoked via this process is touch; in a sense, the touch of the film-maker, which is here somehow still 'in' the film, substitutes for and evokes the impossible, but imagined, touch of the viewer. The sense of touch is further enhanced by the fact that the Clangers are clearly hand-knitted, homemade and fuzzy from being handled and 'played with'. While this might seem fanciful, it is in fact quite common for animators to feel that making the animation 'rough' or deliberately clumsy can evoke a sense of tactility for the viewer and lend a feeling of 'realism' to the animation itself. For example, Richard Morris, a CGI animator, describes how he deliberately engineered elements which he called 'anti-3D' (Stout 2002). Discussing his work on the BBC series, *How to Build a Human*, Morris claims:

> 'I have never been a fan of clean and perfect imagery, so I often try to roughen stuff up in different ways,' he explains. 'For *How to Build* I've written devices to alter some geometry's shading or lighting on the odd frame and also make the floating particle matter jig about and appear alive. Some people might see it and think it's CGI artifacts but it's deliberately there to make the images more genuinely realistic.'

Here, the potentially super-smooth, fluid animation of the computer is deliberately infected by an almost imperceptible human touch, which is designed to make the animation itself seem more real, more tangible to the viewer.

Of course, the kind of tactility I am alluding to here is not unique to television; certain specialist animated films, notably those produced by the Brothers Quay or Jan Svankmajer, also evoke this kind of response. What is interesting, however, is that series such as *Bagpuss* and *The Clangers* were not intended as avant-garde interventions and actually stemmed from an established tradition of charming but rather shabby-looking puppets and models on British children's television (including much-loved characters such as Muffin the Mule and Andy Pandy, as well as the inhabitants of Smallfilms' earlier production, *Poggles' Wood*). These series' limited *mise-en-scène*, visible strings or stuttery stop-motion techniques, perversely seemed to connect with their audience because of, rather than despite, their apparent limitations. This aesthetic continued into the 1980s in series such as *Button Moon* (where puppets were made of ordinary kitchen implements such as wooden spoons) and in stories produced for *Storymakers* (where, again, certain puppets are clearly made from kitchen sponges, brushes and old socks).

It might be tempting to see this tradition as related to a strain of British eccentricity, but, arguably, the tactility of puppets and animation is also present in some aspects of American television. Most notably, the adult animation series, *South Park*, although produced via computer animation, works hard to deliberately evoke its origin as a crude cut-and-paste 'cut-out' animation, made by the series creators, Trey Park and Matt Stone. The cardboard cut-out look of the background and the deliberately economical representation of characters, made out of a few simple shapes and resolutely 2D, recalls, for me at least, memories of Fuzzy Felt kits I played with as a child. In these kits, still sold today, simple, coloured, felt figures of animals and a limited number of felt shapes could be temporarily stuck and restuck wherever you wanted on a flat, felt-covered board that was also supplied. *South Park*'s allusion to this very basic, 'hands-on', childish aesthetic is appropriate to a series which features the extraordinarily foul-mouthed adventures of a group of eight-year-old kids. By using, but also parodying, a visual practice from childhood itself, the series evokes childish games and thus childhood itself, only to subvert this sentiment deliberately for comic effect. In a far less aggressive manner, and for entirely different reasons, I would argue that the American pre-school series, *Sesame Street*, is also successful with its audience because it evokes a tactile response. The series is well known for its eclectic mix of drawn and model animation and live-action shorts, and its use of various fuzzy Muppets and real people. Designed to teach pre-school children about numbers and letters, it draws its viewers in via an abundant sensual experience that emphasizes its tactile qualities as well as visual and aural excitement.

Conclusion

The television image is interesting and worthy of study for its own sake because it is both like and unlike the cinematic image. While it does seem that the television image is unlike the film image in that it is more likely to be functional than beautiful, as I hope I have made clear, it is also sometimes the very restrictions of television – related to budget, technology, and even the conventions of television itself – which produce engaging and evocative images. At points in my discussion, I have indicated that producers and cinematographers working in television are keen to reproduce cinematic effects, but do so within the confines of what the technology and their smaller budgets can facilitate. In other ways, the television image is entirely unlike the film image and can integrate a wide range of visual practices, styles and techniques, without confusing or alienating the viewer. Television, far more commonly than film, makes use of images as evidence and thus expects its audience to accept that the image frequently carries a burden of truth and that, in essence, some things can be known just because they are seen.

In the final section of this chapter I want to produce a case study of *CSI: Crime Scene Investigation* as it rather conveniently articulates, at different points, all these aspects of the television image. First, it is a series that very explicitly reflects the increasing confidence of television producers to imitate cinema. The visual styling of *CSI* is clearly led by the cinematic credentials of its producer, Jerry Bruckheimer, and its main director, Danny Cannon. At the same time, however, in its use of extreme close-ups and image manipulation, the series also relies on the way in which television commonly blurs the distinction between images as evidence and as illustration.

Case study: *CSI: Crime Scene Investigation*

> *There is an intimacy to murder and at CSI we owe it to the families to face that intimacy. I approach with a true reverence. I don't look away. I don't let the camera look away.*
>
> —Ann Donahue, executive producer *CSI* (LaTempa 2002)

CSI: Crime Scene Investigation is a prime-time US drama which follows the activities of a team of forensic experts or 'criminalists' in Las Vegas. Their purpose is to assist investigations into cases of murder or suspicious accidental death. The team is led by Gil Grissom ('Gruesome' Grissom, played by William Petersen) and Catherine Willows (played by Marg Helenberger). They are supported by Warwick Brown (Gary Dourdan, the only black member of the major characters), Nick Stokes (played by George Eads) and Sarah Sidle (played by Jorja Fox). The three other major characters are the police detective, Jim Brass (played by Paul Guilfoyle), the coroner, Dr Robbins (played by disabled actor, Robert David Hall) and the most prominent character among the small group of laboratory analysts, Greg Sanders (played by Eric Szmanda). The basic format of the programme remains the same from week to week – sometimes one, but more often two cases are initiated at the start of each episode. Most episodes begin with one of the crimes being played out before the audience, although it is usually not possible to see the perpetrator(s); alternatively, the episode begins as someone discovers a body or body part. Generally, the team will separate into two smaller groups and resolve the two cases in tandem – often with Catherine leading one sub-group and Grissom leading the other; very occasionally, one of the team may work 'solo'. In many instances, one team member from each group will be seen to lead the investigation because they have a special interest in the case or are directed to do so by Grissom. While most of the crimes are solved in the course of one episode, certain aspects of the narrative, in particular the brief insights we have into the characters' private lives (Warwick's experience as an ex-compulsive gambler, Catherine's status as a single mother and ex-exotic dancer, Grissom's increasing deafness and eventual cure), return from week to week either to inform characters' responses to certain stories or to add increasing colour to their back story.

Key aspects of the show include the investigation of the 'crime scene', which may be any location, including a city street, a suburban living room, a casino, a bar, a restaurant kitchen and, on one occasion, the interior of an airplane. The team members identify and collect a range of different kinds of evidence – bodies, body parts, clothing, hair, dust, bullets, insects, blood, fingerprints, footprints, DNA samples – and take them in to the laboratory to analyse. The series therefore features extensive scenes of characters looking at these items of evidence, as well as other visual evidence, such as photographs, surveillance footage, X-rays and DNA charts, along with phone and bank records read from computer screens. Other key sequences include reconstructive, illustrative flashbacks in which one or more of the team presents their view of events. In addition to this already eclectic visual mix, there is an extensive use of prosthetics, models and CGI in sequences most often associated with the autopsy of the victim(s), where 'snap-zoom' (accelerated zoom) sequences apparently recreate the entry of bullets, knives or even blood cells into the body. These sequences are closely associated with the series and are called '*CSI* shots' by the producers, yet in many ways they echo the visceral close-up and bodily intrusion I have already discussed in the BBC's documentary series, *The Human Body*.

The series was initiated by writer Anthony Zuiker and the producer, Jerry Bruckheimer, who is well known for his slick, high-action feature films, including *Black Hawk Down*. Other influential production personnel include the director/producer Danny Cannon, a British director also known for his work on spectacle films such as *Judge Dredd*. William Petersen, who is both producer and lead actor, is known for his feature film work, particularly for his performance as the troubled detective in *Manhunter*. The series also has two key female producers, Carol Mendelsohn and Ann Donahue. The empirical ground for the programme stems from the information provided by Elizabeth Devine, an ex-criminalist from the LA County Sheriff's Department, who works as a writer and technical consultant. The series is part-funded and transmitted by the CBS network in the United States and co-produced by Alliance Atlantis. (In the UK the series is transmitted by Channel 5.) The initial series, which began transmission in the USA in autumn 2000, has been so successful that, like other US crime series, such as *Law & Order*, it has initiated a franchise; this currently includes *CSI: Miami* (starring David Caruso) and *CSI: New York*, which launched in the United States in the autumn 2004.

As should be evident from my brief description of the series, it is an interesting programme for many reasons: as an example of the relationship between feature film producers and network television; for its ethnic and gender representation; and for its interesting mix of contemporary visual techniques and modern science with 'old-fashioned' storytelling. As John Griffiths (2002: 98) suggests in his profile of the series in *Emmy*, while the setting and presentation may be contemporary, the elements of the narrative are old-fashioned:

> Grissom and gang are the archetypal comic-book good-guys, who, despite lacking supernatural powers, are more *X-Men* than *X-files*. Just when things look dour, elements of day-saving *Quincy* and *Kojak* pop up. 'We're all TV babies,' says Petersen . . . 'So it's fun to be in a show that's kind of a throwback.'

However, in this context I am primarily interested in the visual aspects of the programme: the impact of its visual style and its use of different kinds of image. In relation to my previous discussion, I will explore how the series' mixture of images which *dramatize* with images that (appear to) *demonstrate* produces a particularly televisual aesthetic.

Technological basis

The series is shot primarily on Super 35 mm film, with some 16 mm film used for particular sequences. This is not unusual, as most prime-time American drama is shot on film and then, like *CSI*, transferred to high-definition digital video. The choice of 35 mm from the very beginning does indicate that the series was established as having high production values and a substantial budget, possibly secured via the clout of an established film producer such as

Bruckheimer. It might surprise fans to learn, for example, that the successful cult teen drama, *Buffy the Vampire Slayer*, was shot on 16 mm for its first two series, with 35 mm only being used from series three. The greater expense of 35 mm and its associated prestige was only awarded when *Buffy* had established itself as an ongoing ratings success.

In *CSI*, the telecine and post-production process is organized by Encore Hollywood, who have established a VIP (video-inter-positive) process, designed to avoid the problems of film-to-tape conversion, which can have adverse effects on the range of colour and level of contrast that can be retained and manipulated in post-production. The VIP process, arguably, has allowed the series to preserve a more cinematic palette and texture, as well as encouraging experimentation with colour. *American Cinematographer* (Bankston 2001: 63) quotes Gareth Cook, Encore's senior colourist, who claims: 'Nothing is compressed at all. It's a full, open range, much like the film negative itself, without any clipping or crushing. VIP also gave Roy [Wagner, the original director of photography for the series] and me the ability to take [the look] in any direction we want to go.'

The series is distinguished by a range of post-production digital video effects, including the all but bleach bypass effect I discussed earlier. In general terms, however, the use of 35 mm does ensure that the series' visual image provides a relatively rich, textured and 'deep' look, as opposed to other television programmes, such as studio-bound, videotaped sitcoms or magazine shows characterized by images that are flatter and less textured. This does not mean that *CSI* looks more 'realistic' in terms of its image effect, however. In fact, the use of colour, digital effects and lighting often mean that *CSI* creates an excessively expressionistic and even fantastic impression. Thus, while the use of 35 mm in *CSI* indicates that the quality of the image is important to the series, the fact that the image is then so explicitly manipulated in post-production rather uncannily replicates the manipulation of the visual evidence by the characters in the series itself.

Functions of the image

Images which dramatize

Since *CSI* is a fictional programme, arguably all the images presented function as images which dramatize. Like many drama series, the geography of the images is often deceptive. It is established by dressed theatrical images, which act symbolically and are not generally actual images of the places, spaces and people they appear to represent. Apparently set in Las Vegas, the majority of the series is actually shot in the Los Angeles suburb of Santa Clarita and in studios there. There is, perhaps surprisingly, little location shooting in Las Vegas itself. The relatively anonymous suburb of Santa Clarita is therefore dressed to look like an equivalent suburb in Las Vegas. While the shooting in Las Vegas itself is kept to a minimum for budgetary reasons, prestige episodes or key sequences are shot on location. In many instances, to maximize their impact, these are shot at night, as the neon lights of the hotels and casinos of Vegas are not only key indicators that we are, in fact, in Vegas (and nowhere else), but also fantastic for stylistic reasons – full of colour, glamour, sleaze and visual impact.

Key interior locations – such as the offices and laboratories of the CSI team and, in particular, the coroner's autopsy room/morgue – are studio sets which feature in nearly every episode. The lighting is almost always non-naturalistic and dictated by the dominant emotion in the scene. These sets are characterized by large amounts of glass, chrome, metal and other reflective surfaces, and nearly all the rooms either have glass walls or large windows and glass doors. This means that rooms can be seen from other rooms and characters and extras can be seen to pass behind the main action in the foreground. There are two dominant themes which underwrite the series which are linked to this *mise-en-scène*. First, the layers of glass produce the sense of rooms within rooms, and this enables the directors and cinematographers to set up three or four layers within the scene, thus creating depth. This sense of both depth and transparency at a visual level neatly echoes the push towards 'transparency' and truth in the crime-solving narrative. Second, since they are constantly looking through glass themselves, viewers are reminded that the notion of 'looking' itself is a purposeful action. This is supported by the numerous instances in which we also look at characters looking through windows (or the two-way mirror in the interrogation room) at suspects and victims. 'Looking' as a scientific activity, as examination, whether at X-rays, or through a variety of lenses and with a variety of different screens, is implicit in the *mise-en-scène*. The only room not to feature a large window is the morgue, yet this room is dominated by reflective metallic surfaces and a large light screen at one end, where X-rays are posted. So, like the rest of the laboratory, the morgue is a place of reflection as well as examination.

Within the CSI headquarters, the other most significant room is Grissom's office, which is markedly less open and transparent in its layout and design than the other rooms. In Grissom's office there is, instead, a strong sense of ordered chaos: metallic shelves are filled with specimen jars; there is a fridge with mysterious liquids and yet more glass jars; photographs and posters featuring insects adorn the walls, as well as preserved moths in frames. It is clearly designed to suggest the repressed 'mad scientist' aspect of Grissom. However, his office also recalls the rooms of the serial killer, John Doe, in David Fincher's film, *Seven*, which similarly presented a labyrinth of a meticulous yet crazy display of body parts, photographs, receipts and lists. While it is never indicated that Grissom is potentially a murderer, it is evident that the notion of Grissom mirroring the personality traits of an intellectual serial killer like Thomas Harris' character, Hannibal Lecter, is being played upon here. Grissom, like Lector, is a classical music fan, and Grissom's fascination with insects relates to the moths which are central to the plot of *The Silence of the Lambs*. This doubling of Grissom is again made evident by the occasional storyline which features an elusive serial killer from the first series, who may or may not have had a forensics background. The suggestion of a 'dark shadow' for Grissom is also an indirect homage to the way in which in the original forensic detective, Sherlock Holmes, also had a criminal nemesis – Professor Moriarty – who acted as a distorted mirror to Sherlock Holmes' own scientific intelligence.

Images which demonstrate

As *CSI* is a fictional programme, none of the potentially demonstrative images employed – X-rays, film footage, photographs and microscope slides – are in fact documentary images, as they have all been carefully fabricated for the series. Much of the publicity related to the show insists that these images are carefully constructed so as to seem realistic and authentic. At the same time, within the series, the images are often pushed beyond their actual limits or potential as visual representation. The status of these demonstrative images as visual evidence within the narrative means that they are manipulated quickly and effectively by the characters in ways that, if not always impossible, are, in many instances, implausible. Visual analysis and manipulation of the image is necessarily achieved rather unrealistically within hours or days (and minutes in terms of programme time). Images are often manipulated in ways that are only really possible with much more information or, indeed, more images than appear to be available. Yet these demonstrative images depend upon the audience's willingness to award them both authority and a fantastic amount of information, so that they act convincingly as evidence rather than as illustration. This authority is also awarded to other animated visual sequences in the programme that are clearly artificial – such as the snap-zoom sequences I mentioned above – which similarly borrow their credibility from their increasing use in medical illustration and scientific documentaries.

There are so many different ways in which images are used to 'demonstrate' in *CSI* that a full analysis would be beyond the scope of this limited case study; however, I will use the manipulation of the 'image as evidence' in one particular episode from the third series, 'Snuff', as an example. The episode contains an 'A' story (the murder of a porn actress on film, hence the title 'Snuff', as in the notorious 'snuff film') and a 'B' story (the murder of a young Down's syndrome man, whose body is initially discovered acting as a colony site for red fire ants). It is the investigation of the 'A' story, which inevitably involves the manipulation of the pornographic film image, that most interests me here.

In 'Snuff', the 16 mm film which pictures the murder of the pornographic actress is both a visual and a material artefact, brought to the attention of the CSI team by the film processor. As the episode begins, we first see the film image reversed, as the television camera (and thus the television audience) approaches the image from a position behind a projection screen, which Grissom, Catherine and the film processor (played by a young black actress) are standing in front of. This is the only time in the episode that we see the film as a film, and here, film's difference from television and from video is made clear as we see it as a projected moving image, creating an evocative and disturbing space, made up of the light and shadows that play around the room and over the characters' faces. While the television audience does indeed get to see the murder (though not the initial pornographic activity), the restless movement of the television camera throughout the scene, between and around the projector and the screen, interrupts the potential of a cinematic experience taking place for the television audience. For the television audience, the important elements in the scene are that the action takes place in an unidentified hotel room; that we witness Catherine's emotional response of both disgust and dismay; and that we can confirm Grissom's detached observation that since the blood seen on the lens of the film camera (and hence on the film image) is streaking, it must be 'real' blood.

The next time we see the film, it is as a material object being examined for fingerprints in the lab by Sarah, who is wearing a lab coat, which thus identifies her at this moment as the disinterested, objective scientist. In this way, the disturbing power of the visual images we have just seen are reduced as we literally witness Sarah's control of the material of the image. Interestingly, by this point, the audience knows that Grissom, who was meant to lead this investigation, has been drawn away into the 'B' story, leaving Catherine and Sarah to predominate in this storyline, although Warwick – the most 'sensitive' and hence, perhaps, 'feminized' of the male characters – also helps. This feminization of the image, and also of the detective process itself, is made implicit by the way in which Sarah observes that the film is made of a similar material to Jell-O (jelly in the UK), an incongruous aside that domesticates the object (despite the fact that a regular audience would be aware that Sarah is not 'domestic' at all). This move from an emphasis on the power *of* the visual image to a display of power *over* the visual image is a recurrent shift in the programme, and the stylistic and thematic aspects of this are absolutely integral to one another and to the series. One reason for this may be that the stylistic excess, the gore and spectacle of the programme, is legitimated by the fact that the images are contained by the process of examination, by their status as evidence, enabling the audience to look without compunction, since to look away might mean missing vital information.

Sarah's examination proves fruitless, however, and the film image is then digitized so that it can be manipulated, in the first instance by a male technician and then by Warwick, so that it can be 'read' for clues. A rather implausible sequence including reverse polarization, zooms, close-ups and a triangulation – using a barely perceptible image of a well-known Vegas landmark, the Stratosphere Tower, which can be seen from the window in the hotel room – enable the CSI team to locate the hotel in which the film was shot, and to determine that the man engaged in sex with the victim has, rather fortuitously, a large mole on his neck. This kind of manipulation and compulsive scrutiny of the image is not unusual within *CSI* and it directly relates to the repetitive use of the close-up in documentary that I discussed earlier. However, this process goes one step further than the scrutiny of the still photograph, and literally seems to go 'into' the image as if it were a three-dimensional space. While theoretically possible, this kind of manipulation is actually difficult to achieve. As the image is two-dimensional, even with very high resolution, it must eventually break down into points of light and shade. To actually 'reach in' to the space of the photograph the computer would need a whole range of photographs or film frames from numerous perspectives. In addition, any process of analysis which generates information via speculation (projection) always involves potentially mistaken interpretation, both by the visual system and the analyst. The contested nature of visual interpretation is never referred to within the programme – the pictures are always (eventually) legible even to the amateur sleuth watching at home. What is obscured here, in our desire to see the evidence in the image, is that seeing itself always involves interpretation and is never a neutral, objective activity.

The next time we see the film image it is again being handled as an artefact and not seen as a film. One frame from the film has been blown up into an A4-size transparency and this enables the CSI team to identify the crime scene by holding the image up against three different windows in the hotel (again it is Sarah who finds the right window and thus the right room). Here the film image is made to act as a substitute for another visual representation – the map – and the Stratosphere Tower, helpfully framed by the window, becomes the 'X' which marks the spot. It then seems as though this storyline will come to a quick conclusion as, conveniently, the security guard who has let the CSI team in to the abandoned hotel is seen to have the tell-tale mole on his neck. Unfortunately, while he does admit to having sex with the actress, he claims to have left the room while she was still alive. Returning to the digitized image, the CSI team discover that, in fact, the man who commits the murder is visibly taller than the guard and that there must have been two men.

Since he, too, can be seen, Catherine rather hopefully suggests that, 'This is it – that's our guy', but Warwick is more disillusioned and claims that the visual image has been exhausted in terms of useful evidence. He can find no convenient marks or tattoos for the second man and laments, 'That's it. The film picks up everything there is to see'. This is a fascinating statement, which deliberately reasserts this episode's and the series' explicit faith in the potential of the visual image, just when that image is acknowledged or appears to have a limit as to what can be seen. Luckily, however, Catherine asserts that since the film itself is made out of a 'short end' (that is, a 'cut-off' from film initially used by a mainstream film-maker that has been sold on to smaller companies, such as pornographic film-makers), there will be a 'roll-out' frame – a final frame or a 'hot' frame – that will have been overexposed as the camera is left running as the film runs out. This generates the possibility that there is always something 'more' to be seen. Catherine and Sarah then search for and find the final few frames of film. Once again, the image is digitized and this allows for the discovery of a lamp in the room, which, once retrieved from the hotel, is found still to have traces of the killer's saliva (and hence, apparently, his DNA) on a bulb which has been changed.

From this point, what can be seen in the film image becomes subsidiary to the evidence of DNA and, ultimately, a strain of HIV passed from the actress to the killer as she is stabbed and her blood spray goes into his eyes. However, the film image reappears in two other forms: as a series of slides projected onto a card for Catherine and Warwick to examine and as a photograph, brandished in front of the killer (who is the film-maker). Finally, the climactic, 'blood spatter' frames from the film appear on a slide again, when, repeating her initial encounter with the film itself, Sarah holds up the image to the light. The film image, then, even when it is not used directly as evidence, lurks within the frame of the television image and is returned to compulsively. The notion of an image within the image, and a frame within a frame (and its visual allusion to a puzzle to be solved, as in the concept of 'boxes within boxes'), is played on in this episode, although it recurs throughout the series. In this episode, the image as evidence always appears within a frame (a film screen, a computer console, as a slide) and, therefore, rarely occupies the entirety of the television screen. Characters, too, are frequently 'framed' within the frame of the image, most notably, perhaps, when, in a long shot, we see Warwick, Catherine and Sarah composed within a low arch that is part of the architecture of the hotel room. This effect is also carried over to the 'B' story. For example, at the start of a sequence featuring Grissom and his anthill cadaver, the camera approaches Grissom – who is in the process of boiling the skull clean – through a door window, so that he is initially framed within a large black border, recreating a cinematic 'iris' effect.

The tension between the power of the image and a power over the image is therefore the continual tease of the programme and this episode in particular. There is clearly a complete fascination with the image itself and, as I will discuss briefly below, the programme's own stylistic excess encourages this kind of seduction. At the same time, the ruthless manipulation of the image, and its fragmentation and literal reproduction in different forms, seems to imply that the CSI team and, vicariously, the television audience are in control of it. The demonstrative image is a site of fascination and disgust, but the real frisson of the image (can we believe our eyes?) is safely contained within a narrative intent on deciphering the image and thus obliterating its power to produce shock or dismay.

Qualities

Composition

Framing the image (1) – the aspect ratio

Like many prestige American dramas, CSI is transmitted in the USA in a 4:3 ratio, although the borders of this image are protected for potential future transmission on a wider aspect ratio (16:9). This is not surprising in a series that, in terms of its content and narrative structure, has obvious potential for long-term syndication. As I have indicated, each episode is self-contained in that at least one, if not both storylines are concluded, with the crimes being solved, by the end of the programme. While there are some aspects of continuing narrative (character sub-plots) and continuity issues (Catherine's hairstyles and the fact that Grissom grows a beard in series three), which might trouble the regular viewer if episodes were not shown chronologically, it is entirely feasible that individual episodes could be repeated in any order for many years to come. In the UK, Channel 5 already pairs earlier episodes with programmes from the most recent series. The investment in a wider aspect ratio is therefore likely to be a sensible tactic, particularly as it can already be seen by viewers who purchase the DVDs. Stylistically, however, it also meets with the cinematic ambitions of the programme's makers. Yet, as I will indicate in my discussion of shots, while there is a sense that CSI does feel cinematic, in terms of its composition it is actually indebted to televisual precedents such as the music video, the science documentary and the medical drama. While there are, in any one series, several 'set-piece' locations and crane shots that reach cinematic proportions, the signature visual style of the show is the depth of the shots rather than the breadth or widescreen scale of the image. In particular, the use of the snap-zoom shot as one of the central recurring visual motifs of the programme emphasizes both the graphic and close-up qualities of the images and promotes depth rather than breadth.

Framing the image (2) – choosing the shots

Establishing shot

As I have already discussed, CSI makes use of several different moving aerial views of Las Vegas. These recur but are relatively diverse in terms of content; some are shot in daylight, others at night, and all are distinguished by the use of a saturated colour. A typical sequence might reveal a blanket of whitish suburbs, dominated by a parched orange/yellow desert feel, or a more familiar version of the Las Vegas cityscape, featuring the famous hotels and casinos, lighting up the night sky. These bumpers are edgy and dynamic, made more so by the fact that they are sometimes speeded up or jump-cut and accompanied by an initial white flash. While this flash adds to the visual excitement of these sequences, it also reminds the viewer of a camera flash, recalling, perhaps, the numerous photos taken at the crime scene, a visual cue which again insists upon the notion of looking and the importance of the image to the programme. Aside from these separate sequences, individual scenes often begin with an establishing shot, which is frequently taken not from above, but at eye-level; the camera appears almost to pause and then creep up on the action, moving towards the characters or peering round corners. The intimate, eavesdropping nature of the camera as it moves into each new scene is entirely appropriate to the narrative, which wants to draw the viewer in to a crime-solving plot. While the overall pace of the programme is relatively mobile and fluid, since it frequently employs steadicam shots and some jump-cut sequences, the speed of the show is noticeably slower than either the whip-pan excitements of *NYPD Blue* or the whirling dance of the camera in *ER*. For the most part, the movement of the camera is intimate and non-expressionistic since, necessarily, the 'real world' being pictured needs to be distinguished from the highly stylized 'flashback' sequences, where the camera circles and tilts in a much wilder fashion.

Long shot

Like *The West Wing*, *CSI* commonly employs long shots of characters talking to one another as they walk together and approach the camera down different corridors. In most instances, however, once the scene is fully underway, the shot pattern is resolutely in mid-shot or close-up. Of the regular directors, Danny Cannon does occasionally break up this pattern by shifting back to a long shot, intermittently, in the middle of dialogue which is otherwise framed in mid-shot or close-up, although this tends to be only when the characters are static and carefully composed. In relation to the plot, these brief jumps back to a long shot often serve to imply (or remind the viewer) that the characters are being watched by other interested parties on the scene, who may or may not be able to hear what is being said. Elsewhere in the programme, long shots are often used to create a carefully composed tableau – the scene I have previously described in the hotel bedroom in 'Snuff' is one such example. In most instances, however, the long shot as tableau is employed at the end of a scene, and, frequently, CSI team members will be photographed in silhouette, standing in thoughtful or semi-action poses. In other circumstances, the long shot is used in a montage, which allows the audience to watch as a lone member of the CSI team examines a crime scene. The montage of long shots which dissolve fluidly into one another, unlike the tableau, often stands alone as a sequence and is generally shown without dialogue, accompanied instead by the typically edgy urban dance music used frequently in this series of *CSI*. In the opening episode from series three, 'Revenge is best served cold', there is an extended sequence showing Nick, in long shot, examining an abandoned airstrip for the traces of a car race that ended in murder. Set against the blinding haze of the desert horizon, Nick's figure is seen in silhouette in a sequence of long shots that are edited together to provide a visual ellipsis in time to cover the process of investigation. While, on the one hand, this shot might seem cinematic (the lone cowboy lawman – Nick is Texan – isolated in the vast desert), the contemporary feel to the music which pushes the edit along actually makes the sequence more akin to a music video (the music for this sequence, appropriately, is 'Giving up the ghost' by DJ Shadow). Nick's figure also moves down towards the camera, rather than across the screen, so that the visual trajectory again emphasizes depth rather than breadth. The sequence is also significant because it allows and encourages the audience to look. Simply put, much of *CSI*, here and elsewhere, is about *looking* – the audience *looks* at the investigators as they *look* for clues. Clearly, this emphasis on looking as a purposeful action ties in with the organization of the *mise-en-scène* that I have described in the section on images which dramatize.

Close-up

As in most television dramas, there is a move toward the close-up shot of the face of characters in nearly every scene involving dialogue. In *CSI*, this often culminates in a shot-reverse-shot sequence between the perpetrator and one of the CSI team. However, as I have already indicated, in *CSI* the close-ups can be much more intimate than this. In the '*CSI* shot' (or snap-zoom), a close-up sequence traces a path into the body; mostly traumatic, the camera seemingly travels into the body via a range of different orifices – an ear canal, a bullet or knife wound. Sometimes this intimacy is further increased as the image then shifts into a CGI sequence, showing, perhaps, blood cells moving along veins. In 'Snuff', for example, we have a visual demonstration of how the infected blood of the porn actress goes into the eye of the killer, and we then witness the killer's own blood cells literally being overcome by the HIV virus. The status of the shot within the show is such that it was awarded its own 'bonus feature' on the DVD set for the third series. What is interesting about this short film, which illustrates how the snap-zoom sequences are produced via a mixture of prosthetics, slow-motion capture photography and CGI, is the way in which all of those involved emphasize their concern with 'authenticity', but also acknowledge that this may be compromised due to issues of time and budget. In the film, the only noted origin for the sequences is the kitsch science-fiction film, *The Fantastic Voyage*, in which a ship is made small enough to be injected into a human blood vessel. As in the film, the viewer of *CSI* is being taken on a visual journey, although in this instance (unlike in the film), the entry into the body is accompanied by superbly visceral sound effects, which slurp, pound and hiss as the camera seemingly enters the body. The energy of these sequences is akin to the excitement of the scientific roller-coaster ride also seen in *The Human Body*, and, as with *The Human Body*, there is an implicit understanding that, by seeing more, the viewer will know more.

While the snap-zoom shot is a special effect that perhaps makes *CSI* distinct from other television crime series, the penetration of the body is actually increasingly common as a set piece in public science displays. The most successful exhibit in the notorious Millennium Dome at Greenwich in the UK, for example, was the 'journey' through the human body, where visitors could actually travel through versions of human organs, accompanied by appropriate lighting and sound effects. The acquiring of knowledge is more than pictured or explained, but felt, as a visual and aural 'rush'. The television image is having it both ways, as it were: the almost pornographic penetration implies intimacy and subjectivity, while, at the same time, the point of view of the camera is apparently 'objective' as it follows the inanimate objects into the human body as if it were a scientific or medical exhibit. Many sequences begin with Grissom or the coroner explaining what they think has happened, but once we 'board the ride' the interpretation stops and we are apparently innocent witnesses to the evidence that is before our very eyes.

Graphic effects

As should be clear from my description, *CSI* contains numerous graphic effects, both within the signature snap-zoom sequences and in the creation of more elaborate and difficult locations. What is intriguing about the use of graphic effects is that, especially in the '*CSI* shots', they seldom make up the whole image and, in fact, what is often seen is a layered image, built out of composite parts – prosthetics, slow-motion photography and CGI. Thus, the 'layering' of the image in *CSI* is part of its technical as well as its stylistic design. While the spectacle and obvious artifice of many of these sequences would seem to go against the grain of the programme's ambition to be realistic and authentic, in fact, like the science documentary, the cleverness of the effects supports and celebrates the 'cleverness' of the criminalists and their infallible optical instruments.

Colour

Perhaps the most fantastic stylistic element of the show is its use of colour. As I have already explained, *CSI* relies for much of its look on post-production tweaking. While filters and coloured lights are used in filming, characteristically, in *CSI* whole scenes may be post-produced and appear to be tinted green, blue or, as is frequently the case in the *CSI: Miami* series, orange. In terms of lighting, one of the most characteristic features is the way in which bright, often highly coloured lights are set up in the background of shots: they are usually soft in terms of focus, but relatively bright in terms of hue intensity. Inevitably, this draws the eye, emphasizing, once again, depth, even when the scene is relatively sparse in terms of props or location. The use of a bright hazy light in the background lures the attention of the viewer to move briefly, almost unconsciously, from the foreground to the background and back again. Once more, the direction here is to go into rather than across the screen. The shifts in colour in terms of overall hue – from blueish to greenish tints, from daylight to night and back again – are, Gareth Cook claims, a deliberate strategy: 'Subconsciously, [the colour shifts] stimulate you to keep watching', notes Cook. '[The image] looks normal, but you're not quite sure what's a little unusual about it' (Bankston 2001: 64).

The use of colour in the programme distinguishes it from the expressionistic, but greyer tones of series such as *NYPD Blue* and *Law & Order*. The series is unashamedly loaded with colour, and this is perhaps justified, in part, in both the Vegas and Miami series, since both cities are known as places with high-intensity sunlight, which offer extremes in terms of their climate and environment. It might be argued that the newest series in the *CSI* franchise – *CSI: New York* – demonstrates a much greyer or bluer colour scheme and thus works against the fantastically heightened colour or 'comic-strip palette' of the earlier series. However, some reviewers (Moore 2004) have suggested that its appearance is, in fact, very much in accord with the recognizable and self-conscious 'colour-coding' of the *CSI* 'look':

> With *CSI: New York*, look for a new shade of tell-tale 'CSI' color coding: the chosen filmic look is Urban Blue. *CSI: Miami* will surely stick with Tawny Citrus, while the original series, set in Las Vegas, favors Midnight Chrome. Thus will *CSI* be available in three decorator colors!

Texture

The predominant feel or texture of *CSI* is that it is glossy and smooth and this is, of course, unsurprising, considering that Bruckheimer, as a producer, is known for his glossy, high-action films. However, there are aspects of the texture within the show which make it a more sticky and visceral experience than this 'gloss' or slickness might suggest. For instance, the more uniform application of the all but bleach bypass process in the first series did mean that the image had more grain and that the characters' faces in close-up were more gritty and less perfect than might be expected from glamorous figures in a prime-time American drama. Once Roy Wagner left the show, however, this 'grainy' look was less emphatic, although numerous grainy or fuzzy effects and a play with colour, focus, speed and camera angle are still used in the flashback sequences. In these sequences, the investigators rehearse what may

Fig 1.2 *CSI: Crime Scene Investigation.* CBS-TV/The Kobal Collection

have happened during the course of the crime. For one such scene, one of the current directors of photography, Jonathan West, explains the technical process involved (Wiener 2002: 68):

> For this particular sequence in 'Caged', we darkened the night sky and brought down the blacks considerably. We also shifted the overall tone to a slightly colder, bluer level and forced many of the highlights up to 100 per cent, letting some of them clip. We enhanced the colour of the Wacker lights and took the flashbacks through a couple of versions until we came up with a shift toward the green-orange with extreme contrast.

The visual interruptions of these sequences, in addition to the animation in the snap-zoom sequences, mean that the 'glossiness' of the show is not as uniform as it might seem at first. It is, I would argue, much more of a patchwork of different image textures, an aesthetic that is entirely feasible and appropriate to television, which can integrate (without alienating the viewer) a surprisingly diverse range of visual techniques. (Even aside from its own integration of these different practices, it should also be remembered that the programme is shown on commercial channels in both the USA and the UK, and is thus always already interrupted by a diverse range of images.)

Conclusion

CSI is a programme that is entirely self-conscious about its use and manipulation of the television image and the other visual material used within the programme. Certainly, my brief analysis does not fully exhaust the elaborate composition, qualities and play with the image that takes place in the series. The construction of the television image within the series is seductive and, while it strives for legitimacy by suggesting that the image is to be read as evidence, it also betrays a rather disturbing fascination with what it means to look at and be fascinated by images in this way. At times, the presentation of the image in the series verges on the obscene. Many images in *CSI* reveal things that are gruesome and disgusting or explicitly sexual, yet I would suggest that even when they are not obscene in terms of content, they are stylistically pornographic. In particular, there would seem to be an obvious connection between the infamous 'money shot' in pornographic film (the moment of ejaculation) with the '*CSI* shot'. Pornography, if not always explicit within any one storyline, does seem to me to imbue the visual aesthetic of the show in general. Certainly, Catherine's status as an ex-exotic dancer and Nick's early liaison with a prostitute, along with Grissom's erotic obsession with the madam of a sadomasochistic brothel ('Lady Heather'), suggest, perhaps, that this is not really reading too much into what can be seen on the screen.

chapter two

Sound

This chapter will fall into three parts. In the first section I will outline briefly the ways in which sound functions on television and its relationship to the sounds of other media technologies found in the home, such as CD players, the radio and the telephone. Second, I will go on to discuss, in general terms, categories of sound on television: sound as voice, sound as music, sound as sound and sound as silence. Last, I will demonstrate how thinking about sound through these categories can enable interesting analyses of very different kinds of television programmes. I will conclude the chapter with an investigation, using sound as the primary focus, of the successful pre-school children's programme from the BBC, *Teletubbies*.

Television and sound

Television was not the first medium to introduce electrified or mediated sound into the home. Earlier media technologies – the gramophone, the telephone and the radio – were all sound-based media and all were familiar items and in use in many homes before the mass take-up of television in the 1950s. This means that the significant difference between the sounds that we hear in the real world and the sounds we hear through television had already become accepted before the arrival of television. What I mean by this is that mediated sound is not sound that is simply 'reproduced', but sound that is organized, adjusted and manipulated before we hear it; as Rick Altman (1992) has pointed out, it is always a *representation of sound*, not an 'innocent' reproduction. This is true of all the sounds we hear through the gramophone (or its newer version, the hi-fi or CD player), the telephone, the radio or the television, whether the sounds we hear are recorded to be replayed later or transmitted live. For instance, while it may no longer be the case that you hear your mother, as I did, put on her 'telephone voice' to speak to someone on the telephone, the rise of the voice-activated automated telephone service means that all of us are increasingly obliged to moderate our own speaking tones, whether we are trying to access our bank account details or buy cinema tickets. Aside from these kinds of performance, in which we change and organize our own sound for transmission, we are all familiar with the way in which the telephone changes the voices of those we know well. It can make sisters sound alike and mothers sound like daughters; we may also be aware of the more obvious changes to the voices of friends and loved ones that result from common effects such as distortion, break-up or sound decay. The sound that we hear through these different media,

57

television included, is not, therefore, any more 'real' than the mediated image, despite the fact that sound is often used to provide substance, to aurally 'guarantee' the veracity of the images we see in film and television. The sounds we hear on television are processed, removed from their original source and made into a product that, if recorded, may be repeated at will.

In addition to making different electrified, mediated sounds familiar to the audience, these earlier media were also important in directing the way in which such sounds appeared to function for the listener. The telephone, the gramophone and the radio all brought sound into the home, but, more particularly, they brought sound *to you*. The sounds that you could hear through or via these media were always 'for you', whether it was a telephone call, a piece of music you had chosen or the carefully developed, personalized direct address of the radio. We know the sound is 'there' for us.

Interestingly, however, while the ringing phone is generally answered, the sounds of these media, along with television, are often used in a way that circumvents this direct address. Many people use the radio, the CD player and often the television to 'fill up' their domestic landscape. On first coming home many people often turn on music, the radio or the television, but then leave the room, so that the sound cannot be properly heard (and, of course, in the case of television, the picture cannot be seen). I suspect it is more common for people to leave the television on and leave the room than to do the same with the CD player, but I have no hard evidence for this. However, it does seem to me that since what is playing on the television often represents less of a 'choice' and is less valued, it is likely that it is easier to abandon than a piece of music. Television sound, then, like the sounds from other media, is used as an accompaniment, a companion, in the home. It makes the house seem less 'empty' and, perhaps, less threatening, since unexpected sounds or, of course, the sound of silence itself, are muffled and obscured. Yet the sound we access from television is not always understood as welcome company. The 'blaring' television of noisy neighbours is a source of irritation and when you are tired the relentless chatter of television presenters can make you nauseous; sound can therefore terrorize as much as comfort. Sound's encroaching, overwhelming, even terrifying properties may well be related to the fact that we do not have 'earlids' in the same way we have 'eyelids'. While we can close our eyes or look away, we cannot (without mechanical intervention in the shape of earplugs) close our ears or 'listen away'. Continuous and/or loud sound is a recognized method of torture. Perhaps this is why we do not find it odd that, while we can turn down the sound of the television or even remove the sound exclusively (via the mute button), we cannot, with ease, do the same to the picture.

It is common, and tempting, to present television as a 'sound-led' medium. I think it is a mistake to assess the sounds of television by relying solely on an obvious comparison with radio. While it is certainly true that many of the ways that the voice and other sounds had been organized on the radio were then transported to television, television has always been, from its inception, an *audio-visual* medium, a multimedia form, in which sound and image work with one another in a variety of different ways. A multimedia approach requires an analysis of the particular qualities of each aspect of the audio-visual medium and their interaction with one another. In this chapter I will examine the pitch, tone and timbre of the sound, but I won't be suggesting that it should be understood primarily as manifesting some kind of inherent 'meaning' in and of itself. Instead, I will try to identify what 'sense' particular sounds make in the context of the television medium, which is always sound and image together. In the following section, as I outline four categories of 'sound' on television – sound as voice, sound as music, sound as sound and sound as silence – I will suggest what they are used for and where they are most often heard. However, throughout the chapter, it should be recalled that the sound of television cannot be imagined in isolation, separated from the image; while it is important to learn to listen to television, the meaningfulness of sound and television always depends upon understanding the relationship between what we hear *and* what we see.

Sound as voice

The human voice is probably the most important sound on television. It can be heard everywhere and in nearly every programme on television, in ways that are similar to radio and cinema as well as ways that are unique to television itself. The voice is often attached to people, bodies and objects on screen. However, one of its central functions is as an 'acousmatic' presence, that is, as a voice that is heard by the audience (and, sometimes, by the people in vision), but which does not appear to be attached to a source (a body or an object) that can be seen on-screen.

The voice-over

The most familiar acousmatic presence on television is the 'voice-over', the voice of a person who is not normally seen on the screen, but whom we hear clearly, often driving or describing the events seen on-screen. It serves many different purposes on television and we can hear it in a variety of different modes, as the continuity announcer, the narrator of documentaries, the sports commentator, the voice-over for advertisements or the narrator of public ceremonies, such as state funerals and royal weddings. It is also a familiar device in dramatic fiction. However, in television drama, as in fiction film, the voice-over is used for very specific reasons:

- the voice speaks of events that have already happened, although we may experience them as if they were happening now – here, the voice-over serves simply to describe events seen and/or to encourage a sense of nostalgia
- the voice works humorously and suggests a verbal counterpoint to incidents and characters seen on-screen
- the presence of the voice reminds the audience that what is being seen on-screen is a fiction; in some instances, it may suggest that what is seen is a partial, biased view of a story – thus the voice challenges the assumption that the film is offering an omniscient, 'neutral' viewpoint
- the voice serves to bridge a temporal ellipsis in the narrative, for flashbacks (into the past) or to connect scenes where time has elapsed (a short way into the future) or a flash-forward (into a future time which may or may not have happened).

Some of these functions are similar to the way in which voice-over is used in the different televisual modes I have listed above. However, there is one important difference between the majority of film and television voice-overs. It should be clear from this brief description that, when used in films, the voice-over is nearly always in the past tense. Although the past tense voice-over is found in television – in television drama (the kind of programming closest to film) as well as certain kinds of documentary – it is rare elsewhere on television. So one of the key distinctions between cinema and television's use of the acousmatic voice is that a large proportion of the voice-overs we hear speak to us in the present tense.

The continuity announcer

The most frequent situation in which we hear this voice is from the continuity announcer, the unseen 'master of ceremonies' for the channel. It is now uncommon to see as well as hear the continuity announcer on mainstream television. However, in the early years on television, the 'voice' of the channel would also have a face. This practice has now been largely abandoned in the UK, the last in-vision announcers for regional independent companies disappearing by the mid-1980s. During the early 1990s, Channel 4 did experiment briefly with showing their announcers at work, and they could be seen as well as heard, reading from a script and wearing headphones. It is, of course, still common to see continuity announcers ('video jockeys') on MTV and on various children's channels. Perhaps the acousmatic announcer is seen as more sophisticated, less intrusive and so avoided elsewhere – it may also be that they are less expensive. In fact, as a way of saving money, many channels are increasingly using pre-recorded announcements to bridge the gap between programmes and advertisements, rather than employing on-site personnel to provide live links direct from a television studio. Nonetheless, the pretence remains that the announcer, like the viewer, is (or could be) in front of the set for the duration of the evening (and perhaps the week or viewing season) ahead. This is indicated by the fact that the announcer will routinely say, 'Now on BBC One . . .', 'Coming up later this evening . . .' or 'Next week on . . .', assuming, as the film cannot do, that the audience will still be there in front of the screen for a series of different, and extended, 'futures'. The voice-over as companion and guide is an essential part of what Paddy Scannell (1996) has called television's 'dailiness', the fact that television is there for us, part of our everyday, articulating a sense of time passing and things to come. It is here that television comes closest to radio, for on most stations the DJ or announcer will often give the time and list a forthcoming menu of events.

Sports announcers

In sports commentary, most of the action is related in an excited present tense that looks to the future. However, at certain points there can be a mixture of past, present and future. In the natural lulls between action in play or after an important incident, the sports commentator may refer back (in sound and vision) to earlier incidents in the game – we know this as the 'instant replay'. In this form of narration, as Stephanie Marriott (1996) has shown, there is often an interesting mix of past ('he played that shot well'), present ('look what's happening there') and future ('it's got to be a goal . . . but no!'). The voice-over bridges audibly the disruption experienced visually, since the instant replay takes us away from the live pictures of the game in progress. The replay of the image is anchored and 'cut and pasted' into the 'live' experience of the game by the voice of the commentator, who, by dragging us, aurally, from the past to the future, pretends that we could relive the moment as if it were really happening again. The voice of the commentator is therefore an important element in the way in which the instant replay alters the temporal flow of the game. In these moments the television experience is manipulated, or 'thickened', in terms of what we can hear and see. For the listening audience, the commentator's voice thus often seemingly takes control of events, even the game itself. Over time, the pace, timbre and vocal performance of the commentator may even seem to 'shape' the game for the television viewer. It is certainly true that different commentators' voices, their pitch, pace, resonance and expression, become entwined with the way in which various sports are enjoyed on television. The recent introduction of John McEnroe as a commentator (on-screen and off) for the BBC's coverage of the annual Wimbledon tennis tournament has brought a certain amount of friction to the genteel murmur of the British commentators. Not only does his higher pitched American twang mark him out as distinct, but his polite and damning assessment of different players – particularly the British players – is an interesting rub against years of languid, dry and patriotic commentary by earlier British commentators. In a very different way, it is impossible to imagine television coverage of WWF (World Wrestling Federation) and its various offshoots without the hyper-blown, aggressive, macho style of the commentators – their screams, groans and roars are an essential part of the wrestling's choreography.

Another way of understanding the importance of the voice can be seen through a simple commutation test. If we substitute the commentary on a snooker championship with one provided for a Grand Prix, the sheer volume of the Grand Prix commentary would be startling. Grand Prix commentators often talk very loudly, as if they need to shout over the noise of the cars (this is not necessary, of course, since they could, and often do, provide commentary at some distance from the racetrack). Conversely, snooker commentators often sound as if they are whispering quietly over the players' shoulders, and this is because the arena for snooker tournaments is conventionally 'hushed' to aid the players' concentration. Snooker commentators are also comfortable with long pauses between their different observations on the play and players, a rhythm that would be very much at odds with the practice of Grand Prix commentators, who generally sound as if they are chasing – verbally – the cars and drivers around the track. The voice, therefore, provides more than description and, over time, becomes an implicated and familiar part of the 'play' of the rhythms, textures, tones and pace of the televised experience of individual sports.

Who is talking? The sound of the voice-over

While, as I have indicated, the 'visual essay' or historical documentary often employs voice-overs that speak almost completely in the past tense, newer forms of documentary, particularly the docu-soap, are akin to sports commentary, as they, too, have voice-overs that may slip between past, present and future tense. This is unsurprising, since the narrative of docu-soaps relies on the anticipated, yet apparently spontaneous, incident embedded in a familiar narrative. The increase in the number of reality shows has also helped to increase the number and quality of voice-over artists heard in documentary in the UK. Younger voices, more women and more regional accents can be heard than before. There are, however, clearly fashions for different kinds of voices. Currently, while there are more women than before, they speak in a way that is almost always lower in pitch and slower than many women's voices are naturally. Similarly, while certain regional accents in the UK are very much in favour (Scotland and Newcastle), other accents remain unpopular (Birmingham, Cornwall). These fashions are also mirrored in the voice-overs used in advertisements, which increasingly incorporate a wide range of accent and gender, although it is probably still true that the white male voice tends to predominate.

What every voice-over performance has to negotiate, however, is how *recognizable* the voice is. Will the audience be able to identify the body, face and persona of the voice from previous performances, on-screen and off? In some instances, the possible recognition of a famous actor as the 'performer' of the voice-over may be an added bonus, since their acousmatic presence lends an appropriate 'added value' to the documentary or advertisement. We could think here of Laurence Olivier narrating the landmark documentary series, *The World at War*, or, more infamously, Orson Welles' voice-over for an advertisement for Courvoisier brandy. In other instances, it may be that the programme-makers hope that the identity behind the voice remains uncertain, as previous performances may interfere with their current vocal role. In the UK, for example, it would probably surprise many people to learn that Andrew Sachs has had a long and successful career as a voice-over artist for numerous documentary series, including the BBC's *Children's Hospital*. Sachs' comic performance in *Fawlty Towers*, a well-known and much-repeated sitcom, involves both pathological mugging and an appalling Spanish accent, as he plays the 'waiter from Barcelona', Manuel. This performance and persona is clearly very much at odds with the actor who now narrates the heart-warming and traumatic tales of different children's hospitals. Of course, the fact that his own speaking voice is so much at odds with his best-known performance may enable him to sustain his career. For most of the television audience, while voices are familiar, the faces and bodies of voice-over artists are generally little known.

Nonetheless, it is generally the case that voice-over work tends to make any performer, however well known, relatively invisible, and this can be an advantage. Providing a voice-over is relatively lucrative and short-term, so many well-known actors and presenters are happy to take this kind of work, especially as it would appear to have little consequence for their 'visible' persona. In relation to documentary, for example, actors such as Juliet Stevenson, Zoë Wanamaker, Robert Lindsay and Ian Holm would be fairly expensive to have on-screen. By using their off-screen voices, the programme-maker is able to acquire a resonant impression of these different actors' talents and, perhaps, a hint of their personae, relatively cheaply. Yet there are also less well-known actors, or impersonators, who take on work to 'sound like' favoured voices and thus save advertisers' money. Mariella Frostrup, a British television presenter well known for her husky, seductive voice, has been employed as a voice-over artist for advertisements, but she has also been impersonated closely in others. It seems that, despite the importance and the value of the voice, it is difficult for any performer to demand compensation for infringement of vocal 'copyright', based on sound alone.

For the most part, I am describing an audio landscape that has changed quite radically since the early days of television. It does seem to be the case, for instance, that what was commonly cited as the 'BBC' accent (which was pretty much akin to 'RP' or received pronunciation), with its characteristic South English/Metropolitan, middle-to-upper-class accent, is less dominant than before. Yet, while there is clearly more variety than in the past, accents and voices associated with lower-class markers are still less common. Most mainstream broadcasting continues to insist upon a particular kind of legibility, or audibility, and this, I suspect, is often used as a cover for insisting that the voice-over artist 'speak properly'. And speaking properly is still indelibly tied up with associations with certain kinds of cultural capital that originate in the notion of being from a 'higher' class and having a 'good' education.

The fact that many voice-overs still tend to be tied to increasingly outdated notions of the importance of class and education may be related to the power of the 'unseen' voice. Indeed, some kinds of voice-over, particularly those employed in essay-style, historical documentaries, are referred to as the 'voice of God'. The so-called 'voice of God' refers to the fact that the speaker is invisible, but seemingly all-knowing. He (or, more rarely, she) continues to enjoy a particular authority on television. The remnants of this power, and its previous association with the upper-class tones of the privately educated, white, middle-aged male, is also evident in the relay of major national, ceremonial and public events. On the BBC, David Dimbleby and Tom Fleming often share the voice-over responsibilities for this kind of event, such as Princess Diana's funeral or the annual state opening of Parliament. Dimbleby was, for a long time, the face and voice of the long-running current affairs series, *Panorama*, and now fronts other political programming for the BBC. Perhaps not coincidentally, he is also the son of an equally famous reporter/presenter, and a previous 'voice of the BBC', Richard Dimbleby. David Dimbleby's voice is cultured and clearly upper class, but his speech does have a lighter, more journalistic and energetic feel than that of his father. The deeper and seemingly 'profound' tones of Richard Dimbleby's voice are instead replayed and echoed in Fleming's voice, which, in contrast to David Dimbleby's, resonates with a particularly heavy gravitas and richness, moderated by a slight Scottish lilt. I suspect part of Fleming's authority as voice comes partly from his long association with this kind of event, but also from the fact that his body and face are not well known to the television audience. On the other mainstream channels in the UK it is also generally male newscasters who will take on this role; on ITV, it is often Trevor McDonald who narrates this kind of event. McDonald also has a voice that resonates with the distinctive 'upper-class' accent associated with the privately educated in the UK. Recently, however, there has been a slight move away from this paternalistic dominance and some minor channels have begun to employ women's voices to narrate the live transmission of important public events. In the UK, Kirsty Young, after her brief stint on ITV, returned to Channel 5 to become both their lead newscaster and, in some senses, the official 'voice' (as well as the face) of the channel. Yet her voice, again, interestingly characterized by a slight Scottish lilt, is also very much in tune with the current vogue for female voices that speak relatively slowly and at a low pitch. My point here is to note that although acousmatic voices are increasingly diverse in television, voices that 'speak for' channels at times of national mourning or celebration tend to be recognizably similar in terms of class, pace and pitch.

The speaking body

Most people we see on television have voices attached. We see them speak: their voices are synchronized as their lips move and we are usually justified in believing that it is their voice we are hearing. Michel Chion (1994: 171–2) calls this 'theatrical speech' and these voices, unlike the voice-over, have no external view, nor indeed any apparent control, of events; they speak from within the 'story' being told by the programme. On television, this mode covers the voices of characters in drama, as well as the witness, interviewee or reporter in documentaries and news, the weather presenter and the host, guests and contestants in game shows, variety shows and chat shows. On television, it also refers to the relatively brief appearances of sports men and women in 'after-the-event' interviews and a range of performances in advertisements.

One peculiar aspect of television is that it is not necessarily important for the whole body to be seen, as it is the voice and face that are important – television is full of talking heads. Conventionally, the newscaster, reporter or expert can often appear to be without legs, cut in two by a desk, by the frame of the monitor or, in more complicated visual displays, by the frame of the video. More recently, on British television, since the talking head is often felt to be lifeless, unexciting or lacking in energy, there has been an increase in the 'mobile' presentation of the news. Initiated by Kirsty Young, as the main news anchor for Channel 5 news, this style of presentation has now become more common in many of ITN's news programmes. Jon Snow, for example, usually begins his presentation of Channel 4 news in a full-length shot, as he stands, holding his script, in front of a video wall in the news studio. Yet this form of presentation is generally closed down as the anchor or presenter graduates to the safe haven behind their desk to read the autocue or conduct studio interviews. In television, as in film, it is also common to hear theatrical speech and for it not to be attached to a body at all. Instead, the voice is heard and located to a telephone or some other media technology, such as a radio or cassette player. One of the most familiar examples of this kind of 'speaking body' on television must be the speakerphone which relays Charlie's voice in *Charlie's Angels*.

Theatrical speech is therefore the voice that is synchronized – either to the body, head and lips of the performer or, more loosely, to the image of a suitable technology. In many instances, the sound of the voice will have been recorded simultaneously with the image; yet there is often a deliberate audio-hierarchy as to which voices will be privileged for the listening audience. The most obvious way in which this can be organized in non-fiction programming is via the hand-held microphone: the game show host or reporter holds and 'wields' the microphone, choosing who can speak, when they can speak and for how long. In many instances, the presenter, unlike the vox pop interviewee or contestant, will also have a radio microphone attached to some part of their clothing, ensuring that they may always be heard, even if the hand-held microphone should be torn away from their grasp. Their close proximity to a microphone at all times ensures that their voices are usually transmitted in a way that makes what they say 'drier', clearer and more audible than anyone else who speaks. They are therefore at the top of the hierarchy audibly, even if they seem, in terms of their picture, to be lost in the crowd; and they will dominate aurally even if they appear side by side, visually, with other individuals on-screen. This provides situations where an apparent visual 'democracy' (the 'man in the street', the crowd, the marchers) is seen on-screen, but actually, very few 'ordinary' people are able to speak, and those that do are controlled audibly, even if they are unruly visually. Aside from structured vox pops and reports from mass demonstrations, I am also thinking of the familiar sight of the journalist presenting a live report, where other individuals can be seen jumping around in the background, desperately mugging to the camera. In these instances, it is perhaps surprising that most offenders are generally mute, content to wave or caper in the background of the shot. It may be, of course, that we see these sequences more frequently because these reports can still be used. In other sequences, where the journalist is overwhelmed audibly, the report (unless it becomes news in itself) will have to be filed again. Television therefore often provides the appearance, but not necessarily the *sound* of democracy.

Dialogue

Television drama conventionally privileges the dialogue or speech of characters that serves to drive the narrative of the programme forward. Directional microphones (boom microphones) are used to guarantee audibility, although many American series also require the actors to secrete radio microphones about their persons so that another audio track is available. While audibility is the primary goal of many productions, most directors and sound operators also employ different stylistic tweaks to colour and texture the dialogue and the voices we hear. Most television dramas, for example, will attempt to place the voices of performers in an approximated version of realistic space. If, for example, a character is speaking in a large room, some reverb may be maintained or added so that the character is audibly 'placed' in the scene. In addition, there is also some attempt to match the audience's audio position with their apparent visual positioning in relation to each scene. Audio perspective is therefore mostly dictated by the visual image. Just as what the audience sees gives the impression that we appear to be just behind the camera, we apparently hear as if we were in this position too. If the vision cuts to a camera behind a door, for example, the sound will also be muffled slightly, so that the characters (who may not have moved) also sound as if they are behind that door. This 'sound perspective' is not rigidly maintained, however, and the desire for audibility will often override this kind of audio positioning. In several hospital dramas, for instance, including *ER*, *Casualty* and *Holby City*, the numerous extras that cross over in front of principal characters (thus briefly obscuring them in vision) seldom interrupt the audibility of what these characters are saying. Thus, while visually it may appear that we are 'eavesdropping' on murmured conversations in busy hospital corridors, we can, of course, hear much more than we would be able to in a similar real-life situation. In a drama such as *24*, where split-screen is used as an idiosyncratic visual motif, the sound remains tied firmly to one audio situation. The sound used might be a telephone conversation taking place across two scenes, a piece of non-diegetic music, which bridges the action taking place in the different scenes displayed, or a piece of significant dialogue originating from only one of the scenes shown. So while *24* is visually playful, through its use of split-screen, it remains audibly conventional. Visually spectacular, *24* presents several scenes to the viewer at once, and the scenes may be displayed at different speeds, or from different angles, and originate from different places. Audibly, however, the sound does not 'move around' and instead secures the viewer's (as listener) place in the narrative.

Ventriloquism

As I have suggested, in most instances, the voice of the actor is recorded at the same time as their visual performance. However, in television, as in film, it is also the case that the voices of the actors may be recorded at a different time and place. This performance is then mixed back into location sound and then synched to the visual performance. This process, known as 'looping' or 'automated dialogue replacement' (ADR), is far less common on television than it is in film, since it is costly in terms of studio time and actors' fees. In television, unlike film, ADR is rarely used to improve upon the actor's 'performance' alone. Instead, it generally occurs if there have been technical difficulties or if shooting has taken place in an uncontrollable or 'confusing' sound location, such as a busy road, or a public space, such as an airport. Whatever the reason, ADR is, of course, an explicit form of ventriloquism; a voice produced elsewhere is seen to emanate ('magically') from a body that we believe to be speaking.

Interestingly, while ADR may be limited in television, ventriloquism of another kind is extraordinarily popular. Many music programmes, for example, rely upon lip-synching; that is, the voices and often the music itself are not reproduced or recorded for transmission, but the music and voices are pre-recorded and then synched onto the live visual performance of the artist or band. In the early days of the BBC's long-running chart show, *Top of the Pops*, for instance, viewers would witness the DJ placing a needle on the record as an expected preliminary to the visual appearance of the band, who would then proceed to mime to the record. More recently, *Top of the Pops* has required performers to pre-record their performance in the studio, but then asked them to mime 'live' to the playback of their earlier recording. In genres of music that value the exhibition of the technical ability of the musicians and are, in some senses, dependent for their credibility on the guaranteed 'authorship' of the musician, miming or lip-synching is seen as a dubious and potentially duplicitous activity. Miming carries with it the possibility that the band cannot actually sing or play the music they appear to be performing. The initial furore around the Spice Girls' early appearances on television was tied up with whether or not the girls themselves could actually 'sing'.

The unresolved tension around the common practice of lip-synching underwrites part of the success of the different pop reality shows, such as *Pop Idol* and the American programme, *Making the Band*. Both programmes spend a great deal of time on the auditioning process, in which the thousands of hopeful wannabes perform, without the aid of microphones or music, in front of the panel of judges. These sequences, which reveal how well or badly people actually sing, are enjoyed by the audience with a degree of sadistic pleasure, as numerous participants obviously cannot sing at all. However, the auditions are also a guarantee that the individuals ultimately selected *can* sing. This is despite the fact that, if ultimately successful, the individual performers will later appear on other music programmes miming to their own records. Some performers, particularly those who wish to promote their 'credibility', may refuse to mime for television and, if forced, will deliberately mime so 'badly' that the artifice is evident. Despite the apparent controversy involved, it is important to remember that industry scandals (such as the one involving the duo, Milli Vanilli) are relatively rare. There are artists who mime freely without the same kind of penalty. While Milli Vanilli were ultimately revealed to be a 'fraud', since they claimed to, but did not actually sing on any of the records they promoted through their extraordinarily successful 'live' appearances and music videos, other performers lip-synch quite openly. For instance, the male 'singer' in Boney M did not actually sing on any of the records, and his voice was actually provided by the German record producer who wrote and produced the band's long run of hit singles.

Ventriloquism of a different order is another common device on television. What should perhaps be considered a rather odd aspect of television is that there are numerous animals, objects and drawings that appear to speak on television. In cinema, animals, drawings and objects also talk, but they are still largely confined to specialized niche markets – animated films or films generally aimed at a child audience. While it is true that in television, as in film, the majority of non-human and inanimate objects that talk are also aimed at the child audience, adults are similarly talked at or appealed to through ventriloquism in advertisements which feature talking dogs, animated telephones and even foodstuffs. In one advertisement currently running on British television, a high-pitched, giggly and seductive female voice is attached to a Kinder chocolate bar. Set in a newsagent, the bar hovers above a display of sweets and chocolate, teasing a bemused male customer into selecting 'her', urging him to 'lick my ripples'. Another immensely popular campaign involved the comedian Johnny Vegas and his 'monkey' (a knitted toy monkey). While their 'odd couple' repartee began a national craze for the monkey doll, it failed to save the product they were advertising (ITV Digital).

Michel Chion provocatively suggests that all film or television images which seem 'to speak for themselves' are acts of ventriloquism. It does seem that sound, especially the human voice, appears to animate the television image. The voice gives expression, individuality and, perhaps, even a 'soul' to the body seen on-screen. The human voice on television is therefore a powerful force, both emotionally and metaphorically speaking. Unsurprisingly, therefore, there have been instances when the voice as 'presence', and its animating qualities, has become a political issue on television. During the 1980s in the UK, the Thatcher government decreed that no 'voice' should be given to terrorism on British television, as it was argued that terrorism should not be given the 'oxygen of publicity'. Specifically, this meant 'silencing' the Provisional IRA and spokesmen from the political party closely associated with it, Sinn Fein, including the high-profile Sinn Fein politician, Gerry Adams. In effect, this meant that on news reports, Adams was either seen speaking, with subtitles provided, or, more commonly, an actor was employed to dub his speech. If dubbing took place, the image would be captioned with an explanation that it was an 'actor's voice' that was being heard. This created a rather peculiar audio effect, which subverted (and, in some ways, deliberately flouted) the

Thatcher government's intention of disabling the voice of Sinn Fein. If subtitles were used, this necessarily made Adams' 'speech act' different, and, while inaudible, what he had to say was perhaps more noticeable than what other people in the same report were saying. A sudden silence, the break in the rhythm of sound, might well have caused the audience to look up or simply to pay more rather than less attention to the screen. Equally, if dubbing took place, the actor's voice recorded in a studio would be much drier, clearer and more coherent than speech recorded on location, and, in terms of the audio-hierarchy I outlined earlier, the substitution for Adams' voice would be privileged since it was audibly 'closer' to the listening audience.

While the dubbing of US and UK television programmes in Europe is relatively common, few live-action European programmes are dubbed for American or British television audiences. Many children's cartoons, in particular Japanese cartoons, are dubbed and often given different musical soundtracks for transmission in the UK and USA. Somewhat strangely, in the United States, many of the UK's best-known children's animated programmes, such as *Bob the Builder*, are dubbed by American voices, even though, presumably, the original English accents would be reasonably comprehensible to the audience. In some children's programmes, the commercial strain the 'language barrier' causes for the global marketing of television is cleverly avoided when certain programmes employ invented 'languages' for their characters. One of the most famous of these invented languages has to be the rich vocal patterning provided by the Italian clown, Carlo Bonomi, for the original series of the Swiss-produced children's programme *Pingu*. Pingu, a plasticine-model penguin, lives with his mother, father and baby sister, Pinga, and experiences the joys, trials and tribulations common to young children everywhere. Bonomi's wide range of vocal inflections and his musical burbling of half-words and exclamations fit the antics of Pingu and his friends fantastically well. Interestingly, the density and range of emotion his 'language' manifested was reputed to have convinced a wide range of different nationalities (German, Italian, Finnish) that 'Pinguish' originated from their own language. Of course, as I will discuss in relation to *Teletubbies* below, this 'half-language' has a particular appeal and usefulness for the young audience. Conveniently, however, it also removes the need for a new soundtrack for each new national market. 'Pinguish' makes the same kind of sense or the same 'non-sense' in any language.

While dubbing is common in animation, very few live-action programmes are dubbed and subtitles are associated with programmes that could be said to be highbrow or are seemingly aimed at clearly defined niche audiences. This includes programmes such as Fassbinder's landmark series, *Berlin Alexanderplatz*, and the Indian epic, *Mahabharata*. Only the unsuccessful screening of the French soap, *Chateauvallion*, by the BBC in the 1980s could be said to have gone against this particular trend.

Dubbing or subtitles – why does it matter?

Curiously, though, dubbing for certain kinds of imported programming has crept into the margins of UK television. Increasingly, some advertisements for global products (shampoos, medical creams and cleaning products) are rather clumsily dubbed into English. However, it is usually rare to actually *see* the dubbing in practice. So, for instance, we will not often see the model/actor speak to us directly, since then we would be conscious of the mismatch between the way their lips move and the words being said. Instead, the advertisement is usually carefully edited so that the voice *appears* to be originating from the body we see on-screen, but we do not necessarily see the person speak. For British audiences, arrogant in the belief that English is the predominant global language, this kind of dubbing is often held up for ridicule. In fact, one dubbed advertisement, for Ferrero Rocher chocolates, became a minor comic cult in the UK. Apparently set in the glamorous environment of an embassy party, its bizarre mix of pseudo-*Dynasty* glitz and bad dubbing made it an easy object of ridicule ('Ah, Monsieur, with these chocolates you are really spoiling us'). Dubbing, therefore, is rarely watched comfortably by English-speaking audiences, who have come to expect that the 'norm' will be that voices will always be in synch with the visual performance. Non-British European audiences have not always had this luxury, but this may not be the disadvantage it seems, as the practice of dubbing can have surprising effects. For example, dubbing allows individual countries the freedom to interpret or remodel the overwhelming dominance of American programming in a way that is not dissimilar to the redubbing of *Bob the Builder* for American audiences. Revoicing characters makes them 'belong' to the new national viewing context. Seeing *Starsky and Hutch* dubbed into French, for instance, where the two main characters' voices become deeper and more identifiably mature, gives a very different tempo and feel to the original programme. It may not make it less obviously 'American', but the sound of the voice is an audible 'lens' through which the programme may be interpreted within a different national culture and context.

Dubbing actuality

In certain domestically produced programmes, dubbing and subtitles are used regularly: in news reports, magazine items and documentaries. This process might seem unremarkable, in that most of the audience will require an interpretation for any individual who does not speak English. Nonetheless, I want to consider this in a little more detail, particularly in relation to understanding that the voice – its cadence, tone, timbre and pace – is clearly important and exceptionally powerful on television. I want to do this by asking some provocative questions.

What if Hitler spoke in English? What if, in the infamous videotapes screened since the events of 11 September 2001, Osama Bin Laden spoke in English (which he clearly could if he wished)? Would they be more or less compelling or threatening for English-speaking viewers? Is it better to dub the voice, so that we can concentrate on the visual aspects of the speaker and their words? Or is it better to use subtitles so that the individual qualities of the speaker's voice can be heard, even if this means distracting some viewers from the image?

For many programme-makers and broadcasters, the choice is straightforward: dubbing is preferred as subtitles are often seen as difficult, clumsy and irritating for the audience. Many people do not like subtitles or find them inaccessible, making the programme (or, indeed, the film) hard to follow if they are obliged to read as well as look. Dubbing voices makes the speaker coherent and accessible. Dubbing can look odd and there is, perhaps, something a little strange or uncanny about watching a dubbed performance, usually because of a perceptible mismatch between how the lips of the performer move and what is being said. Equally, it can mean that the expression or emotional content of the voice does not comfortably concur with the visual performance; for instance, if the voice is excited it may be that the visual performance seems inappropriately static and impassive. In some instances this could work in the programme's favour, however. *The Singing Ringing Tree* – a children's fantasy produced in Europe – was a slightly spooky fairytale, only enhanced by the added confusion and mystery of the dubbed voice, which contributed to the 'other-worldly' charm of the series. This was unintentional, but in *Twin Peaks*, the surreal, grotesque adult drama series created by David Lynch, dubbing was employed deliberately to unsettle the viewer. In this series, during certain dream and fantasy sequences, the actors' voices are played backwards and dubbed on to their visual image, thereby creating a fittingly disturbing and eerie impression. It is difficult to avoid the fact that dubbing often makes the speaker look odd, somehow 'wrong'.

Dubbing can also make the performer's speech act seem ridiculous. This comic effect is used deliberately on *Eurotrash*, a British magazine show, screened late at night on Channel 4. The French presenter of the show, Antoine de Caunes, speaks with an accent that is (deliberately) a parody of a 'French accent'. The programme features items on different pornographers, risqué performance artists and 'celebrities' from other parts of Europe. While de Caunes and the female voice-over in the show, performed by Maria McFarlane, both speak in English, the items themselves are dubbed, as most of the filmed participants do not speak English. The comic effect of this is further heightened by the fact that the voices used are not the 'neutral' tones of 'middle-class' translators. Instead, the show uses a range of 'performed' voices, which employ heavily exaggerated accents, often a version of the cockney accent (a London accent that is commonly understood to be working class and 'vulgar'). It also has strong associations with a certain kind of British 'blue' humour, articulated through the iconic performances of actors such as Barbara Windsor and Sid James, whose distinctive voices are well known from the *Carry on . . .* films and their television work. Therefore, the voices serve to emphasize the lewd and often exhibitionist behaviour of the speakers and to exaggerate the disrupting effects of dubbing. Although the effect of these dubbed voices in *Eurotrash* is comic, it also seems, to me at least, that the participants are being 'spoken for' and their words are being turned against them. Such is the power of the voice that the mouthing body seen on-screen, if obviously distinct from the voice, can appear almost as if it were a ventriloquist's dummy, as if the speaker has little control over what they say. Seeming like a 'dummy' not only carries connotations of being inhuman or 'lifeless', but also of stupidity, and neither of these associations would allow the television viewer to empathize effectively with the speaker.

Subtitles

Subtitles, which preserve the tone, inflection and rhythm of the original speech act (through what we can hear of the voice, even if we do not understand what is being said), are therefore often preferred by programme-makers who wish to retain the colour and authority of the speaker's voice. The speaker-as-real-person remains intact when subtitles are used, and what is lost in this process is not empathy, as in dubbing, but often semantics – *what* is being said, rather than *how* it is being said – although both are affected, as I will go on to illustrate. As subtitles will necessarily be read at a much slower pace than the person seen on-screen is speaking, the subtitle will often approximate what is actually being said. Subtitles therefore regularly leave out parts of what is being said; for example, hesitation, stumbles, pauses and 'unnecessary' stylistic traits, such as 'um', 'er', may not be included, as they are not strictly needed for understanding. Yet these vocal tics or mannerisms, which relate to *how* things are being said, are often crucial for our emotional and affective understanding of *what* is being said. How would we understand a speaker like Martin Luther King if we only *saw* the repetition in what he says, and were thus not fully able to understand the power of his speech through relating his words directly to the sounds and rhythms that are peculiar to his vocal technique? If an aural connection cannot be made between understanding *what* is being said and *how* it is being said, some of the power of the voice will still be missing.

It is also the case that many people whose first language is English have firmly held prejudices about the sound of other languages. German, Arabic and Slavonic languages are often thought to sound 'harsh' or guttural to English audiences – a cultural assumption generated through years of the negative representation of these accents in film and television. Other languages, the Romance languages, such as French, Italian and Spanish, are seen as musical and seductive. The Japanese language is seen as entirely foreign, strange and sometimes intimidating. Thus, the way in which 'language as sound' is heard by audiences is tied up with the creation of national stereotypes. When we cannot understand, hearing language becomes a much more abstract experience and one that many people find intimidating and disorientating. I remember first moving to Scotland and half-watching a children's cartoon on television, one I was familiar with. After a short time I began to worry for my sanity as I could not seem to understand what was going on. It was a little while, in fact, before I shamefully realized that I could not understand because the cartoon was dubbed into Gaelic, the native Scottish language, as part of an attempt to preserve the language and aimed at young Gaelic speakers. Despite the fact that I had only made a journey of 300 miles over the border to Scotland, I was surprised by how alienated (and stupid) this made me feel.

Sound as music

Music, like the human voice, is everywhere on television. It is ubiquitous – it can be seen to emanate from a visual source, an instrument, a radio or a jukebox on-screen (diegetic), but it is more often sourceless, coming from somewhere, 'nowhere' off-screen (non-diegetic). Programme-makers, advertisers and individual channels seem to use music almost as if it were simply convenient background sound or aural wallpaper. I say almost, but not entirely, since music on television is also used instrumentally, as it is in film, to 'thicken' the audio-visual experience. Music colours, provides mood and atmosphere and imparts a 'meaningfulness' (if not always a concrete meaning) to events and images seen on-screen. It can generate a particular temporality to the image as music can make and mark time in phrases or beats. Yet music also works to establish the spatial aspects of the image as well. The presence of music may suggest volume though its pitch, loudness and timbre, giving weight or apparent breadth to large objects or open vistas, or fragility and a sense of confinement to tiny objects and tight spaces. And, as in film, music often serves as an aural bridge, sonic glue that welds different visual scenes together.

Television also relays many different kinds of musical performance: popular music videos on MTV and VH1, rock performances in the studio or at open-air festivals, classical concerts, dance and, occasionally, opera. Music is essential to variety shows and many chat shows, as well as karaoke-reality shows such as *Pop Idol* and *Stars in their Eyes*. In fiction programmes, characters may also burst into song, both appropriately and inappropriately, depending on the conventional confines of the genre. Obviously the 'kids' will sing and dance in *Fame*, but characters also sing and dance in *Ally McBeal*. While the series employed its own regular chanteuse – Vonda Shephard – one of the characters would, and often did, sing, or they might find themselves serenaded by singing hallucinations, featuring well-known artists such as Barry White or Al Green. Interestingly, the 'song as hallucination' has an established place in British television through the work of the writer Dennis Potter. In several series – *Pennies from Heaven*, *The Singing Detective* and *Lipstick on my Collar* – Potter employed the device of characters bursting into song during moments of stress, excitement or reflection. Although this is conventional for musicals, the drive of the narrative in each series was otherwise distinguished by straight drama, creating an interesting rub between the 'excess' of the music and the apparent naturalism of the drama. In a further twist, the songs heard were existing recordings, often performed by well-known artists. They were clearly and deliberately dubbed onto the on-screen actors, creating a curiously compelling and, at times, quite disturbing effect. In another, more recent, American series, *Buffy the Vampire Slayer*, characters were forced to do nothing *but* sing for themselves. Thus, the usually non-singing familiar characters seemed understandably bewildered during the special musical episode, 'Once more with feeling'. Another less successful experiment, produced by Steven Bochco, known for his work on the seminal police series *Hill Street Blues*, was *Cop Rock*, an otherwise conventional police drama that was distinguished by the characters bursting into song. In other genres of television, such as children's television, music is such a fundamental part of the programming that it is unremarkable. Here, children and adults, as well as the trained performers in purple dinosaur suits in *Barney*, sing and dance *all the time* and often specifically encourage their audience to do the same.

On the one hand, then, television uses music, as film does, to support and enhance the visual stories being told, whether as a score or as in a musical. On the other hand, music on television is also presented as an event in itself and television often uses music to reach out to its audience and literally demand a response. In this chapter, however, I will concentrate on music as score, since I am more interested here in music as 'sound' rather than as an 'event'.

Television music as soundtrack

Listened to as a continuous soundtrack, music on television is chaotic and fragmented. If experienced or listened to without the pictures, music on television rarely develops in a way that would seem consistent with a musically determined narrative or sensibility. Music stops and starts all the time on television. In most instances, it is clear that it is the images that direct the musical soundscape. It can seem as if there is no perceptible organization to the music of television and the passage from one piece of music to another can be surprisingly abrupt. In any one two-minute commercial break on British television there might be more than eight separate fragments of music. Some of the music will be faded down under the voices of continuity announcers or programme presenters, while other pieces will be loud and ostentatious, adding sophistication or sex appeal to motor cars, chocolate bars or forthcoming programmes. Much of the music used will originate from elsewhere, from a wide range of recent and existing recordings, including rock, pop, classical and 'world' music. Musical recordings are made available to programme-makers and advertisers through the acquisition of 'synch rights'. Previously the 'poor relation' of music publishing and promotion, it has now become as 'important as A&R', according to Tracie London-Rowell, the director of film, television and advertising licensing for Universal Music. Synch rights are effectively temporary licences allowing programme-makers, advertisers and broadcasters to use a particular version of a piece of music. The licence enables them to use the music either within the programme for perpetuity (as background music or as a theme tune) or for a stated time period (often a year), for use in continuity announcements and trailers. In addition to the fact that this kind of licensing has now evidently proved extremely lucrative for both music companies and their artists, it is also successful as a promotional ploy. London-Rowell (2003), for instance, argues that one of her recent achievements was in relation to the band Feeder: 'It's not all ads, it's even things like the caff scenes in *EastEnders*. It's all promotion and convinces the acts you're doing something. When the last Feeder single came out, it was practically back-to-back in *EastEnders* and on trailers for cricket and *Cutting It*.'

Television companies also have access to recordings of music that can be used much more cheaply. Certain companies, such as the BBC, will have established libraries, but even smaller independent companies will have access to an extensive range of commercially produced stock music. This stock music offers a wide range of 'soundalikes', where music known from another source (such as a feature film) is effectively pastiched. The music will sound enough 'like' the original music so that the audience may be cued to remember the initial context and associated mood, but will be essentially different enough to avoid issues of plagiarism and copyright. Companies such as Koka Media, De Wolf and Bruton Music will regularly send out promotional copies of recordings to television directors and producers. Frequently, the music is organized onto different CDs, with titles such as 'Directors' Cuts'. Sometimes the music will be composed to 'sound like' the music and theme of a specific feature film, or it will evoke a particular genre of films, such as the spaghetti western. It may also be generated to imply a particular historical period, such as the 1930s. The difference between licensing this kind of music and the real thing can be considerable. Whereas it could cost up to £1,300 per minute to use the original music composed by John Williams for the Harry Potter films, similar-sounding music, licensed from a CD such as 'Directors' Cuts – Fantasy', will cost as little as £50 for unlimited use within a 40-minute television programme. Even for some classical music, where issues of copyright do not apply, some recordings of music may be cheaper to license than others, obligating producers or directors operating under particular financial restrictions to select certain performances and artists over others.

Television music as score: interludes and theme tunes

Some music, of course, is composed specifically for use on television. As in film, television employs composers to write theme tunes and incidental music for many genres of television programme and commissions full musical scores for big-budget television dramas or documentaries. A peculiar aspect of the scoring for television programmes is the need for specially composed musical interludes. These interludes feature either as a way in or out of commercial breaks, or as a simple device to cover a scene change where time and space is 'bridged' in the course of the narrative. Listened to as music alone, they would seem to make little sense. In the context of television, however, the music is indelibly tied to what is seen in vision. This might be the exterior of Roseanne's house, or an 'across-the-street' shot showing the entrance to Sam's bar in *Cheers*. The sitcom, *Friends*, for example, frequently uses a stock shot of a brownstone apartment building in New York (which signifies the friends' apartment block). The brief visual sequence, often a gentle pan up the building, is always accompanied by a short phrase of music and is frequently employed to move the characters from one location (the café, Central Perk) to another (one of the friends' apartments). The use of music here is unremarkable, despite the fact that *Friends* does not generally use non-diegetic music as 'score' anywhere else in the programme. In other programmes, such as *Charlie's Angels*, the exterior of a familiar building can be dispensed with; instead, there may be a simple videographic twisting of the television frame itself, plus an accompanying trill of music, which enables the shift in scene. In a more frenetic series, such as *Homicide: Life on the Streets*, the visual aspect will be much more mobile, with the camera scanning across a cityscape or freeway, and the 'music' may be more akin to sound effects that implicitly suggest police work. Thus we may hear distorted ambient sounds of sirens, helicopters and cars, arranged with syncopated beats from a drum machine.

It is clear that these audio-visual sequences are similar to the theme tune, which is designed to herald the viewer, call them to attention or silence them (Altman 1987). Yet, while it might seem obvious that these short musical interludes are designed to be impertinent, demanding that the audience 'look up', I am not convinced that they always *feel* like that for the regular viewer. Certainly, when US programmes are shown in the UK, the interludes do not always 'fit' appropriately into commercial breaks and, indeed, if seen on the BBC, which does not feature any advertisement breaks at all, they may even seem entirely redundant. However, if we stop thinking about the soundtrack and image as entirely separate from one another, as if the sound and music's only effect is to make us concentrate on the image, then we can understand the audio-visual interlude as a more organic part of the 'choreography' of the programme. The movement implied by the music, whether or not any movement within the visual sequence supports it, can become part of the established rhythm, or the temporally organized emotional experience of the programme. The audience's feelings about the programme, and their participation in the emotions generated by it, can be related, in part, to the repetition of these musical interludes. The repetition of the music enables particular emotions to be consistently and continually accumulated or alluded to as the individual programme, or the ongoing series of related programmes, is viewed. Importantly, this accumulated effect is *in addition to* the specific content of any two scenes that the interlude may actually 'bridge' in any one programme. These musical interludes thus become symptomatic of the experience, the sensibility or atmosphere of the programme itself, and function as a kind of musical 'uber-motif'. For example, the musical phrase that supports the scene change in *Charlie's Angels* is a perky, flirty trill, generally ending on an upbeat high note, which says a great deal about the tone of the programme itself. In stark contrast, the complex sonic buzz of the sound effects used in *Homicide* creates a completely different kind of rhythm and experience. Clearly, despite the fact that both dramas involve detective work and solving 'crimes', they are very different and this can be heard even in these short musical interludes. The happy 'trill' of *Charlie's Angels* suggests a costume change as much as it does a scene change ('give us a twirl'). And, of course, the hairstyles (Farrah Fawcett-Majors' famous 'flicks') and costumes (bikinis, jumpsuits and shiny dresses) were very much part of this show's particular appeal. In contrast, *Homicide's* sonic buzz foregrounds the city, and provides an echo of the cool but threatening urban soundscape also reproduced in 'gangsta' rap music. *Homicide's* audio-visual bridges thus encourage the audience to accumulate (in terms of what they hear, as well as what they see) a feeling of tension appropriate to a narrative that features policemen and women who must do their work in an overwhelming and uncontrollable urban environment. The city streets are never empty, since the audio-visual interlude 'fills in' as an aural substitute for the people and places we pass over as we move from one intense scene to another.

Similarly, theme tunes also do much more than simply herald the viewer and are, in fact, often quite complex audio signifiers of the style, pace and structuring narrative of the programmes they identify. In his analysis of the opening sequence of *ER*, Jason Jacobs (2001) has demonstrated that the many-layered texture of the theme tune not only works to complement the visual images, but also signals other aspects of the programme. The 'variations on a siren theme' indicate that it is a hospital drama; the abrupt percussive sounds of the drum machine indicate action, of trolleys bearing critically ill patients being crashed through hospital doors. The main theme is bold, featuring short, high-pitched sounds suggesting urgency, as well as the sound of electronic medical equipment; but the cadence of the melody itself is implicitly mournful as it rises and falls away. The effect is to create a complex and seductive musical texture that is at once modern (as Jacobs notes, it owes much to ambient and trance music) and generically appropriate. The music complements and is supported by the visual montage of the title sequence. More than this, however, the theme music also identifies the particular narrative structure of the programme, suggesting the presence of interweaving storylines and multiple characters. In some senses, the theme can also be heard to express what Jacobs suggests is the particular problematic of the hospital drama – the tension between 'morbidity' (tales of trauma, illness and death) and 'glamour' (doctors and nurses saving lives and their personal and romantic entanglements).

Television idents

Music also features regularly on television as a way of 'branding' channel identities. All television channels employ 'idents', different audio-visual interludes screened in between the transmission of programmes and/or advertising. These sequences, which can be as short as one or two seconds or run for several minutes, are promotional trailers for the channel itself. Their primary function is to identify the channel (via its number '4', name 'Nickelodeon' or acronym 'BBC One') and they commonly involve a live-action or graphic image sequence, supported or driven by music. Mark Brownrigg and Peter Meech, in their analysis of the music from a range of past and current idents, suggest that on British television there has been a move away from the 'fanfare' model previously heard in these sequences to an ambient, music as 'funfair' accompaniment (Brownrigg and Meech 2002). The fanfare model, they note, is closely associated with music used by Hollywood studios, such as the famous trumpet-based fanfare that is used to support the display of the logo for Twentieth Century Fox. Variations on this theme continue to be popular in America, possibly due to the closer relationship between Hollywood studios and the television networks in the USA. However, in the UK, particularly since the success of the animated '2' logo for BBC Two in the 1990s, more diffuse and less ostentatious music and sounds have been used.

The popular '2' logo was introduced onto BBC Two in 1991, and was designed by the company Lambie-Nairn. The 2 appeared in a variety of guises, including a furry, somersaulting, three-dimensional figure and a metallic, flat design, 'artfully' splashed by paint. One of its major innovations was to adapt itself to the programming context. For instance, as a preview to a horror film, the 2 might appear with the top arch of the number 2 weaving towards the camera, cutting through the floor. This was clearly a clever pastiche of the famous sequence from the film *Jaws*, where the fin of the shark is seen cutting through the surface of

Fig 2.1 BBC Two '2' logo © BBC

the sea. For food programmes, the 2 might appear covered in baked beans or as batter in a frying pan. The series of idents were so successful they were credited with changing the public's opinion of BBC Two; previously perceived as an elite channel aimed at 'stuffy', older viewers, Lambie-Nairn claim that within six months the idents had changed popular perception to such an extent that the channel was now identified as a cutting-edge channel that appealed to a much younger audience. Significantly, the idents were not accompanied by one endlessly repeated musical phrase, but featured a range of different kinds of music or sound effect. For instance, the furry, somersaulting 2 squeaked like a mechanical toy as it bounced, and the shark-like 2 was accompanied by a pastiche of the famous *Jaws'* rhythmic bass sounds ('der-duh, der-duh, der-duh'). The use of the sound effect to complement or substantiate the ident as animated graphic had been established by MTV and it was this association, perhaps, that allowed the idents to connect to younger audiences.

After several design changes in the 1990s, the BBC have recently (2003) introduced a new range of idents on BBC One, which, for the first time, abandon the 'globe' as a central visual motif. Instead, the idents, again designed and produced by Lambie-Nairn, are, it is claimed, based on 'the universal theme of rhythm, dance and music and are designed to represent the vibrancy and diversity of both the channel and its viewers'. The idents, which feature ballet dancers, tap dancers, people dancing in wheelchairs, salsa dancers, acrobats and figures performing t'ai chi, are interesting in this context because each of the idents is now supported by a different musical arrangement, appropriate to the dance or movements being performed. Significantly, the musical phrase itself is essentially the same across the idents, but has been rearranged to fit the mood and environment of each visual sequence. Thus, the tap dancers have an arrangement which features a strong percussive element, while the acrobats are supported by one which employs strings, to create a lighter and more elegant feel to the music. ITV has also finally succeeded in creating a 'global' brand identity across all the regional companies, all of which now use similar idents that use people as an essential element. Personalities and actors associated with ITV programming are shown in ostensibly 'off-duty' moments, accompanied by a particular phrase of music. The musical phrase used for each sequence is not the same for all idents, but the celebrities are 'grouped' through an association with a particular kind of music and setting. Younger presenters, such as Ant and Dec or Davina McCall, are associated with an upbeat, 'funky' phrase, whereas older celebrities, such as the sports presenter, Des Lynam, have a slower, more jazz-inspired accompaniment. For the BBC, then, music is a way of establishing a brand identity across the 'diversity' implied by the visual sequences, whereas ITV's idents offer a variety that is organized by the music and setting into identifiable 'groups' for the viewer. The branding for the BBC therefore implies representation; the essential elements of the programming are the same for everyone, but the audience is implicitly diverse and the programmes are about you. ITV's idents, however, emphasize variety as consumption, since, even though ostensibly off-duty, the celebrities are clearly on display, as if they were in a shop window. In terms of what can be heard, the music is an important signal to the audience as to how certain personalities offer similar kinds of viewing experience, and therefore indicate which parts of ITV's programming schedule different parts of the audience might want to 'buy into'. In other words, if you like Ant and Dec, you might like Davina, too.

Brownrigg and Meech suggest that the move towards more ambient, multi-layered music or eclectic sound effects for idents can be associated with the trend for ambient, dance-oriented music that is associated with the contemporary music scene. They also argue that the idents are now composed to allow the audience to 'catch their breath' between programmes. While not disputing this, I feel that the change in the sonic accompaniment of idents also relates to their changing role in the new broadcasting landscape. Previously, idents might be used as part of 'start-up' sequences, where channels which had been off-air would restart transmission. The 'look-at-me', herald sound of the fanfare was clearly designed to say, 'here I am again'. The idents were also used previously to 'fill' the passing of time between programmes as the audience waited for the next programme to begin. However, since 24-hour programming is now firmly established in the UK, there are rarely instances of channels needing to signal their arrival back on the television screen. Similarly, there are now few instances where any channel would be confident enough to believe that the audience is patiently 'waiting around' for the next programme rather than flicking between channels with the remote control. Instead, television channels now wish to emphasize their qualities as an ongoing, habitable and comfortable environment. This means that the music is used emphatically to allude to the spatial rather than temporal qualities of individual television channels. In some senses, the music used in ident sequences is now more akin to a sophisticated version of 'muzak' or the carefully programmed selections of music heard in shopping malls and in global franchises such as Starbucks. You are 'here', the music says; isn't that a good place to be? Sound effects, which effectively 'realize' the animations or graphic sequences, equally establish the channel as a place, a three-dimensional environment. The channel is now, metaphorically, or sonically speaking, no longer a flat (two-dimensional) electronic signal, but a place or a home where people and objects can walk, dance or zoom about. Crucially, it is music, or 'sound as music', which enables the visuals to become fully realized. It is the music that makes the dancing figures move, and the sound which establishes the personality and solidity of the 2 as we hear it whirr, bubble or squeak.

Clearly, there is more that could be said about music on television, and I have limited myself, as far as possible, to examples that are peculiar to television. In the case study that concludes this chapter I will explore some of the ways that music as score is used within one television programme. In the next section, I will concentrate on the potentially tautological concept of sound as sound. However, as my concluding remarks here suggest, it is important to note that there is a definite categorical 'blur' which exists between what can be understood purely as 'music' and what can be identified as solely or exclusively 'sound' on television.

Sound as sound

In this section, I want to concentrate on the different ways in which we hear sound as sound on television. Sound as sound refers to the various noises, effects and environmental sounds that occur on television. As I suggested in my introduction to the chapter, it is important to establish that sound as sound does not unproblematically refer to sounds that are simply lifted or recorded from real life. Just as the human voice is manipulated, edited and mediated by television, so, too, are the sounds that we hear. One of the most obvious ways that this occurs is that, as in film, many sounds heard on television are artificially reproduced in a foley studio or sourced from sound libraries or production archives. The BBC, for example, in their annual presentation of the Wimbledon tennis tournament, has used the same background sound, a track of atmospheric 'birdsong', for at least 30 years. Specific sounds required in a visual sequence – such as footsteps in gravel or the sound of a whale breaking the surface of the sea – may well have been created with, or enhanced by, sounds recorded in a foley studio. Although many of these sounds could have been recorded at the same time as the visual track, the image is frequently post-dubbed with these 'artificial' sounds or enhanced during post-production. Ultimately, the sound heard by the audience may be designed specifically to be louder, clearer or more 'appropriate' (so that, for instance, a *big* whale makes a *big* splash). If we can understand that the speaking body on television is an act of ventriloquism, we should note that this is equally true of all sounds that we hear on television.

Concrete sounds

These sounds are heard in synch with specific events or objects that are seen on-screen. In almost all cases, this persuades the audience that the object or event is indeed producing that sound. Concrete sounds give substance or weight to the actions of people, animals and objects. This may be the door slamming, a car screeching to a halt or the sound of someone being punched in the face. We see the action and have learnt to expect that the sound will seem appropriate to the action or object we are seeing. The whale goes 'splash!' and the gravel goes 'crunch!' Concrete sounds on television are therefore nearly always *appropriate* and rarely confound our expectations. Sound mismatch does occur, but it is generally for deliberate comic effect, taking place most frequently in cartoons, but also in 'home video' shows, such as *Who's Been Framed?* Here, inappropriate sounds or the intermittent absence of concrete sound and the substitution of a pop/rock soundtrack ensures that the people, animals and objects are seen to perform (accidentally) as if they were in a cartoon or slapstick comedy. The lack of 'real' sound makes their possible pain less real and, therefore, allowably funny to the watching audience. Interestingly, in *Jackass*, an MTV programme that has had cult and popular success both in the UK and in the USA, this rule is sometimes subverted. The show is basically a series of semi-professional capers, involving a group of young men, led by the charismatic Johnny Knoxville. The group perform a selection of stunts similar to those traditionally used in many different 'candid camera' shows, as well as some deliberately imbecilic activities, such as fashioning live bee underpants, throwing balls at each other's genitals or simply throwing themselves downstairs. Part of the programme's appeal actually stems from the real pain of its protagonists and there is a deliberate emphasis on their masochistic machismo. Accordingly, while rock music is sometimes used to soundtrack their activities, the concrete sound (the slapping of bare flesh with raw fish, the buzz of the bees or the thud of someone falling downstairs) is often enhanced to exaggerate the physical impact and demonstrably real pain involved.

Concrete sounds in context

What this exaggeration demonstrates is that, while concrete sounds, like the human voice, are generally appropriate, they are always made *approximate* to their context and adjusted to fit the overall soundscape of the programme. Concrete sounds are thus contained on television and, although they are used to substantiate events and objects and, as I have suggested, to 'realize' the images we see on-screen, they do not reflect or reproduce how we would actually hear those sounds in real life. In effect, concrete sounds are often diminished, despite the fact that they may appear to leap out from the soundtrack at times. For example, a gunshot at close quarters, in a closed environment like a car, would be incredibly loud – loud enough to have a physical effect (for example, your ears might 'ring' for some time). Heard in the context of a television programme, the sound of a gunshot may well be loud, but the effect of the sound cannot be said to be similar to the way the sound would be heard in real life. However realistic the sound appears to be, it can never reproduce the specific sound context that determines how that particular sound will be heard or felt by the auditor or replicate the particular environments which affect the way in which sound decays as it approaches the listener. The specific sound qualities, the relationship between impact and decay, cannot be perfectly reproduced. For example, the sound we hear when someone is being punched in the face might, theoretically, be satisfactorily recorded and reproduced in the context of a boxing match. Then, however, the sound will have to travel from microphones in the ring, from the speakers of your television, over the carpet, over this evening's dinner and finally reach your ears as you sit on the sofa. Thus the sound of the punch must travel over and be affected by a very different environment to the sweaty, raucous boxing crowd who are an instrumental part of the environment of the event. Evidently, your 'ringside' seat at home does not concur sonically, even if may appear (at times) to do so visually.

The sound of sport

Different sports tend to have different ways of incorporating the concrete sound of play into the programme. Televised football, for example, tends to privilege the sound of the crowd over other sounds, since this appears to enhance the 'live' atmosphere of the game. The sound of the ball being kicked is only heard at moments where there seems to be a natural lull in the crowd noise, such as when the goalkeeper kicks the ball up the field. The voices, panting and grunting of the players are rarely heard. In tennis, however, the crowd is effectively silenced ('quiet, please') and, aside from the regular sound of the ball being hit from one side of the court to the other, the grunting and panting of the players is clearly audible. Obviously, this distinction is partly related to the fact that tennis is more contained as a sport and covers less space, so that fixed microphones can be sure of picking up all the sound with limited ambient disruption. However, it is also the case that the sound is bound into the perception of the sport itself. Football, as a team event, is strongly associated with unified groups of supporters, whose presence is at least as significant as that of the individual players; the goalkeeper's free kick is therefore more akin to punctuation, marking the rhythm of the game rather than being a display of virtuosity. Otherwise, the swell and roar of the crowd washes over the action as an accompaniment, or the 'ground' to the 'figure' of the commentator's patter. In tennis, the focus is on the individual and how they are coping psychologically, as well as physically, with the demands of the game.

Although the way in which concrete sounds in sport are heard may seem to be inevitable and tied into the structure and environment of the game, there is actually no reason why the soundscape of individual sports on television cannot be changed. In the UK, Sky Television's coverage of Premier League football has clearly altered the sound of the sport on television, so that the sound of the ball being kicked is more audible than before. At the same time, there has been an increase in the number of camera angles available to the viewer, and the various attempts to increase interactivity for the home viewer, who now has to pay directly for access to the sport. The changes to the sound and visual aspects of the game prioritize the position and status of the individual viewer at home as spectator, rather than attempting to pull the television viewer into a vicarious position as part of the crowd at the event itself. Changes have also been made to other televised sports. Part of Channel 4's revamping of televised cricket has involved the introduction of mini-cameras and microphones on the wickets. This means that sounds previously unheard in the televised version of the game – the tapping of the batsman's bat against the ground as he waits for the bowler's delivery, the bowler's approach and the thud as the ball bounces before it reaches the batsman – are all potentially audible. The microphone (and camera) at the stump places the audience audibly (and visually) right at the heart of the action and emphasizes the visceral, physical element of the game. It is now difficult to ignore, for instance, the fact that the cricket ball is extremely hard and is approaching 'you' at up to 90 miles an hour – surprising, perhaps, for a game previously associated with 'middle England' and as a genteel, gentleman's game. Clearly, this audible disruption is an important element in the repositioning of the game by Channel 4, and one of the distinctive aspects of Channel 4's coverage, when cricket as a sport moved from its original position on the BBC, was its redefinition as a 'post-colonial' global sport. Cricket's post-colonial status and *global* identity was openly signalled by the initial Channel 4 trailers promoting the move, which featured children from a range of different backgrounds and different parts of the world playing the game in their home environment. Ownership of the game of cricket is obviously no longer the preserve of a mythical, imperial 'England'. Metaphorically, and literally, therefore, the place of the 'English' viewer-as-listener in relation to cricket is no longer as secure as it once seemed to be.

The disgusting sound of nature

Another important television genre that relies upon concrete sounds to create a particular, visceral response in its audience is the nature documentary. Natural history programmes are known for their spectacular sequences of wildlife and landscape, and their visual aspects would seem to dominate the audience's experience and appreciation of this kind of programme. One of the fascinating aspects of these programmes, however, is how they sound. As high-budget, prestige productions, many of these programmes, especially those produced by the BBC, such as *The Blue Planet* and *Life on Earth*, have a specially composed classical music score, and a compelling, patrician voice-over from David Attenborough. What they also feature, of course, is a range of disgusting sound effects. While sequences of birds flying, fish swimming and gazelles leaping may be associated with the evocative, and conventionally beautiful, rise and fall of the musical soundtrack, the audience also hears, very clearly, when animals are eating, giving birth, fighting and fornicating. Animals squelch, slurp and, if they are underwater, bubble very distinctly on television. Of course, in most instances, the sound is entirely appropriate to their activity: the sound of hyenas snuffling, grunting, ripping and slurping their way through a felled zebra is crucial to the audience's fascination with this sight. The way these sounds are used is obviously in accordance with the use of concrete sounds elsewhere on television, since they help to fully 'realize' the events seen. This is also true, for instance, of some scenes of human sexual activity. Sound, particularly the intimate sounds of sucking, grunting and slurping, increases the visceral impact of such scenes, generating an audible proximity, even if the visual aspects are sometimes – through necessity – taken at a distance. Sound's ability to suggest touch can make the programme thrilling in a way that visual spectacle alone might not: for while we can see the hyenas eating, we will 'feel' the sound of a slurp or a squelch in a much more intimate manner.

Musical sounds

In addition to concrete sounds that are visibly attached to particular events or objects on-screen, other sounds as sound that can be heard are those perceived as 'atmosphere'. As ambient sounds, made louder or faded under dialogue or commentary, these kinds of sounds might be understood as 'musical sounds'. In drama, the barely audible hubbub of voices often serves as the background for dialogue spoken by central characters. One of the innovations of the much-lauded American police series, *Hill Street Blues*, was its inclusion of a specially recorded 'atmos' track, involving actors improvising murmuring and conversations that would serve to audibly thicken the 'realism' of the show, set in a busy police station. Most drama series in the UK and the USA now conventionally use this kind of sound as sound. For scenes that are shot outside, appropriate atmos is also important. Series that are set in an urban environment will be supported with 'city sounds', such as cars, sirens and dogs barking. Just as the music or 'musical sound' that supports the bridging between scenes can provide an audible signature for a programme, the atmos track also subtly places the viewer-as-listener in the visual scene.

The sound of the crowd

One of the most distinctive aspects of television sound is the audible inclusion of an audience that may either be seen (at times) on-screen or is never seen at all. As I have already noted, in the televised presentation of sport, the crowd's roars, chants and cheers are crucial to the experience and atmosphere of the game. The sound of the audience, however, is also important to a range of different television genres – it can be heard in game shows, sitcoms, variety shows, music programmes, current affairs programmes, chat shows and live public events. In the majority of programmes that might be categorized loosely as light entertainment, the sound of the audience is included to cue the audience at home as to the kind of affective response the actions of the actors and entertainers should generate. The sound of the audience – laughing, coughing, screaming – both *suggests* a response ('Don't you think it's funny, too?') and *confirms* and *allows* for the audience's own reaction ('It is meant to be funny'). Of course, the sound of the audience heard in this way is rarely spontaneous or actual, even if the sitcom or game show is overtly recorded before a 'live' studio audience. Laughter, cheers and boos are manipulated initially through a 'warm-up man' – a comedian or actor who does not appear on-screen – who is employed to loosen the audience's inhibitions, explain to them what is expected and generate anticipation and excitement for when the central performers finally appear. Second, after the recording of the programme, the sound of the crowd will be manipulated in post-production, so that the laughter, for instance, will be appropriate, in the right place and suitably audible. This is because the business of filming, with its necessary stops and starts, when, for example, the actors fluff lines and move between sets, will mean that the audience's actual build towards the 'biggest laugh' may not concur with the finished narrative of the programme. One name for this kind of sound is the 'laughter track', something which in itself reveals the mediated aspect of the sound. As its appearance is often seen as being a result of manipulation, along with its association with vulgar light-entertainment genres, the sound of the crowd signals a lack of 'quality'. Certain sitcoms (for example, the American sitcom *M*A*S*H* when it was shown in the UK, and the British sitcoms, *The Royle Family* and *The Office*) do not have laugh tracks and, consequently, their humour is judged to be more subtle and intellectual. Audiences at home are supposedly left to make up their own minds as to what is funny and to experience moments of pathos and empathy as well as humour. The laugh track is one of television's most explicit attempts to promote the illusion of sociability, to suggest that television viewing is a social rather than an individual encounter. While it is one of the most obvious aspects of television, sound is surprisingly easy not to hear consciously. The sound of the audience, then, is often present and important in terms of atmosphere and environment (hearing as feeling), but is rarely listened to (as if it were directly communicating).

One interesting incident in the UK, however, illustrates the potential significance and communicative potential of crowd noise. In September 2001, Major Charles Ingram apparently won the million pound prize in an episode of *Who Wants to be a Millionaire?* that was due to be screened on 10 September. However, during and after the recording, members of the studio audience and production crew became convinced he was cheating. It appeared that another contestant, a college lecturer, Tecwen Whittock, had been coughing to guide Ingram's answers. Ultimately, Ingram, his wife, Diana, and Whittock were all convicted of fraud in April 2003. Central to the prosecution of the trial was the recording of the programme, which did appear to confirm that Whittock was coughing on cue. In particular, it was argued that the Major's odd playing strategy, his continued repetition of potential answers and the coughing were not accidental, but clearly part of a strategy to direct him towards the right answers. Aside from the coughing, it also became evident that when the major was noticeably wavering on the answer to the £500,000 question, Whittock could be heard audibly blowing his nose and uttering the word 'No'. Whittock claimed that there had been no deliberate coughing and that his attack had been caused by hay fever, exacerbated by the hot studio environment. The Ingrams, in turn, claimed that the tape had been edited to make it seem as if there had been a direct link between the coughs and correct answers. Unconvinced by their arguments, a jury convicted all three via a majority verdict. For this, they received suspended sentences and were ordered to pay legal costs. Celador and ITV, the channel that transmits the programme in the UK, were also able to profit from the scandal by producing a hugely successful documentary about the affair, *Millionaire: A Major Fraud*.

This incident demonstrates that the conventionally 'unheard' sounds made by the audience can be vitally important. Interestingly, while Whittock's coughs were suspected by the production crew and some audience members, Chris Tarrant, the host of the show, did not 'hear' them during the recording process. The coughs clearly had to be listened for to make sense as communication rather than emanation. Another interesting element that became evident from the recording of the episode was that the audience themselves had also unwittingly helped Ingram. Having already used his 'ask the audience' facility, the major was struggling to decide which of two pop acts had released a particular album. Finally, he appeared to select one of the artists. At this point, the studio audience could be heard gasping with surprise; unsurprisingly, perhaps, the major changed his mind.

In the context of the game show, emanation as communication is not unusual. After all, audible support or direction from the on-screen audience is an important aspect of other game shows, most notably, perhaps, in *The Price is Right*. In this programme, the on-screen audience is actively encouraged to scream support to the contestants choosing prices for different consumer goods ('Higher, higher!' 'Lower, lower!'). Similarly, in *Blind Date*, the audience noise often directs the final selection of the date. What is interesting about *Who Wants to be a Millionaire?*, however, is how the programme tries to contain this response. First, it does so through the official 'ask the audience' facility, as one of the 'lifelines' a contestant may opt for as they progress through the questions – here, the audience does not shout out, but records their answers electronically through individual keypads. Second, the audience is disempowered through the lighting design, as they are effectively made invisible while questions are being asked and answers sought. During this oft-repeated sequence in the show, the studio lights dim down so that only the quizmaster and the contestant can be seen, although there are occasional cutaways to an anxious relative or friend of the contestant, who is lit by a small sidelight. Even the other potential contestants, who await the next round of 'fastest finger first', are in darkness. The sound of the audience is therefore discouraged – they are waiting 'in the dark', with 'bated breath', and are explicitly silenced. Unlike the audience at home, who are likely to be shouting at the screen with the answer, the on-screen audience is limited to inadvertent sounds, such as gasps, coughs and sneezes. In this context, it is not surprising that someone caught up in the midst of the excitement – such as Tarrant – would miss what would seem all too obvious to the ultimate viewers and listeners of the televised version of the show. Once it became *television*, the sound of the audience in the programme could be understood more readily as an abstract rather than material event. Separating the sound from the body (a fundamental aspect of recorded sound), without reattaching it to a visible body, revealed that the coughs and snuffle were not simply, or innocently, ambient noise. Television's separation of the cough from the body, or the nose from the sound of its blowing, meant that the sounds could be recognized more easily as deliberate, as communication rather than emanation. In contrast, hearing the sounds in the context of the set would mean that the sounds Whittock made would still have been visibly attached to a real body, and the material origin of the sound still apparent. Sitting 10 feet away and distracted by the narrative of the game, Tarrant's awareness of Whittock's physical and still visible presence would have consolidated his assumption that any sound it emanated was natural, inadvertent and non communicative.

Hearing problems

It should be clear that the relative audibility of concrete sound on television is an important aspect of the viewer's understanding and relationship to the content of individual programmes. It is also the case that the position and audibility of such sounds is now increasingly open to revision by the individual viewer. Television viewers have always been able to control the loudness of television sound and, increasingly, they are now able to determine the 'dimensional' qualities of television's sound as well. Via their remote control, many viewers can now select options which will manipulate the sound so that it reverberates as though the sound were being heard in a particular space, such as a 'concert hall' or a 'cathedral'. Or they may simply increase or decrease certain aspects of the sound, such as the dialogue, music, echo or bass effects, to enhance or even override the mix of sound provided by the programme. This means that, even more unpredictably than in the cinema, television producers must negotiate the fact that each viewer can modify how they hear each programme. And even if it were possible, objectively speaking, to reproduce accurately the sound in a way that was ideal professionally, it is also the case that sound has an important subjective element as well. Individual listeners will have their own idiosyncratic ways of responding to particular sounds.

However, with the introduction of digital television and widescreen technology, there has been increasing pressure to develop a depth and breadth of sound that seems to fit the wider screen better and that attempts to replicate the quality of sound found in cinema. The development and marketing of the different technologies needed to construct 'home theatres' is key here. Not surprisingly, it is seeing films on DVD in the home, rather than the development of television programming, that seems to be the driving force. However, the shift towards increasing sound quality has encouraged television producers to develop a richer, broader, deeper soundscape. In programmes such as *The Sopranos*, and other dramas such as *Six Feet Under* and *CSI: Crime Scene Investigation*, increasing attention is paid to sound perspective, the layering of sound and some attempt to develop notional sound 'subjectivity'.

Sound as silence

When is television ever silent? Popularly, television is sometimes seen as an 'idiot box', chattering away endlessly, never pausing for breath. Actually, this is not really true of television, at least in the UK. Several British channels, such as Channel 5 and Channel 4, provide an audible 'blink' as a bumper between a programme and a selection of advertisements and trailers. This moment of silence, associated with a visual 'break bumper' (sometimes the name of the channel sliding across the screen), disrupts the audible flow of noise and acts as punctuation for the flow of programming. Otherwise, when television is silent, it would seem that it is either a deliberate intervention by the home viewer – via the mute button – or an accidental, technical fault in transmission. Even during a technical fault, however, it is rare to hear nothing, as usually the first thing viewers note is the sound of music, accompanied by an explanatory sign, which promises that 'normal service' will be resumed shortly.

Is it true, then, that television is 'normally' audible? Perhaps it would be more accurate to say that it nearly always has the *potential* to be heard, but, in fact, it is surprisingly often seen and not heard. One of the most obvious ways that television is silenced is through its increasing use and display outside the home. In bars, cafés, urinals, in shopping malls and on large screens in city centres, television is often visible without being audible (although it can be both). This can produce some interesting contrasts. In my local café, for example, MTV or VH1 is often displayed on the two televisions on view, yet the staff generally prefer their own music, allowing for a happy combination of Van Morrison apparently being danced to by Christina Aguilera. More recently, the café staff have tended to select and mute Sky News. Previously, television news would have seemed bereft without sound, as it is traditionally so dominated by detailed commentary and voice-over. However, Sky News, along with other newer channels (and, increasingly, the major terrestrial networks in the USA, following the lead of CNN) are distinguished by their heavy rotation of rolling captions and subtitles. These channels also regularly employ large written headlines or (inaudible) 'soundbites' that float behind the news talking heads. When important news breaks, the café staff are thus able to mute their music and turn up the sound on the television. As I suggested in the chapter on image, the increasingly caption-heavy presentation of television news may well be linked to the silent reception of television in a wide range of places and spaces outside the home.

Other kinds of non-domestic television are also more 'usually' silent. Closed-circuit television (CCTV) used in malls, stores, airports and, increasingly, in most public spaces, such as city streets and sports grounds, is conventionally silent. This kind of television is rarely viewed by a non-specialist audience and is used mainly by the police and security forces. When it is seen on television, however, it is usually accompanied by an explanatory voice-over, directing the viewer where to look or asking for the viewer to identify individuals who may be lost or in the process of committing a crime. The lack of sound, however, can lend a peculiar ambience to some of these images. In the UK, two particular sequences have been shown frequently without sound or with limited commentary. The first of these is the footage of the toddler, James Bulger, being led away from a shopping mall in Liverpool by two young boys. This is the last footage of James alive, since the two young boys, tragically, went on to kill James later that day. The public horror and shock at the murder meant that the sequence was shown so frequently on television (in news programmes and documentaries) that an explanation became redundant. The silence of television in relation to this particular sequence seemed to make the blurred images resonant with the future tragic consequences of the boys' meeting. The second sequence shows Princess Diana and her lover, Dodi Fayed, leaving the Ritz Hotel in Paris via the back entrance. Again, this is the last sequence showing Diana alive, since it was taken immediately before her car crashed and she, Dodi and the driver were killed. The sequence shows the time and, although sometimes accompanied by commentary (pointing out the driver, for example), its repetition was often silent, again, audibly distinguishing this visual sequence from the rest of television.

On television, then, silence commonly heralds or reflects upon death. Certain specific ceremonies in the UK call for silence in relation to death and are televised accordingly. Remembrance Sunday (which recalls the sacrifice of servicemen and women from the two world wars) calls for three minutes of silence. When broadcasting the official public ceremony from London, both ITV and the BBC necessarily screen three minutes of 'silence', although visually there is still movement, as the camera scans the public faces among the mourners. Similarly, before certain sporting events, a minute's silence is sometimes organized, either to remember recently deceased sporting heroes or, occasionally, tragic news events (such as the murder of the two Soham schoolgirls in the UK in 2002). Infrequently, certain news events are seen as so significant that certain images or sequences are also shown without sound. After Princess Diana's death, sequences of her life and charitable works were frequently added into news reports, and these were either accompanied with mournful music or the original sound. However, on ITV, a still image of Diana was also shown at the end of one news report for two minutes, without sound, presumably to allow the audience time to reflect upon her death. Similarly, the now iconic footage of the aeroplanes crashing into the World Trade Center towers in New York was shown without sound. Interestingly, when ITN presented an edited visual sequence of the 'events' of 11 September 2001, with music by the composer Gounod, they were criticized heavily. The music, although classical, was seen as too obviously dramatic, and was synchronized to the events (planes crashing, cymbals clashing), so that the sequence seemed a little like a music video. Silence, presumably, would have been more appropriate. In fact, much of the visual footage from the events of 11 September had a problematic relationship to sound. Actual sound was either too incoherent or potentially distressing. I remember, for instance, the shock I felt when, in a documentary made and shown much later, I actually heard, for the first time, the sound of the bodies when they hit the ground outside one of the towers. I had, like most of the rest of the world, seen pictures of people leaping and bodies falling when the events were in process and this had seemed shocking enough. The sound, however, was far more powerful in realizing the event and the fact that these bodies were people; it is not surprising, therefore, that, initially at least, the use of actual sound (live sound recorded on location) was intermittent, and that certain image sequences were often shown without any sound at all.

The absence of sound on television is often related to the missing sound's potential to cause offence. As I have suggested, this is because the sound of voices, or even apparently innocent concrete sounds, might cause distress. More commonly, however, sound may also be removed for legal reasons. In *Big Brother*, for example, in both the 'ordinary' and celebrity versions, live sound is often faded out or replaced by white noise to drown out what the contestants are saying. This usually takes place when individuals are discussing people and events in such a way that it may make them and the programme-makers open to allegations of libel. While understandable, for the viewer it can be very frustrating, particularly in *Celebrity Big Brother* or, indeed, in the similar programme, *I'm A Celebrity: Get Me Out of Here!* In both these programmes, significant parts of their live transmission are effectively silent. Presumably, the celebrities are discussing other well-known individuals, perhaps from their own private perspective and knowledge. What is frustrating is that this kind of conversation is part of the reason the audience is interested in the programme in the first place, as they hope to hear celebrity 'secrets' that are not in the public domain. Ultimately, while the absence of sound is frustrating, it can also increase the voyeuristic atmosphere of the show. Since it is frequently silent, the live footage becomes more akin to surveillance from CCTV cameras, and the audience is obliged (if they are willing) to work harder to make sense of the images. Without sound, they are forced to imagine what might be being said, and witness how contestants are relating to one another or 'being themselves', through body language alone.

In *Big Brother* the potentially offensive aspect of sound can work in two ways. In the UK version, the house is situated alongside an extensive garden, with a high fence, which both protects and incarcerates the contestants. Just beyond this is the relatively public space of the recording studio and an arena where the public, friends and family gather on eviction nights. It is possible for either individuals or a crowd to make enough noise from this quasi-public space to be heard by the contestants when they are in the garden. Infamously, in *Big Brother 3*, one contestant – Jade Goody – was taunted with cries of 'Pig! Pig!' from the crowd, who were inspired by misogynist tabloid coverage. In *Big Brother 4*, one contestant, Anouska ('Nush'), was told, via a megaphone, that her boyfriend had called an end to their relationship. In fact, sound from the outside became such a problem in *Big Brother 4* that contestants frequently were either ordered to stay indoors or played loud music to cover such sounds as the boos of the crowd as certain contestants were evicted.

Conclusion

As I suggested at the beginning of this chapter, sound is a powerful force, and one of its most important aspects is that it can seem more aggressive and more intimate than the image. Television, unlike the crowd in *Big Brother*, rarely uses sound to try to intimidate its audience. Instead, as I have shown, aside from a few exceptional instances, television organizes a carefully moderated wash of sound for the viewer-as-listener. In the same way, silence is employed carefully so it fits the context. On several channels and in many programmes, intermittent audible blinks or pauses are essential to the rhythm of presentation or the atmosphere of specific sports (particularly golf and snooker). Longer periods of silence occur far more rarely, although they are used both to signify events of great importance and for events that are too awful, perhaps, for anything to be heard at all.

Case study: *Teletubbies*

Teletubbies was originally a 30-minute programme, shown daily, aimed at children between one and three years of age. Created and produced by Ragdoll Ltd for the BBC, the programme first ran on the BBC in the UK in 1997. Since its inception, *Teletubbies* has become a global phenomenon, screened in slightly different versions in more than 120 countries. There is also a wide range of attached merchandise, including toys, board games, books, PC games, video and audiocassettes and clothing. The programme's main protagonists are four large, alien 'toddlers', Tinky Winky, Dipsy, Laa-Laa and Po, who are, respectively, purple, green, yellow and red. The Tubbies have large round faces, baggy bottoms and individually shaped antennae on their heads; each one also has a screen situated on their stomach. They live and play in Teletubbyland, a land of rolling green hills, plastic flowers, large rabbits, blue skies and fluffy clouds. They share their dome-like, metallic home (the 'Tubbytronic superdome') with a mechanical vacuum cleaner-like creature, the 'Noo-noo'. Their world is also populated by a mechanical windmill, which spins to alert the Tubbies to tune into a video from the 'real world', which is then displayed to the Tubbies and the audience at home via one of their 'tummy-televisions'. The videos feature children between two and four years old, engaged in a variety of different activities, from washing cars and making cakes to rolling down hills. In addition, voice trumpets frequently push up, like periscopes, from the ground, to sing songs, tell nursery rhymes or suggest activities to the Tubbies. Their world is overlooked by a yellow sun, which frames the face of a baby, about nine months old, who looks down on the events with a mixture of interest, amusement or surprise.

Teletubbies was an immediate and controversial success. It is indisputably successful in attracting the attention of, and generating pleasure for, its very young audience. Much has already been written about the way in which the programme captivates or supposedly exploits its audience, but this is not my concern here (Buckingham 2002). Equally, the programme's use of colour and space, as well as the pacing and structure of its narrative, are obviously central to the show's popularity. In this context, however, it is the soundscape of *Teletubbies* that I wish to discuss.

For younger generations, at least in the UK, I think *Teletubbies* will be seen to have taught children how to watch and listen to television. The soundscape of *Teletubbies* – its use of music, sound effects and language – is very carefully planned and integrated into the global aim of the programme itself. The programme overtly aims to support fundamental learning processes that are important to the very young, such as language development and sociability. Anne Wood (1998), one of the series creators, claimed:

> The series is crafted with the understanding that little children watch television
> in a radically different way than older children and grown-ups watch. Teletubbies
> make liberal use of repetition, large movement, bright colours, and deliberate
> pace to nurture and reinforce the development of children's listening and
> thinking skills.

In other comments made in interviews, both Wood and her co-creator, Andrew Davenport, continually insist on the fact that the pedagogical style of *Teletubbies* is explicitly child-centred. In this model, children are believed to learn most effectively by gradually building an understanding of how the world works through a process of testing, repetition and imitation. They progress by grasping one element (a sound, for instance) and then connecting it to another feature of the world around them (the object which makes the sound). Learning is therefore implicitly structured around a narrative that is generated via a series of questions and answers; answers are recalled through repetition and imitation is constantly encouraged. Both Wood and Davenport also stress the importance of humour and

Fig 2.2 The Teletubbies © BBC

playfulness in the programme. For instance, on the BBC's *Teletubbies* website, they respond to a question that is concerned with the 'babyish' language used by the Tubbies, arguing, 'Children love to play with language – hence nursery rhymes and nonsense verse – and playing with something is by far the best way to learn about it' (Wood and Davenport).

So how does the sound in *Teletubbies* facilitate these ambitions? First, we can examine the different voices we hear in the programme. Perhaps surprisingly, given the concern the Tubbies' own voices have caused, the most dominant voice heard in the UK version of the programme is actually that of the unseen narrator, Tim Whitnall. His voice, distinctively adult, male and with an accent that is close to RP, is heard explaining events ('One day in Teletubbyland, something appeared from far away'). Alternatively, he can be heard telling the Tubbies to do something ('One day the Teletubbies went for a walk', 'Now it's time for Teletubbies to say goodbye'). While he remains unseen, the proximity of his voice is ensured through a slight deepening of the bass element, so that the narrator seems (audibly) to be sitting at the child's shoulder. In contrast, the Tubbies' own voices are clearly located in the space of the programme itself. Although Whitnall's voice is the main narrator of the programme, his authority only exists within the confines of Teletubbyland, since in the recognizably 'real' world, shown via the video inserts, it is a child's voice which acts as the narrator and it is the child, therefore, who explains what is happening ('Getting up in the morning', 'Going to the beach'). The children's voices are clearly coached and carefully edited, but they are recognizably *real* children's voices in terms of their pitch, dynamics and sometimes fragmented pace. The voices are not 'performed' and therefore feel and sound much less artificial than other children's voices on television, such as the children who sing and talk in a programme such as *Barney*. It is also significant that the children's voices are not 'impersonated' by anyone, as they are, for example, by adult actors in the majority of children's animation. In the *Teletubbies*, children's voices are recognizably authentic and, thus, perhaps more akin to children's speech when they are talking to one another than when they are performing for adults. So while the programme retains the 'schoolteacher' or parental narrator, he is regularly usurped by a real child, who is audibly placed as the 'author' of an accessible 'real-world' experience.

There is a surprisingly large number of voices heard in the programme. Aside from the Tubbies, the flowers, too, have voices, modelled, it seems to me, on the talking flowers from Lewis Caroll's *Alice in Wonderland* and an earlier children's programme in the UK, *Bill and Ben*. Speaking in a high-pitched, almost inaudible burble, the flowers can be slightly acerbic or patronizing, or simply rather camp, as they frequently comment on the Tubbies' behaviour ('How silly!' 'How lovely!'). The flowers do not speak very often, partly, I suspect, since their tone is not really in keeping with the overwhelmingly positive and innocent nature of the programme. Of the visitors to Teletubbyland, the most interesting voices are those of the Bear and the Scary Lion – cut-out animal figures on wheels that chase each other over the hills. The Bear's voice, while not credited, clearly belongs to the actress, Penelope Keith, while the Lion has a gruff male voice. Keith's voice is simply one of several (credited and uncredited) 'cameo' vocal appearances in the programme, which also features well-known British actors, such as Eric Sykes and Toyah Wilcox, both of whom are heard regularly in the opening sequence. The voices are only likely to be recognized by the parents listening and not the child. However, the range of voices – in terms of age, gender and class – is significant; Keith's voice, for instance, is definitively upper class and 'white', yet the programme also regularly uses another actor whose voice has a distinctive Afro-Caribbean texture and pitch (he is also seen in one of the video inserts, reading a story to a mother and baby group). Evidently, the diversity implied by the colour, size and apparently different gender of the Tubbies themselves is supported by the variety of different voices used in the programme.

The way in which the Tubbies themselves speak has provoked some of the most intense debate about the programme. All four speak in a 'babyish' way, that is, they mispronounce words, most infamously saying 'Eh-oh' for 'Hello'. Po, the smallest of the Tubbies, also occasionally speaks in Cantonese (Po was played by the Chinese actor/presenter Pui Fan Lee). Many critics suggested that the babyish language of the Tubbies was bad for children and that children's programmes had a responsibility to employ voices that speak 'properly'. This was actually a rather old debate in children's television, as earlier programmes such as *Morph*, *Bill and Ben* and *The Clangers* all involved characters who did not speak 'properly'. However, it became central to arguments around the 'dumbing down' of children's programmes and, ultimately, even the BBC itself. Thus, in a series of understandably defensive statements designed to counter these opinions, Wood defended the Tubbies' speech. In doing so, she reiterates one of the central aspects of the programme – 'playfulness': 'Andy and I compiled a list of the words and phrases that children first make their own and this comprises the

Teletubbies' own vocabulary. Like children, they also imitate what they hear, so they will attempt to speak like the narrator and, sometimes, like the voice trumpets' (Wood and Davenport). Davenport, in turn, returns to the 'child-centred' perspective of the programme: 'Adults speak like adults, children speak like children and Teletubbies speak like Teletubbies. Children understand a lot more about language than we credit them for' (Wood and Davenport). The Tubbies' voices, therefore, are central to both the pedagogical and entertaining aspects of the programme. As the Tubbies copy the other speakers, get excited or (rarely) cross, they demonstrate both repetition and imitation and they are accessible to the very young child, who may also struggle to speak 'properly'. The Tubbies' voices are also funny, playful and musical.

Another important element of the soundscape of the programme is the way in which the Tubbies sing and often hum to each other and themselves. Each Tubby has an individual vocal, musical 'motif', which enables the viewer-as-listener to identify the particular Tubby before they are seen. Po can be heard murmuring 'Fi-dit, fi-dit, fi-dit' ('Faster, faster' in Cantonese), before she appears riding her scooter, and Tinky Winky burbles, 'Tinkle-winkle, tinkle-winkle' to himself before he comes into view. Crucially, then, the child learns to anticipate the visual arrival of any one Tubby through an audio cue. In this, the voices are in total accordance with the other aspects of the sound as sound in the programme. Sound effects (animal noises, music, technological sounds, squeaking wheels or bouncing balls) all conform to a carefully organized sound hermeneutic, so that the sound always represents and indicates a specific object and/or event. This is important pedagogically for the programme, as Wood suggests: 'The way the sound is placed becomes something a child can predict. It is all to do with anticipating action.' Equally, Davenport claims, 'The sound is to do with making predictions from clues as well as from what a child can see on the screen' (Wood and Davenport). In other words, *hearing* Po will cue her appearance; or, in relation to Laa-Laa's ball, the following will occur: 'Boing, boing!' 'What's that?' 'It's a ball!' Knowledge is achieved through close attention, through listening, questioning and then being rewarded with a visual response. This kind of audibly directed narrative is repeated endlessly throughout the programme in various different contexts. The voices and the sound effects in the programme, therefore, are organized carefully to meet with the pedagogical ambitions of the programme's producers.

The sonic universe of Teletubbyland is fully realized, but it is also, perhaps, claustrophobic – it is designed to be immersive, which means that it becomes hermetically, as much as hermeneutically, sealed. In fact, the only aspect of the sound that may encourage the child to look away from the screen is the atmospheric birdsong that can sometimes be heard when the programme is moving from one sequence to another. An avid fan of the programme, my very young daughter would only turn away from the screen when the birdsong alone could be heard. At these moments she would turn her head in some confusion and look out of the window. This makes perfect sense, since the birdsong, after all, is the only sound 'question' that is never 'answered' visually, on-screen, as the birdsong does not result in or relate to any visual representation of birds. While birds are seen elsewhere, in computer animations and in the video inserts, the 'birds' of the birdsong are never seen. This audible presence, but visual absence, is entirely familiar to adult viewers, who are used to hearing things on television and not seeing them, but in Teletubbyland, only the rabbits are silent, since even the clouds can make sounds.

At its inception, another remarkable aspect of the programme was its pacing; unlike the conventional approach to the child audience, *Teletubbies* deliberately slowed the pace of its visual and audible narrative. Aside from certain sequences where the Tubbies are clearly artificially speeded up (in a manner borrowed from *The Benny Hill Show*), in general, the programme was clearly slower than other kinds of pre-school television. In many ways, its pace was the antithesis of the speedy, advertisement-like structure of a programme such as *Sesame Street*. One significant way in which this was achieved was through the inclusion of frequent, silent pauses in the soundtrack. While, as I have suggested, birdsong might be used to bridge the shift from one location to another or to cover a tracking shot through Teletubbyland, the soundscape was also punctuated at specific points by silence. For instance, in the short, frequently repeated sequences featuring the baby's face in the sun, there are often several moments of silence and the audience necessarily waits for the baby to react to the events below and, by doing so, make a sound. Thus, the silence in *Teletubbies* is nearly always about anticipation (what is baby going to do? what are the trumpets going to say?), but, as audible breaks, they also act as brief sonic vacuums, practically sucking the listener-as-viewer's attention back into the events on-screen. The sound in *Teletubbies*, then, rather than 'washing over' the viewer, is always designed to provoke a physical response in the audience, all but issuing direct instructions. Audibly, the programme presents its audience with a series of unspoken requests: 'sing along', 'dance', 'look there', and questions: 'what's that?' In the moments of silence, the implicit suggestion is that 'you had better look, as you cannot hear it, and where do you think it has gone?'

Another important aspect of the soundscape is that each sound is carefully placed in terms of audio perspective. Objects, animals and Tubbies that are nearer to the screen are always louder than those situated further away; while this might seem obvious, in fact, as I indicated above, not even the most apparently 'realistic' television dramas adhere to the rules of sound perspective all the time. *Teletubbies*, however, not only consistently conforms to these rules, but also frequently demonstrates how sound perspective works to the child who is looking and listening. Frequently, the Tubbies themselves can be heard (faintly, at first) before they are seen on-screen; if they are coming from some way in the distance, the sound will remain low until they are closer to the screen. In one sequence, featuring a 'little lamb', his plaintive 'baa' is carefully contrasted with the 'baa' of his lamb friend, which becomes gradually more audible as the second lamb comes closer to the screen. Similarly, if and when the Tubbies enter the Tubbytronic superdome and the camera remains on the outside, their voices can often be heard, but are relayed with both a slight muffle and echo effect. This is clearly designed to illustrate the fact that the Tubbies have gone indoors (hence muffled), but also to remind the viewer of the spacious dimensions of the drome itself (hence the echo).

Like the sound of the voices and the sound effects, the music is also carefully designed to meet with the pedagogical drive of the programme. Like many children's programmes, the music heard is predominantly sung or played on instruments such as the piano, or on 'comic' instruments that have very distinctive sounds (such as the xylophone, the triangle, the tuba, cymbals and whistles). Much of the music is based around the repetition of the short melody that supports the introduction of the Tubbies, which echoes the vocal rhythm and natural pitch of the introductory phrase when it is spoken in the programme ('Tel-e-tubb-ies, Tel-e-tubb-ies, say, hel-lo!'). Elsewhere in the programme the music is generally simple and unsophisticated, in that its arrangement accentuates the aspects of melody and percussion, giving the child the opportunity to become familiar with the (catchy) melody and dance along in time with the rhythm. The programme also features numerous nursery rhymes, folk songs and, when appropriate, Christmas carols. Clearly the musical soundscape is as diverse as other aspects of the programme in terms of content; and this is also true not only in relation to the number of different songs, but also to how they are heard. Nursery rhymes, for instance, are often given different kinds of treatment within the same programme, so that the 'Grand Old Duke of York' is heard spoken by one of the voice trumpets and acted out by the Tubbies, but is then repeated in a video insert in a 'jazz' version.

On occasions, however, the musical score develops in a relatively sophisticated and complex way. In certain sequences, the music builds and develops a considerable depth through the repetition and layering of different phrases and a diverse range of instruments. In the sell-through video, *Teletubbies and the Snow*, that was made up of a series of episodes shown in the run-up to Christmas 1998, a variety of different songs and carols are heard. These include folk songs originating from Finland and Spain, as well as carols traditionally heard in the UK context, such as 'Away in a manger'. While all the songs are initially performed by Finnish, Spanish and British children, the specific melody from each song, along with a more 'Christmas-like' rendition of the theme tune (heard as if it were played on hand bells), is incorporated into the climactic score. In the visual climax to the video, the Tubbies finish building their 'snow-tubby'. The way in which the music accompanying this sequence gradually builds explicitly responds to the question-and-answer pedagogical structure that is so dominant elsewhere in the programme. Featuring repetition, layering and a 'call-and-response' strategy means that the music develops into a surprisingly sophisticated arrangement, creating an audible flourish which concurs with the increasing visual excitement as it begins to snow once again.

Teletubbies, therefore, demonstrates that all the aspects of the sound of television that I have discussed may be orchestrated carefully to support the educational as well as the entertaining ambitions of a specific television programme. Despite the fact that the programme is perhaps best known for its now iconic visual style, my analysis should have indicated that the design and orchestration of the sound effects, silence and music is fundamental to its integrity and success.

chapter three

Time

Introduction

In this chapter, I will be looking at the relationship of television to time. In this brief introduction I want to present three ways in which television as a medium expresses time. First, capturing time as a recording; second, relaying time, as in a direct transmission; and last, through the construction of liveness on television, which, paradoxically perhaps, most often combines both the recording and relaying of time. Later sections of the chapter will look in more detail at the way in which time is *organized* by television: the recent development and changes to television *schedules* and scheduling practices, through *technologies* such as the video recorder, within both fictional and non-fiction *narrative*, and as an *economy*, where the duration of television programmes and the viewing time of the audience are calculated in monetary terms. Within this, the perception of time by the audience is understood as experience; this may be recognized as *repetition* in both programmes and formats, generated through *anticipation and retrospection* of events that are constantly just ahead or just past, and felt in relation to the *duration* of viewing in terms of minutes, weeks and years; or expressed through *participation* when time seems immediate and filled with purpose.

Recording time

Television, like film, radio and other media which can archive sounds and/or images, is able to 'record' time. In effect, it dislocates time by capturing sounds and images from one time and place and is then able to re-present these images and sounds to the viewer 'as if' they were happening again, or even 'as if' it were the first time they were taking place. Unlike photography, but like film and audiotape, television records *moving* images and sound, and this means that the events recorded 'take time' to be replayed. However, what is actually heard and seen will not necessarily take the same amount of time or be the same duration as the original event.

Thus we have two temporalities here: the initial duration of the original event and the secondary duration of the recorded event. In both factual and fictional television, the original duration can be manipulated, making the time of replaying shorter or longer. The most common manipulation is through editing, through which time can be cut up, condensed or expanded. In most fictional television programmes, editing is used to contract the amount of time recorded, as the extensive period of shooting is reduced to a series of usable scenes which push the narrative along. Alternatively, televisual technologies, such as the instant replay in slow motion, commonly used in sports coverage, can seem to extend or expand the original time of an event (whether this is the 3 or 4 seconds taken by a penalty or a 10-second gold medal sprint). On television, the time it takes to view the events recorded also varies in terms of the actual length of time the programme takes (the programme time measured in seconds, minutes or hours). Not all programmes – even the same kind of programmes – are the same length; a news programme may be anything from 60 seconds to 50 minutes, or a repeating cycle of 30-minute episodes, 24 hours a day, 7 days a week. Aside from the actual length of time the programme takes, time as it is experienced by the viewer will also vary and may be measured subjectively as fast, slow, tedious or exciting. These differing responses of the audience are managed in part by the director and editor's selection of various visual and audible strategies, such as the use of particular music and sound effects, long takes, whip pans, and fast cutting, all of which may serve to alter the perception of time passing for the viewer.

There is, of course, a third temporality present within recorded television and this is the perceived 'period of time' or 'historical time' that is implicit or explicit in the content of material that has been filmed. This historical time is always in the past, but it will vary in terms of how near it seems to be in relation to the actual time of the viewer – that is, how contemporary it feels. In fictional television, historical time may appear to be contemporary (as in most British soap operas) or refer entirely to a period situated clearly in the past (as in a Jane Austen adaptation, for example). The integrity of this illusory historical time may depend on whether the programme is viewed near to the actual time of its production. Old episodes of *Coronation Street* no longer look 'of the now' to the viewer, not just because they refer to past events in the narrative of the soap, but because camera angles, composition and even the presence or absence of colour marks the aesthetics of the programme as distinctive from the contemporary conventions of television drama and the soap itself. The programme can then be recognized by the viewer as an object that has aged, that has become 'dated' in terms of its formal strategies. Ironically, perhaps, 'period' dramas are also affected by the passage of time in this way. Re-viewing the BBC's 1980 version of *Pride and Prejudice* at the time of the more recent adaptation in 1995, it was clear to me that, while both programmes referred to the same time period (the eighteenth century), equally obviously, the programmes had been made at different times. The earlier adaptation expressed this most explicitly in the way it used a mixture of sparse exterior scenes, shot on film, with extensive studio-bound sequences, shot on video. Formally, therefore, there was a visible mismatch in lighting and in the quality of the image between these two kinds of visual material, which made it seem old-fashioned. In contrast, the larger budget and improved technology made available to the producers in 1995 meant that the more recent adaptation employed extensive location shooting and was shot entirely on film. The illusory reproduction of the eighteenth century felt authentic and coherent, but it also fitted with the conventions of television drama in 1995, as it used many of the same visual and aural techniques as other popular drama being shown on television at that time. Unlike the earlier adaptation, it did not employ certain scripting aspects – such as interior monologues – that were no longer in fashion. (Now, of course, re-viewing the 1995 adaptation in 2004, it, too, has dated, despite its filmic lushness.) I do not mean to suggest that the 1995 adaptation was necessarily more effective at describing the eighteenth century; in fact, it could be argued that the introspective and mannered narrative of the earlier adaptation was more appropriate to the novel and the period. Rather, my point is that the time of production and the time of reception always have repercussions for the simulation and perception of the illusory 'historical time' of television fiction.

In historical documentary, the historical time that is the subject of the documentary may be represented either through dramatic re-enactments or through the use of archive film (if any is available). What happens to the perception of historical time in this context? On the one hand, the historical time that is simulated via re-enactment will remain unchanged, no matter how 'old' the documentary becomes (the simulation of a battle in the First World War will always primarily refer to the historical period that is the First World War). On the other hand, the aesthetics of the dramatic re-enactment will date in the same way that the 'period drama' does. While this is problematic in relation to its ability to seem authentic, this is offset by the fact that, since the re-enactment is generally made at the same time as the documentary, it will age in the same way and at the same rate as the formal aspects of the documentary narrative itself do. The effectiveness of the re-enactment, its apparent ability to show us the past, is, then, for better or worse, closely bound up in the authority of the documentary narrative itself.

In contrast to this, archive film is actuality and therefore refers to and reproduces historical time differently (since it is, literally, from another time). Therefore, it has a more complicated relationship to the historical time of the documentary narrative than the dramatic re-enactment. Since archive film is distinct from the perceived historical time of the documentary (recognized via methods of filming and conventions of presentation), its presence is potentially disruptive and confusing. Archive material cannot be controlled in the same way as the dramatic re-enactment. Its temporal qualities – how long it is, the actual detail and pace of the events recorded, its perceived historical status – are not under the control of the documentary director. Thus, when archive material is used, it is often carefully manipulated to fit within the contemporary context or 'historical time' of the documentary. It may be edited, looped, speeded up, slowed down, re-voiced or played with non-synchronous sound and music. Commonly, archive material is set into the context of the documentary through a voice-over that was not produced at the same time as the archive's own historical time of production, but which acts to confirm the status of the historical content of the images. Yet the history referred to is rarely specific; the narrator rarely comments on the particular qualities, characters or events taking place, unless the place, image or individual is very famous. Pictures of trenches in the First World War are used generally to refer to the First World War and rarely to specific battles, dates or the individuals we see scrambling in the mud. A sequence of Adolf Hitler delivering a speech may always be recognizable as Hitler, but when or where it is or what he is saying or, indeed, how long he speaks for, is often not made clear. Therefore, the contemporary manipulation of archive footage can result in a contradiction, for while archive material is used because it 'really is' from the historical time that the documentary is referring to, the contemporary remodelling of the material can affect its authentic status and dissolve the temporal specificity of the scenes and sounds that have been recorded. The way in which archive footage is used in the documentary means that its relationship to time is not only dislocated (meaning that it is from another time and place), but also 'unlocated' (meaning that, while it still refers generally to a historical time, its specific origin and duration has become mysterious). Even archive material that seems indelibly historically specific and of an exact duration, such as material from certain video cameras, surveillance cameras and closed-circuit television – all of which seemingly carry the exact time and date of production on the image itself – may still have its temporal specificity altered or diluted by the context in which it is shown.

Relaying time

Television, like radio, distinguishes itself from film in that it has the ability to relay time. As it has the ability to transmit images and sounds from events as they are happening, television has the potential to be a 'live' medium. 'Liveness' implies temporal simultaneity with the audience – the time being relayed by the television is the 'same' time as that of the watching audience and events unfold at the same pace for the audience as they do for the television cameras (it is 'now', it is 'live'). The time of production, transmission and reception are one and the same. Television, therefore, cannot only 'keep' time (record time), but also 'tell' time (relay time). This potential may be experienced by the audience at the most epic and most intimate of scales.

In his extensive writing on the subject, Paddy Scannell (1988) has carefully described how television and radio have functioned as both calendar and clock for modern societies in the West. At the grandest scale, television marks the passing of years, and of each year – television's relaying of seasons (Christmas, summer) echoes and confirms the passing of the real seasons for the television viewer. Special national events – such as Wimbledon or the Superbowl – are marked and happen on television at the same time that they take place in the everyday of the viewer. Every year, the passing of the year at midnight on 31 December is relayed by television. On a slightly smaller scale, the passing of weeks, the days of the week and the hours of the day are marked out, relayed to the audience at home by television. When the newscaster states, 'This is the 10 o'clock news from the BBC', it is likely to be at the same 10 o'clock, on the same day, for all viewers watching in the UK. While this time-telling function of broadcasting continues to exist within contemporary television, in the era of global expansion some aspects of this capacity are changing. With a greater number of channels and more channels which are no longer exclusively local, but have an increasingly global reach, television's role as timekeeper has changed from the established pattern originally described by Scannell in relation to the UK.

Paradoxically, in some instances, telling the time has become a more explicit function, while in other contexts it is now largely irrelevant. On 24-hour news channels, for example, time is continuously present and a clock on-screen tells the time all the time. Part of these news channels' authority stems from the fact that they situate, and relay, the 'time of the world' to the viewer. On other channels, such as an 'auction' shopping channel, such as

Chase-it.tv, while there is an absolutely immediate, even frenzied connection to the time of the viewer (presenters exhort viewers to 'Buy it now! Press the button now!'), the relay of calendar time, or actual clock time, is far less evident. It might not be ridiculous to suggest that for this channel, the 'real' time of the world and the viewer is deliberately obscured; otherwise it might become evident how much time is being 'used up' or wasted by watching a channel that does nothing but attempt to sell you things.

Liveness: relay and record

In both 24-hour news channels and shopping channels, the fact that television is live (or appears to be so) is an important aspect of their address and relationship to the viewer. Yet this raw transmission is most often an illusion and 'live' programmes are often a mix of different temporalities. In a televised football game there will be a mix of live visuals, recorded visuals, live commentary, live sounds and recorded sounds. As Stephanie Marriott has explained, in an article examining sports programming (Marriott 1996), the layering of different image and sound tracks, some of which are live, some of which are recorded, produces a narrative that can refer, simultaneously, to the immediate unfolding of events, to the just past or to the past of 30 minutes ago. In addition, multiple perspectives, slow motion and excitable commentary also serve to subjectively manipulate time, making the temporal feel of the programme more 'lively', but not necessarily 'just' live.

As Marriott explains, part of the reason that television is able to produce several 'temporalities' simultaneously is that it offers two channels of potentially live communication – image and sound. This duality of image and sound, either of which might be recorded or live, means that they can be used to create temporalities specific to television: recorded images anchored by live sound (common in news reports) or live images accompanied by recorded sound (common in 'live' music performances), or live images accompanied by live sound (as in some aspects of sports programmes). The actual characteristics within a 'live presentation', therefore, frequently connect my two initial categories of time on television – the record and the relay. I will return to the characteristics of liveness later in my exploration of time and television, but now I want to describe in more specific detail how the organization of time relates to the formal aspects of television.

The schedule

The television schedule appears in a variety of formats. In the UK, the BBC first published times of their radio programmes in their own magazine – the *Radio Times* – in 1923. This magazine first ran a 'television number' in November 1936, when television broadcasting began (in the UK) from Alexandria Palace in London. Since programmes could not be received outside a small area, the edition including television programmes was for the London area only, and other regional editions took little notice of the metropolitan 'experiment'. The inclusion of television programmes in the London edition continued until the television service was closed for the duration of the Second World War. After the war, television programmes were again listed in the London editions and it was not until the early 1950s that other regional editions began including television programmes in their listings, as television broadcasting began to develop nationally. ITV, the UK's commercial network, began transmission in 1955 and its programme schedules were published exclusively in another magazine – the *TV Times*. For well over 30 years in the UK, if you wanted to have schedules for all programming for the forthcoming week, it was necessary to buy two weekly magazines. It was not until 1 March 1991 that both magazines were allowed to publish all scheduling information for all channels, including the emergent satellite and digital channels, and that other magazines could be published to do the same. In addition, newspapers were allowed to print television guides for the entire forthcoming week in their Saturday or Sunday editions. In terms of sales, both broadcaster-related magazines suffered a radical drop in circulation and were overtaken rapidly by a newer publication, *What's On TV?* However, both the *Radio Times* (which now publishes the radio programmes in its back pages) and the *TV Times* continue to this day. Today, the television schedule, or, more accurately, various different kinds of schedule, can be found in a variety of contexts: in newspapers, as an electronic programme guide available via satellite or digital handsets, on websites and in a wide variety of specialist (*What's On TV?*, *TV Quick*) and non-specialist magazines (*Heat*, *OK!*).

Literally, the schedule represents the organization of time by television since it publishes the times at which particular programmes will be screened. It indicates how long the programme will take and usually provides a brief summary of content. Most obviously, at least on the terrestrial channels, the potential 24 hours of a broadcasting day are divided into periods of time, identified in various ways. It may be related to the presumed domestic routines of viewers ('Breakfast-time', after the likely activity of the audience at that time in the morning, 6 a.m. to 9 a.m.), the target audience (CBBC – Children's BBC – named after the target audience, watching either in the early morning, 6 a.m. to 9 a.m., or in the early afternoon, 3.15 p.m. to 5 p.m.) or the fact that it offers the highest numbers of viewers ('Peak-time', when the largest audience is likely to be watching, 7.30 p.m. to 10.30 p.m.). As Scannell has pointed out, the domestic routines of households, the everyday of the viewer, is, in some sense, mirrored and incorporated by the television schedule. Even with the advent of numerous satellite and digital channels, the fit between the schedule time of programmes, the content of the programmes and the everyday time of the viewer remains consistent. Certain non-terrestrial channels continue to replicate the conventional broadcast day – for instance, both Living TV and ITV2 offer children's programming early in the morning. Additionally, other channels clearly relate themselves to the routines of their particular viewers, at least at certain points. For example, CBeebies, the BBC's pre-school channel, closes down after its 'bedtime hour', 6 p.m. to 7 p.m., presumably since its audience is believed to have gone to bed. Rather neatly, this is echoed by the fact that the BBC's 'youth and entertainment' digital channel, BBC Three, only begins transmission at 7 p.m., perhaps when its audience is presumed to have woken up or at least be available to view.

Yet a change does become evident if we look at other channels, such as UKTV Gold and Hallmark, which offer programmes early in the morning that are not really distinct from those they offer later in the day. Sitcoms, such as *Man about the House* (shown on UKTV Gold), or courtroom dramas, such as *Perry Mason* (shown on Hallmark), were produced for peak-time viewing; now they can be seen on these channels at 6 a.m. And unlike BBC Three, other channels aimed at the youth audience, such as MTV and Trouble, either broadcast programmes 24 hours a day (MTV) or begin their schedule at 6 a.m. (Trouble). In addition, certain channels actually loop their programmes (Cartoon Playhouse Disney, Nick Jr., CBeebies), so that an entire schedule is repeated as a cycle throughout the day. The repeat of the schedule seems to indicate that these channels no longer believe in creating a varied, developing sequence of programmes that loosely mirrors an imagined 'day' in the life of the viewer, since their particular television audience is unlikely to be watching all day. Fifteen-year-olds and three-year-olds may well share the same house (and sometimes the same television), but their individual temporal routines (such as what time they get up, when they sleep and when they watch TV) will be very different. Thus, although terrestrial television is, at present, holding fast to the conventional temporal qualities of the broadcast day, for many satellite and digital channels the scheduling of television is no longer tied indelibly to the constructed day of the 'average' family, but to individuals. As a result, the organization of time on television presents a kind of paradox: on individual channels, time has become more regimented and condensed, so that, on some channels, there are now three-hour schedules, tightly packed with specific programming aimed at a particular audience. However, looked at in its entirety, the schedule of different channels provides a more expansive and less obviously constructed 'viewing day', as there are, increasingly, more kinds of programmes available at a range of different times throughout the day and night.

Currently, programmes are still related primarily to the channel on which they appear ('on BBC One at 8 p.m. there is . . .'), rather than to the type of programme available at a particular time ('where can I find a documentary about wildlife at 8 p.m.?'). However, there are signs that a shift – from channel-based to programme-based scheduling – is emerging. For example, in a listing magazine such as *What's on TV?*, one day's schedule describing the mainstream terrestrial channels (BBC One, BBC Two, ITV and Channels 4 and 5) takes up two pages and is presented in a layout where they can be seen side by side (backed by a separate colour for each channel), with the different programmes listed one after another, vertically down the page, as in a restaurant menu. While the times of the various programmes on different channels do loosely appear side by side (with the evening or peak-time viewing appearing in larger and bolder print), generally, when reading the schedule, the eye is naturally drawn down the page for each individual channel. The choice of viewing, therefore, is understood as a sequence of programmes offered on each channel. One aspect of this means that it would take some effort to see which programmes I might miss on other channels should I choose to watch, say, *The Weakest Link* on BBC One at 8 p.m. In this layout, the mini-schedule (or menu) for each channel's programming still predominates. However, for the satellite and digital channels (not of all which are included) listed on the following four pages in the magazine, the channels are grouped according to category and identified as 'entertainment', 'sport', 'movies', 'kids', 'factual' and 'music & teens'. Here the listings are much reduced, with only programme titles and times being included (with the exception of the major movie channels, for which a little more detail in relation to the films being screened is provided). The way in which the viewer treats this part of the schedule will have to be different to the mainstream schedule. Thirty years ago my father used to use the traditionally printed schedule in the *Radio Times* to methodically 'ring round' programmes he would like to watch in the week ahead. Now, in terms of planning ahead in relation to programmes on the digital channels, unless the viewer has some prior knowledge of the programmes, the fact that the magazines simply list the titles makes this practice increasingly difficult. Thus, some knowledge of the programmes prior to their inclusion in the schedule is increasingly necessary. For example, because of my domestic circumstances I know what the *Fimbles* is and I know that my two-year-old likes it; therefore I may well highlight its appearance in the schedule (where, perhaps confusingly, it appears on more than one channel). However, I have no idea what the programme *Pimp my Ride* is about and, thus, have no idea whether I would like to watch it, although, just from the title, I am pretty certain it would not be suitable for my kids.

If this form of schedule no longer functions primarily to allow the viewer to identify specific programmes of potential interest in the week ahead what can it do? Despite its proliferation and summary status, this schedule does retain some propensity to guide its audience. By grouping channels together, it allows even the potential first-time viewer to make an educated guess at the programme type. *Pimp my Ride*, for example, is on MTV and categorized as 'music & teens', so both the likely content and target audience are made clear, and I would have to be pretty dense to expect it to be suitable for a pre-school child. This broad categorization of channels allows viewers to seek out a particular type of programme and then see what is on offer at the time they wish to view. The channels, to an extent, become subordinate to the category. This schedule also allows viewers to avoid programmes that are 'not for them'. Yet the large number of channels, and the fact that they are lumped together, puts pressure on controllers and producers to make their particular programmes (and thus their channels) the most accessible and apparently interesting to the viewer at the time they wish to watch. To aid this process, it seems evident that programme titles are now increasingly literal (telling the viewer exactly what is in the programme) and often explicitly sensational (in order to direct attention to themselves). As one television critic (Wollaston 2004) remarked: 'With so much out there on so many channels, titles need to be sexed-up for a programme to get noticed at all. Hence *When Dingoes Attack* (Sky Travel), *Junkyard Mega-Wars* (Discovery) and *Chris Barrie's Massive Engines* (Discovery).' As he goes on to observe, the attachment of words such as 'extreme' or 'from hell' (as in *Builders from Hell*, *Neighbours from Hell*) are now common, on both satellite and terrestrial channels, as yet another way of suggesting that the programmes offer that something 'extra' over those of their rivals.

This thematic grouping of the schedule is also possible since, by and large, the digital and satellite channels are specialist or 'niche'. Specialist channels such as Discovery (documentaries) and Nickelodeon (kids) schedule programming either of the same genre or for the same target audience. The main terrestrial channels continue to produce a schedule that has too much variety to allow them to be grouped (except perhaps as 'entertainment'); how long this will continue is perhaps open to question, as it seems clear that schedules and the associated sense of programming is shifting as the take-up of digital and satellite channels increases. An indication of this shift becomes clear when satellite channels are given the same weight as the terrestrial channels. One magazine – *TV & Satellite Week* – advertises itself as 'The Clearest Listings Ever', relating, perhaps, to the current confusion experienced by the audience as viewing possibilities change. Here, an important feature is the full-page, 'at-a-glance' schedule for each evening's viewing. In this schedule, the time is presented horizontally across the page, from 7 p.m. to 10.30 p.m., broken up into half-hour intervals (7 p.m., 7.30 p.m., etc.). Thirty-nine different channels are then grouped into a series of categories: 'favourites' (including satellite channels as well as terrestrial channels), 'entertainment', 'documentaries', 'films' and 'sport'. These are then arranged vertically, running down the side of the page. In this kind of layout, time is no longer presented haphazardly, but regimented, blocked out clearly in alternate columns of blue and white. Using this layout, the viewer who is looking for their evening's programmes is likely to look down the page according to the time (what is on at that time?), rather than being lured into the narrative of a particular channel's schedule (what's on BBC One tonight?). The choice of what is on at the same time becomes much more evident – I can immediately see, even just within 'favourites', that by watching *The Weakest Link* at 8 p.m. I might miss (or could choose to watch instead) a range of programmes that might also be my favourite, such as, *Would Like To Meet . . .*, *The Bill*, *How Clean Is Your House?*, *Piranha Attack*, *Joe versus the Volcano* (film), *Kirsty's Home Videos*, *Trauma*, *Holiday Airport* and *Big Brother's Little Brother*.

The layout of this schedule is also significant as it follows the format of the electronic programme guide on Sky Digital. Here, using a remote control, the viewer can access an

	7.00pm	7.30pm	8.00pm	8.30pm	9.00pm	9.30pm	10.00pm	10.30pm	SKY
FAVOURITES									
BBC1	◂ Match of the Day	The National Lottery: Wright Around the World	Casualty		Sea of Souls		Billy Connolly's World Tour of New Zealand	News	101
BBC2	Abroad Again in Britain		Timewatch		Ruby Wax Meets... Jerry Springer	The Story of the Musical	Jerry Springer: The Opera		102
ITV1	Scream! If You Want to Get Off		Who Wants to Be a Millionaire?		Ultimate Force		News	Film: The Eiger...	103
Channel 4	Force of Nature	The End of the World As We Know It			Celebrity Big Brother		Film: Jackie Brown		104
Five	Film: Jungle 2 Jungle				CSI		Law & Order: Special Victims Unit		105
Sky One	Malcolm in the Middle	Oliver Beene	Stargate SG-1		Stargate Atlantis		Day of Destruction		106
BBC3	The Story of Bohemian Rhapsody		Fantasy		Film: Bird on a Wire			Two Pints...	115
ITV2	Celebrity Fit Club		Scream! If You Want to Get Off		Film: The Ghost and the Darkness				118
E4	Big Brother Panto		Big Brother: Living with Evil		Celebrity Punch-Ups of 2004		Celebrity Big Brother Live		163
ITV3	The Bill				Agatha Christie's Marple				119
ENTERTAINMENT									
LivingTV	Charmed						Film: Madonna: Truth or Dare		112
UKTV Gold	'Allo 'Allo!				Only Fools and Horses				109
Paramount	M*A*S*H		Seinfeld	Becker	Scrubs	Everybody Loves...	Frasier	Film: Roxanne	127
Hallmark	The District				Film: Second Nature				190
Sci-Fi	The Invisible Man		Dark Angel				Film: Cyborg		130
FX	King of the Hill		The X-Files		The Man Show	Kenny v Spenny	Carnivàle		289
Bravo	Knight Rider				Carrott's Commercial Breakdown				124
DOCUMENTARIES									
Discovery	The Tower		Why Intelligence Fails		Scene of the Crime		FBI Files		551
Nat Geographic	Seconds from Disaster		The Real Alexander the Great		Film: The Nelson Affair				558
Animal Planet	◂ King of the Jungle		Jungle Orphans		In the Wild With		Venom ER		570
History	World's Deadliest Aircraft		The Great Escape		Ted Bundy		Crime Stories		561
UKTV History	Time Flyers								582
FILMS									
Sky Movies 1	◂ Harry Potter and the Chamber of Secrets		The Lord of the Rings: The Two Towers						301
Sky Movies 2	◂ Beautiful Girl	Movie News	Intolerable Cruelty				The Banger Sisters		302
Sky Movies 3	◂ Jackie Bouvier...	Peacemakers			The Fourth Angel			Punch-Drunk...	303
Sky Movies 4	Columbo Cries Wolf				Intolerable Cruelty			Transporter	304
Sky Movies 5	◂ An American Tail		The Core				Jason X		305
Sky Movies 6	◂ Prelude to a Kiss			Signs			Road Kill		306
Sky Movies 7	◂ A Wrinkle in Time			Catch Me If You Can					307
Sky Movies 8	◂ My Big Fat Greek Wedding		Ripley's Game				Rollerball		308
Sky Movies 9	◂ Going Ape!		Dirty Pretty Things			Sunshine State			309
TCM	Meet Me in St Louis				The Purple Rose of Cairo			Dr. Zhivago	327
Sky Cinema 1	◂ A Matter of Life and Death		The King of Comedy				The Wild Bunch		310
Sky Cinema 2	◂ The Grapes of Wrath				The Night of the Hunter			Lost...	311
SPORT									
Sky Sports 1	◂ Rugby Union – Live Football				Spanish Football – Live: A La Liga match				401
Sky Sports 2	◂ Golf – Live: Mercedes Championship						Badminton		402
Sky Sports 3	WWE – Bottom Line		Tennis						403
Sky Sports Xtra	◂ NFL Weekly Review	NBA Basketball					American Football – Live: A double-header of wildcard play-offs		404
Eurosport	Football – Live: Coverage of a match from the Efes Pilsen Cup				Watts	Rallying	Youth Only Zone	News	410

◂ Programme begins before 7.00pm   * These channels also have a +1 hour timeshift service

SATURDAY AT A GLANCE **31**

Fig 3.1 'At a glance' page from *TV & Satellite Week* © TV & Satellite Week/IPC+ Syndication

on-screen programme guide at any time. Initially, you are presented with a list of categories, broadly similar to those of the print magazines (although the electronic programme guide includes other categories, such as 'news', which the print magazines do not). Once a category has been chosen, the different grouped channels' offerings are laid out in a similar manner to *TV and Satellite Week*, so that the time proceeds horizontally across the screen, with the channels listed vertically down the screen. While the time remains fixed, of course, the order in which the channels may be listed down the screen (according to their number) and the category in which they are put is determined by the generator of the programme guide, whether this is BSkyB, Freeview, Telewest or NTL. The increasing importance of the electronic programme guide (EPG), and its new layout, has created some tension between broadcasters as to how and in which order channels are listed. In 2003 the BBC decided to broadcast its services from a new satellite, meaning that it would no longer have to pay for the encryption services provided by Sky. Because of this, there was initially some concern at the BBC that Sky would relegate the two main public service channels, BBC One and BBC Two, to 'obscure' slots on their EPG. While it might seem to be a trivial dispute, in fact, the location and assignment of numbers to channels within programme guides becomes increasingly important as the number of channels continues to expand. Even in its more abbreviated form, the schedule on the EPG may have at least two screen pages full of different channels to scroll through (within each category), so the order in which channels are listed is obviously significant. BSkyB has every right to list and categorize programmes and channels in any way it sees fit (just as the BBC has done for years in its own print listings magazine, the *Radio Times*). The BBC holds fast to the belief that, as a public service and a national institution, it should have a particular status and presence within any schedule. Yet since the schedule is, by default, a kind of advertising (and since the BBC is still a much better known 'brand' than Sky), it is not in BSkyB's interest to promote its public service rival. This tension has only become more explicit as the BBC develops its own niche channels for digital television. In the end, Sky did not relegate the BBC channels to 'obscure' slots, but in 2004 the television regulator, OfCom, began a consultation process as to how EPGs should be organized. Although this kind of layout is obviously a space-saving requirement, regimenting time and apparently promoting programmes over channels, it can also reveal how something as apparently simple as the schedule (the presentation to the viewer of what is on at what time) becomes a political and corporate issue.

In terms of the temporal qualities of the programmes themselves, this new schedule layout is also supported by the way in which programme times and programme duration have become organized increasingly to meet at what is called a 'hard' junction – a specific time period, often on the half-hour or hour, where the majority of channels start and finish their programmes. Here, time – both of the programmes and in terms of when they appear – is becoming regimented. This is encouraged by the fact that if I look down the screen or page to see what is on at 8 p.m., if a programme began at 7.20 p.m. or starts at 8.15 p.m., I may well only register the end or the beginning of the programme title, and thus fail to notice it; in addition, it also looks 'wrong', out of synch, disorganized. The fact that it does not fall into place or line up with the majority of other programmes will suggest that I might miss the beginning of other programmes or that I might already have missed the start of the programme itself.

Once again, what this implies is that if audiences do act in the way that the schedule seems to encourage – that is, to select programmes across the schedule at a particular time, rather than selecting a channel to view – they will be making choices organized by their own (established) tastes and the time *they* are available to view, rather than being directed by an individual channel's programme sequence. Equally, if channels choose to ignore the impact of a hard junction taken up by over 20 other channels, they may well lose the audience at that point, or at least frustrate them if programme times overlap. This also seems to have had an impact on the duration of programmes. For example, the majority of programmes now have an apparent running time of 30 or 60 minutes. It is increasingly rare for 'non-standard' programme times – programmes of 15, 40 and 50 minutes – to be produced domestically. Of course, the actual running time of any programme will not be 30 or 60 minutes; even on a public service channel, the actual programme may be as short as 26 or 56 minutes, to allow for continuity announcements and trailers. On commercial channels, 1 programme hour will actually include up to 14 minutes for advertisements and announcements.

This can make the scheduling of American imports on non-commercial channels problematic. One of the most obvious ways this can be seen is in relation to the American drama, *24*, which famously features the key narrative motif that each episode covers exactly '1 hour' of the 24 hours in 1 day in the life of a beleaguered secret agent. The temporal specificity of the programme – that the events apparently taking place in each episode are occurring as they would in real time – is emphasized by the fact that the time passing is frequently shown via a digital clock on-screen. In fact, the programme is actually only 45 minutes of drama. Designed to be screened on an American commercial channel, the advertisement breaks are included in the hour, and counted as 'minutes' which pass, although the events in the drama are unseen. On the BBC, however, there are no commercial breaks, so the programme does only last 45 minutes – not only does this rather shatter the elaborate temporal illusion present in the narrative, but it is also an inconvenient length of time if programmes are increasingly scheduled to begin on the hour or half-hour. In terms of managing this mismatch, the BBC appears to have countered this problem by screening the programme either late at night (after 11 p.m.) or by screening two episodes back to back, making the programme-block up to a more convenient length of 90 minutes.

Technologies

I have already suggested how one technology – the EPG – has affected aspects such as programme duration and programme titles. In this section, I want to examine in more detail how other technologies, both old and new, affect the way in which time is organized on television.

The remote control

This now familiar technological tool is a handset that allows viewers to change channels and, increasingly, to interact with the television itself and with certain specifically designed programmes. Since its primary function is to allow the viewer rapid access to different channels or to different parts of an interactive presentation, its influence may have a more directly spatial (where does it get you?) than temporal dimension. Nonetheless, perhaps the most obvious temporal quality of the remote is that it does seem to be 'instant' and it can get you there – to another channel, another programme or more information – 'now'. The remote control is about speed. While one of the activities associated with the remote does imply a more leisurely pace ('grazing' suggests a relaxed approach), the more common practices associated with the device are termed 'zapping', 'zipping' or 'surfing'.

In his book, *Faster*, James Gleick (2000) provides some useful observations about the effect of the remote control on television, for both television producers and the audience. One of his central points is that the remote control can act, in effect, as a kind of editing device for the audience. Switching from channel to channel produces a sequence of images from different programmes and advertisements that creates an individual narrative of images, carved out, as it were, from the range of programming available. This narrative, of course, has its own temporal logic, which will be different to the temporal logic and narrative of the programmes involved. Coming in at the start or the end, halfway through a variety of programmes, moving back and forth between the same two or three channels, perhaps, the viewer could construct a narrative that has no clear chronology and which mixes up the different rhythms of the programmes themselves. Gleick, in his generally negative assessment of the effects of speed on modern life, seems to agree with Saul Bellow, who believes that this practice is destructive and ultimately causes 'distraction', which 'catches us all in the end and makes mental mincemeat' (Gleick 2000: 181). Yet even Gleick also acknowledges that the remote control does offer some power to the viewer and an immediate escape from the tyranny of programmes and advertisements they find dull.

Gleick's most relevant observation, perhaps, for my purposes, is that the remote control does seem to have encouraged a change to the beginning and ending of programmes. One of the key potential uses of the remote control is that it enables audiences to zap out of credit sequences or advertisement breaks and move on to parts of programmes elsewhere that they find more interesting. To try to convince audiences that they are not 'wasting time' by staying with the credit sequence, a common practice is the 'squeeze and tease'. The squeeze relates to the way in which, at the end of a programme, channels are now increasingly likely to squeeze the credits into part of the frame (to one side, or even smaller) and use the remaining space on the screen to display a variety of different lures to the audience, whether it is to promote upcoming programmes, offer a preview of next week's episode, advertise related products, such as CDs or DVDs, or even direct viewers to a helpline telephone number that offers information related to issues raised by the programme. This practice is clearly designed to keep audiences tuned to that channel and to prevent them 'zipping' away. The related tactic, the tease, is generated by programme-makers. Here, the closing credit sequence is used either to offer a hook for the next episode or to provide an extra scene for viewers who stay tuned. Commonly, in the sitcom, the practice is to include an 'extra' gag; three well-known sitcoms – *Seinfeld, Friends* and *Frasier* – all produced a final 'add-on' for their loyal audiences. In a slightly different way, the animated sitcom, *The Simpsons*, draws its audience in to its familiar title sequence by offering a new 'in-joke' for each individual episode. This occurs in two places: in the instruction (or punishment lines) that Bart writes on the blackboard at his school and, second, in the way in which the family arranges themselves on the sofa in front of the television at the end of the title sequence itself. This visual gag might involve the family resolving their seating positions via an American football scrum, evolving into a song-and-dance routine or even disappearing into the sofa itself. Rather neatly, of course, the gag refers directly to the fact that the title sequence is the invitation to the 'real' television audience to arrange themselves on their own sofa to watch the programme.

In addition to the squeeze and tease, many programmes now increasingly break up their opening by offering a short prologue and then following this with a generic title sequence that can be relatively brief, as it does not include all the information relevant to that particular episode. Information such as the specific director and writer for each individual episode will instead be subtitled over the actual programme (this can be seen in *CSI* and *ER*). What this produces is a sense in which the break – the separation – between programmes or for advertising and/or continuity announcements is effaced. Thus, the conventional temporal markers of the television programme – the titles which begin each episode and the closing credits which end it – seem, at least for a substantial number of fictional programmes, to increasingly merge the narrative of the programmes into the overall narrative of the channel context. In effect, the practice of merging credits, or using jokes to reward viewers for hanging around, tries to ensure that each minute, or perhaps each second, of television is equally useful or valuable to the audience (just as it is already valuable to advertisers). Gleick (2000: 183–4) quotes John Miller of the American network NBC:

> Every station looks at every second of air time and uses it to the best of their ability. We're all bound by the laws of physics. There are only 24 hours in a day and 60 minutes in an hour and 60 seconds in a minute. Everybody looks at their time with a microscope to get the best utilization they can. It is the only real estate we have.

Other similar practices visible on British television include the way in which, in many instances, news bulletins now feature the newscaster presenting the opening headlines of the news before the title sequence, effectively 'advertising' the news to audience, rather than expecting that they will be waiting patiently in their seats once they have been called to attention. As Gleick notes, perhaps the most telling aspect of the remote control is that its presence means that there need be no 'dead' time on television, and that, in response, television itself may need to be increasingly immediate in its impact, both to attract and hold on to its viewers. Arguably, the kind of tactics I have described work to create a 'stickier' and increasingly seamless television environment, which attempts to dampen the audience's desire to speed from one channel to the next.

The video recorder

The video recorder (VCR) is, in the domestic context, now as ubiquitous as the remote control. The machine allows viewers to record programmes off-air to replay at another time. Specifically, then, this is a technology that allows the viewer to 'time-shift' – that is, to override the schedule and choose to watch the programme at a later date and time than it was initially screened. Through the facility of the fast-forward, rewind and pause button controls it is also possible for viewers to impose their own chronology and temporal control on the programme that has been recorded. They can interrupt, speed through or revisit aspects of the programme at will, thereby potentially disrupting the temporal continuity and coherence established by the programme-makers and channel controllers.

There are three common assumptions about off-air video recording: one which may still be true for many people is that individuals tend to record much more television than they ever actually watch, and, in addition, they may choose to watch programmes that are on television rather than those they have recorded. This means that video recording has actually been less of a threat to the established schedule than was first anticipated. Related to this is the assumption that programmes recorded are often summarily taped over, whether they have been watched or not. In my experience, the relentless way in which television seems to move on means that viewers may simply give up on, or lose interest in, tapes they have recorded. I remember one of my colleagues remarking that although he had carefully recorded episodes of his favourite soap while away on a two-week holiday, he had begun to feel that he would never have time to 'catch up' on his viewing and so had given up watching the soap altogether – this is perhaps surprising given the fact that the soap narrative actually allows for intermittent viewing. Nonetheless, he clearly felt duty-bound to actually watch the programmes he had saved; rather ironically, this led to a situation where he seemed condemned continually to lag behind the ongoing soap narrative. Ultimately, it seemed that he might be doomed to record the soap for ever, as he would always be attempting to catch up. Here it is possible to see that the simple fact that there is so much television available, and that it could take so much time to actually view it, makes the practice of recording and reviewing off-air recordings a time-consuming one, which can sometimes seem burdensome rather than pleasurable.

Another dominant assumption is that the fast-forward button means that viewers who do watch recordings will fast-forward through parts of the programme they are not interested in, such as title sequences and advertising. This may be the case for the large majority of viewers who use their VCR in a relatively random and partial fashion (recording favourite programmes to keep or favourite programmes they will miss). However, in a fascinating article about the activities of 'TV collectors', Kim Bjarkman provides evidence of how these archivists – individuals who seek out and then archive specific programmes or appearances by particular stars – approach the recording and reviewing of television in quite surprising ways that reveal a particular temporal sensitivity to television as a medium.

The first aspect I want to draw out of Bjarkman's research is that, for a self-advertising 'obsessed' fan, the video collection can act as an indicator to consolidate their status as a 'true' fan and, thus, give them some standing in relation to their peers. In the following quote from one of her collectors, Bjarkman (2004: 229) demonstrates how the 'history' of a collection can award a particular authority to the individual concerned:

> In order to be a 'true' fan or to have stuff that other fans might care about, you need to have the actors' appearances elsewhere – the ones before they were famous, before they were on that show, or their appearance on an obscure

channel or in another country . . . from ten years ago on some talk show that nobody's ever heard of, so that you can show that you were a *true* fan – not only that, but you were a true fan *way back when.*

As Bjarkman observes, not only does the videotape here act as a store for memory and proof of a long-term 'authentic' interest in personalities and programmes, but it is also a way of holding on to the otherwise transient television appearances. Bjarkman's research, therefore, suggests that, for a few viewers, the programmes or programme snippets recorded on tape are not summarily dismissed once they have been viewed. They become prized objects, which, within specific communities, have a clearly understood exchange value, whether this is money or a barter value for different programme-tapes. Their age, their genuine 'antiquity', becomes an accredited aspect of their value.

Bjarkman also demonstrates that even aspects of programmes that other audiences might regard as wasted time are, in fact, valued by these collectors. She writes (Bjarkman 2004:234):

> Collectors recognize first runs, complete with original commercials, as somehow more authentic. John calls these recordings, 'the closest thing we have to time travel' . . . Unlike movie collectors for whom video is merely a packaging, or a vehicle transporting the text from the big screen to the small, for the television collector video recordings are themselves objects of historical interest that seem to seal in traces of the televised 'event'.

Even for the less disciplined or obsessed collector, certain off-air recordings – featuring advertisements, channel idents and other voices and images no longer regularly seen 'incidentally' on television – can make certain recordings unique and memorable. For example, as a television studies lecturer, I frequently used to ask my mother to record programmes for me. Since my mother's death, several of these tapes have become a reminder of her kindness (and tolerance), but also of her tastes and aspects of the time I had spent viewing television with her. While, of course, her handwriting on the video sleeve provides its own reminder, the off-air quality of the content of certain tapes is also significant. On one such tape, on which she had duly recorded a documentary for me, there are, incidentally, two snippets of other programmes, including now dated channel idents, from a time when she used to watch television regularly, which I would watch with her when visiting. Oddly, perhaps, I find their presence affecting, touching, and would not remove them; in fact, I enjoy glimpsing that 'past' when I re-view that tape. As Bjarkman notes, 'video collecting blurs notions of public broadcast and private property by transforming such events into personal possessions' (Bjarkman 2004: 234). Significantly, therefore, videotapes recorded on the domestic VCR can act to preserve moments where the 'public time' of the original broadcast is preserved in such a way that it can shore up memories of 'private times' spent with friends and family.

Digital video recorders (DVR)

The digital video recorder differs from the earlier analogue video cassette recorder in that it records material on a hard disk, rather than on videotape. This allows for two major differences from the conventional VCR. First, since it stores material on hard disk, it can record and store more material, using up a much smaller amount of space. As the programmes are captured as computer data they remain tidily located within the machine rather than developing into piles of videotapes. Second, the way in which the recorder receives data means that it can both record and replay material at the same time. This allows the recorder to apparently 'pause' live television. The viewer who steps out of the room, or is interrupted by a phone call, can simply 'pause/record' the live transmission; the DVR will then record the on-air programming, although the image and sound on the television screen will appear to have stopped. Once the viewer comes back to the set and presses play, the programme will apparently start up where the viewer left off. The key aspect is that the programme being viewed will carry on recording, even as the viewer is replaying the recorded element. This means that the apparently live transmission of the television programme will continue, with a time delay instigated by the activities of the individual DVR user. This means that live television – television's time – can apparently be interrupted at the whim of the viewer. In addition, if this facility has been used, the viewer can also fast-forward through parts of the apparently live transmission they do not wish to see, such as advertisements, and 'catch up' with the live transmission.

Other aspects of the various DVRs currently available allow for a variety of different activities. All DVRs provide the viewer with up-to-date schedules, downloaded overnight, from which the viewer can make a selection of programmes to record. In some instances (on Sky+, for example) more than one digital/satellite channel can be recorded at one time (a facility not currently available via the analogue VCR). In addition to this, if one episode from a season of programmes is selected (an episode of a sitcom, for example), the recorder can, if requested, record all episodes from that season without needing to be reminded. TiVo, one of the most high-profile versions of the DVR, launched in 1999, has an additional feature which allows viewers to rate programmes – 'Thumbs up' or 'Thumbs down' – and to identify particular programmes, actors, directors or categories that it would like the recorder to seek out. TiVo then 'learns' from this 'wish list' and will produce a list of recorded programmes for the viewer to select from in a suggestions (the 'now playing') schedule. For the viewer, therefore, the DVR's advantages over the conventional VCR include: a substantial increase in the number of programmes that can be stored and recorded; the presence of an on-screen, automatic catalogue of what has been recorded (so that boxes and labels do not have to be rummaged through); and, in some versions, the ability to 'personalize' future recording activities automatically, creating, in effect, individual schedules.

The DVR has the potential to impact on the relationship of time to television in two ways. First, by apparently 'pausing' live television, the DVR can effectively detach the viewer's individual experience of 'live' television from the actual transmission of the 'live' broadcast. Second, it allows viewers to ignore the vast range of scheduled programming by the individual channels and develop their own personalized schedule, tailored to their own particular tastes and routines of viewing. However, although it is easier to manage, it is not actually new. By careful use of the published schedule and the traditional VCR, it was always perfectly possible for any dedicated viewer to construct their own schedule. I am not convinced that a DVR would fundamentally alter my relationship to television. There might be certain programmes

I would watch later (whether this is five minutes or five days later) and programmes I would have forgotten to record which the machine would have 'remembered' for me. Yet it should be remembered that the various different television companies/channels (whether commercial or publicly funded) are not in the business of perverse scheduling. By and large, conventional scheduling still offers appropriate programmes at appropriate times for the kinds of audiences that might want to watch them. Despite the much-touted fragmentation of lifestyles and associated media-related activities (the impact of computer games, the internet, sell-through DVDs and mobile phone technologies), it is still the case that large swathes of the television audience continue to have relatively predictable domestic routines, which involve some time spent watching television. While television schedules may become increasingly programme-led, there are still tastes, pleasures and, more specifically, viewing *times* that I will share with people 'like me'. Television controllers and television companies *want* me to watch television; they want to make it easy for me. Therefore, programmes that I might like to watch, at times I am likely to be available to view, still exist. Clumsily, perhaps, in the multi-channel environment, companies are even attempting to pre-empt the DVR and increase flexibility within their existing schedules. One established feature of several satellite channels, for example, is the +1 channel, where programmes from a particular channel (such as E4, Discovery and UKTV Gold) are re-screened one hour after their original transmission, in effect, providing a crude 'pause' to the published schedule.

What the DVR does do, however, is focus attention on what exactly 'live' television actually means. Once the viewer using their DVR pauses 'live' television and turns away from the screen, they are no longer really watching 'live' television. This means that they are not watching at the same time as the programme is being broadcast and, more significantly, it means that they are not watching at the same time as other audience members. Even if it seems as though the programme is waiting for them, the DVR viewer still has time (minutes, hours) to make up in order to catch up with the 'live' transmission (and with everybody else). What the DVR makes explicit is that 'liveness' on television is not really, or not simply, about the experience of individual viewers (liveness as something that is unfolding, still about to happen *for me*), but is significant because it is a *shared* experience. Liveness, therefore, is a broadcast 'now' that is, simultaneously, inescapably, the now of the individual viewer, but which, crucially, is also a 'now' that is shared by other audience members watching television somewhere else. It is also the 'now' that is often being lived through by those individuals seen on the television screen itself. On the one hand, this characteristic of 'liveness' can seem like a dictatorship, and is often expressed as a kind of chronic neediness (as the television commentator pleads, 'stay with us now', 'don't miss'), from which the DVR may release the viewer. On the other hand, by refusing to take part in the actual, shared 'now', the viewer is refusing to participate in a shared present with those on-screen and the television audience in general. While you might be able to imagine interrupting a live sporting event and going back to it after a break for a cup of tea or a phone call, it is unlikely that it would seem appropriate to interrupt the live transmission of a disaster, such as the events of 11 September 2001. It is at times like these, as Paddy Scannell notes, that the 'bridging' quality of live television – a bridge between the world 'out there' and the individual viewer, who is also part of a larger community – becomes paramount. 'Radio and television are powerful bridging media that span the times of societies and the times of individual existences, bringing them into an available, public world now-of-concern' (Scannell 2002: 273).

Thus, despite its increased capabilities, the DVR cannot circumvent the most significant (and, perhaps, one of the most ironic) aspect relating to time on television. It is precisely the *unscheduled* time and the unpredicted timing of the live event – particularly the initially unexpected and then unfolding time of a disaster being transmitted live – that can be the most valuable to the television audience.

Satellite news gathering (SNG)

The previous three technologies I have discussed – the remote control, the VCR and the DVR – all involve the use of television by the viewer at home. In contrast, the last technology I wish to investigate in this section – the facility for satellite news gathering (SNG) – has a direct impact on the way in which a particular television genre – news – reaches the viewer. It also encourages different kinds of news presentation and, therefore, also has consequences for the next aspect of organization I want to focus on – narrative.

SNG is simply the ability to transmit television news pictures and sound from practically any location, via satellite, to the television newsroom. Sounds and images are shot on location, and may be edited by the reporter/producer on the scene, and are then sent via a telephone/satellite link to the home base of the news channel. Many satellite link-ups (via satphones) can offer two-way communication between the reporter at the news scene and the news anchor on-air, enabling them to speak to each other 'live' – a process known as a 'two-way'. It is now possible to incorporate all aspects of news production – recording, editing and transmission – either from a temporary land station or a mobile SNG truck. A typical SNG truck consists of a Land Rover-sized vehicle, with a satellite dish attached and computer hardware designed to edit and send video and audio data. Temporary land stations may be set up in convenient locations, such as hotel rooftops – for example, the Palestine Hotel in central Baghdad during the second Gulf War. Initially, SNG trucks/centres would have needed to book and schedule transmission time on satellites. The inconvenience and necessary time delay involved in the need to pre-book satellite transmission times has led major television companies – such as CBS, ITN and the BBC – to organize deals where they can have 24-hour access to satellites and, thus, unlimited facility for two-ways and live transmission. SNG is not just used for news pictures, of course; major sporting events, such as the Olympics, are now increasingly covered by this technology. For example, for their coverage of the 2004 Olympics, the BBC employed three mobile SNG units, as well as a satellite-link vehicle as a command and control centre.

What does this technology do for news presentation? Overwhelmingly, SNG means that news can seem to be instantaneous and it can be 'live'. In terms of time, SNG speeds up the reporting of news – events can seem to unfold for the anchors in the newsroom almost at the same time as they unfold for the viewers at home. Paddy Scannell (2004: 578) describes this kind of news production as a 'snowballing narrative', where the continuous unfolding of events is narrated on-screen by anchors, experts and reporters on the scene. Some critics have suggested that this pressure to be first and the need to provide speculation and commentary at once and on demand can cause problems, in terms of both getting facts right and analysis. Scannell (2004: 583), along with other analysts, suggests that this is moderated by the fact that the very duration of a 24-hour news channel means that it has time to go back to and 'worry over' facts and events until the story is confirmed. Whether this is seen as liberating or confusing for the viewer, it is clear that the flexible, 'open' news narrative is no longer confined to minor satellite news channels, but is now being taken up increasingly by larger companies, such as the BBC and ITN. Yet, in many instances, this notion of events unfolding as they happen is an illusion – real-world events do not follow a set, convenient pattern and, sometimes, literally, 'nothing' happens. In the early days of the BBC's coverage of the second Gulf War, for example, images were continually shown of a major road in Baghdad, labelled 'live', yet for days on end nothing more memorable than a few cars was seen on this road. Brent MacGregor's excellent analysis of the recent developments in news presentation quotes a CNN correspondent who also discusses the problem of live news presentation when nothing is happening: 'It's great if you have a Berlin Wall falling, but that doesn't happen very often. Most of the time you've got a parked car' (MacGregor 1997: 186).

The ubiquity of the live two-way has fundamentally altered how news reports are presented; in almost all instances, for each major news item, the news anchor will communicate directly with a reporter at the scene via a monitor. The reporter will then reintroduce the news event and often present a short pre-recorded report. At the end of the report, the news anchor and reporter will conclude with a brief two-way, where, inevitably, the news anchor generally asks what the 'latest' is. Presumably, the live presence on-screen of the reporter adds credibility to the report and the live two-way seemingly enables viewers to keep on top of any current developments. Yet, once again, a mismatch between the organized time of the news narrative and the disorganized time of the real world (where incidents start and stop, nothing happens or there is nothing but confusion) has to be obscured, sometimes to the exasperation of the reporters themselves. For example, MacGregor (1997: 185–6) cites a source whom he calls a 'veteran correspondent', who vividly illustrates what the problems are when live witness is privileged over the carefully edited, but previously recorded report:

> Recently when I was in Sarajevo I'd sent over a report, quite a long one, and the newscaster came and said 'What's the latest?' I said 'you've just seen the latest, I've just said it to you, I've got nothing to add to that'. There was a kind of a long pause.

The 'rolling' news narrative enabled by SNG has a particular order of time: time is now; events unfold in an exciting but comprehensible manner; and being live and being there are the most effective ways in which television companies can bring the news directly to the viewer. In some instances – the World Trade Center disaster, for example – this might seem to be the case. Most of the time, however, the 'time of events' in the real world stutters, confuses or drags on the ordered time of the news so that much of the information viewers receive is redundant, repetitive or pointless. And, ironically, the demand that the reporter be there for the television camera can actually make the business of finding out the news difficult; trapped by the demands of hourly bulletins, the reporter may have limited time to actually go out and find out what is going on.

Even when reporters are directly on the scene and viewers at home can apparently see and hear events unfolding 'as they happen', the relationship between time, sound and image enabled by SNG can be quite disorientating. As Stephanie Marriott (2001: 726) has noted, one of the key problems for broadcasters of live events is that while the presence of the situated eyewitness (in this instance, the reporter) is a crucial element which authenticates the broadcast, their actual limited point of view means that the totality of the event (and, perhaps, the parts which are most significant) may be missed:

> To produce the event from the point of view of an individual with a limited mobility and only a partial outlook on the scene is not to produce it as eventful. If television, in order to deliver a sense of 'being there' must produce for the viewer the kind of intense bursts of *hereness* which would realize the standpoint of a situated observer, then it must also perform the event in the totality of its unfolding.

As she goes on to observe, this means that live television broadcasts of real-world events somehow have to bridge the distinction between *being here* and *being everywhere*. Yet in travelling from place to place, from vantage point to vantage point, there is, inevitably, some temporal confusion or distortion as sounds and images – all apparently live – reach the viewer at different times.

Early on in their coverage of the second Gulf War (21 March 2003), the BBC *News at 6 O'clock* had a live two-way (sound-only) link with their world affairs correspondent, Rageh Omah. Introduced by the male news anchor, George Alagiah, it was announced that, 'while on-air', news of a bombardment of Baghdad had been received. The picture of Alagiah, who had left his desk to stand by the large video screen in the studio, was then displaced by a 'live' image of Baghdad, initially showing a nondescript deserted street scene at night. He then commenced a telephone conversation with Omah, who proceeded (in an understandably rather breathless manner) to try to describe the city being bombed. The original pictures of the street scene (presumably from a BBC feed) were then displaced by greenish night-vision shots (unlabelled but, presumably, again, from the BBC and possibly from near to Omah's actual position in the Palestine Hotel), which were then also intercut with other night sky scenes (this time labelled clearly as being from Abu Dhabi TV – 'exclusive' – showing a different city skyline to the night-vision shots). Both the BBC and the Abu Dhabi TV feeds showed little 'action' at first, but were then increasingly inundated with explosions. Obviously, what the viewers could see at home was not actually the same as the version of events that Omah could see (presumably from the hotel). Nonetheless, the 'live' quality of the two different picture feeds and the 'live' quality of the sound of Omah's voice, echoing and breaking up, unavoidably merged the three different instances of the 'live'. Here, then, the apparent temporal simultaneity overcame the different spatial locations of the visual and audio material being transmitted and there was a sense of both 'being here', with Omah, and 'being everywhere', visualized through the different night scenes. Bizarrely, however, at one point, as the action intensified and Omah announced, 'Hang on a minute, there's a huge explosion . . . I think you can hear that', the vision and ambient sound switched from the relatively uneventful night-vision scene to the Abu Dhabi TV feed, where, indeed, an explosion was then heard and seen. The slight time delay between Omah's voice on the telephone and the live, but not as immediate, pictures and sounds from the Abu Dhabi TV feed awarded Omah a rather spooky prescience as we heard the sound of the explosion *after* he announced that we should be able to hear it. Fractionally, therefore, the 'real time' of the world and the 'live' pictures and sounds transmitted by television news failed to coincide. The seemingly authentic 'hereness' of real-world events is revealed as inauthentic, ironically, because the reporter's eyewitness account (of what he can see and hear) reaches us *before* we see and hear the 'everywhere' live pictures and sounds from another source. What this slippage demonstrates is that even when the news cameras are apparently allowing viewers to watch events unfolding in 'real time' (producing an authentic sense of *hereness*), the unpredictability and the different places in which the events happen (which may be here, but also there and everywhere) can all too easily disrupt the illusion of the perpetual 'now' seemingly facilitated by SNG.

Narrative

Narrative is the way in which events, stories, ideas, image and sound sequences are organized on television. As a narrative unfolds, ideas, arguments and stories are 'told' and this telling takes up time (the duration of the programme in minutes and, perhaps, over days and even years). Narrative, therefore, is made up of two aspects: conventionally, these are known as 'story' (the events, plot or ideas that are the content of the narrative related to one another chronologically) and 'discourse' (the way in which this content is explained, told, shown or demonstrated). Initially, therefore, we have two different time periods. First, we have the 'time' of the story, which may cover decades in a family epic, or seconds in a 100-metre race. Second, there is the time taken up by the narrative itself – this might be 6 successive hour-long episodes or 20 minutes of 'live' television, involving the anticipation, the race itself, instant replays and in-studio analysis. In terms of time, the 'story' is nearly always moving forward from the present into the future ('this happened, then this', or, 'if this, then that'). Discourse, however, is not tied to any temporal regime and can move from the present, to the past, to the future or repeat events all over again and do so at different speeds (via flashbacks or flash-forwards, through still images or in split-screen, as well as instant replays in slow motion or fast-forward).

It is not my intention to outline all the existing narrative forms on television; despite their notorious reputation as formulaic, repetitive and unchallenging, they are still too many and too various for me to do them justice in this context. Instead, I will concentrate on a few different tendencies within television narratives that are distinctive in the way in which they manipulate or refer to time.

Repetition

In a narrative incorporating repetition, the same event (a pole vault jump, for example) will be seen in a series of repeated scenes; in each scene the actual event (the jump) remains the same, but the viewpoint and, sometimes, the speed of the image sequence will differ (the jump may be seen from the side, from above and in slow motion.) Repetition is common in sporting narratives, and in terms of time this means two things. First, the time of the event, as it is experienced by viewers, is extended for a longer duration than the actual event itself. Second, the notion of time continuing (events proceeding as they would in real time and in real life) is partly abandoned as we go back over the same period of time again and again. As other writers have noted (Morse 1983), this practice is, perhaps, an attempt by television to produce a spatial abundance (lots of different angles) as a substitute for the fact that the viewer is not actually there at the live event. It also allows viewers to catch up on an event that may have been too fleeting for them to experience fully.

This kind of repetition (where the same event is seen again but from a different perspective) also occurs in other genres, such as news programmes – most vividly in coverage of the World Trade Center disaster. In a short item presented at the end of the ITN *Ten O'clock News* on 12 September 2001, the traumatic events of the last 30 hours were reproduced for viewers in a kind of super-condensed mini-narrative (which some disparagingly called a music video). In this sequence, 2 minutes and 30 seconds long, the 'story' of the disaster was presented in a series of images. The sequence begins with shots of the clear blue sky over the familiar New York cityscape (incorporating the Twin Towers); moves on to the planes crashing and pictures of the towers falling; edits in the Pentagon being attacked; returns to the huge clouds of dust over New York; shows the start of the clear-up; and culminates with the sun setting on the ruins and the fractured skyline of the city. Pictured events were arranged in a loosely chronological and sequential order. However, in the first part of the sequence, in which the planes crashed into the towers, what was the pivotal event for many (when the second plane crashed and it became evident that it could not simply be an accident) was repeated several times from different perspectives. While this was, of course, made possible by the fact that, 30 hours after the disaster, news teams now had access to a wide variety of professional and amateur footage, it also produced a brief interlude where the temporal verisimilitude of an otherwise conventional narrative structure was abandoned. Repetition fractures this form of temporality – which presents events only once and in the order in which they originally occurred – and awards the moment of the second plane crash a particular status. As in sporting narratives, its repetition meant that the plane crash was experienced for a longer time than it actually took in 'real time', and that spatial abundance was, in part, a substitute for not actually 'being there'. In addition, however, this brief temporal immobility (where events did not advance) seemed to suggest that the audience would want to see it again (since they would not believe their eyes), but also that it was an event that was already 'outside' of time. Its incorporation into a mini-narrative that was otherwise dominated by conventional storytelling practice led to some dismayed critics insinuating that the sequence (set to classical music, as I discussed in the chapter on sound) was inappropriate – transmitted too soon, in indecent haste, after the events had actually occurred.

Repetition of this sort occurs less frequently in fictional narratives, where the demands of story-time (which push ever onwards) tend to take precedence over the aesthetics of discourse. However, as a device, repetition is sometimes used in comic narratives, where repeating events from a different perspective can reveal a comic truth about a mysterious incident. It is also occasionally used as a device in drama to illustrate a misunderstanding or create a moment of poignancy. In a romantic drama, *NY-Lon*, transmitted on Channel 4 in the UK, temporality was a key motif in the programme; among other formal conceits it employed an on-screen digital clock and split-screen – practices clearly borrowed and adapted from the American series, *24*. It also employed occasional bouts of 'stuttering temporality', albeit in this instance within a single screen image. In the second episode, 'Excess baggage', Edie (an American woman living in New York, and one half of the 'will-they-won't-they' romantic couple) is attending a ceremony at which her ex-boyfriend is to throw the ashes of his recently deceased brother into the Brooklyn River. In panoramic split-screen, we see the small party get out of a car and approach the river; below, in another panoramic split-screen, we see the scene start again (in the scene, Edie opens a red umbrella, which acts as a clear visible signal that the event is repeating itself). While clearly part of the series' attempt to play with time stylistically (just as, in terms of content, the time difference between New York and London was a central part of the story), the repetition here can be linked, a little awkwardly perhaps, to the repetition of the World Trade Center footage – in part, because of the location, but, more importantly, through the connection with death. Repetition, here, is meant, perhaps, to suggest, once more, a moment 'outside' time; the story-time deliberately 'trips up' and, in doing so, attempts to suggest to the viewer that the repeated event is a significant, meaningful moment.

One recent drama series from NBC/DreamWorks – *Boomtown* – employs repetition as a key stylistic device in an even more emphatic manner. The crime series set in Los Angeles promotes itself as a cross between Akira Kurosawa's *Rashomon* (1950; where a murder/rape/ambush is seen from four different perspectives) and Quentin Tarantino's *Pulp Fiction* (1994; which interweaves three different storylines and pushes forwards and backwards in time). Of course, this fictional repetition is different to the factual repetition in sports and news programming, as the incident that is repeated is not actually the same event – it just appears to be. In *Boomtown*, the device is used explicitly to introduce a different character's perspective, and the actual element that is repeated in vision tends to be very brief. For example, in the pilot episode, in clear homage to *Pulp Fiction*, there is a short 'irrelevant' conversation between the two main plain-clothes detectives – 'Fearless' and 'Joel Stevens'. Fearless asks Stevens whether he knows what the French word is for orgasm (*la petit mort* – the little death). The scene is clearly a coy reminder of the famous exchange in *Pulp Fiction* between Jules Winnfield (Samuel L. Jackson) and Vincent Vega (John Travolta), where Vincent asks Jules whether he knows what the French call 'a quarter pounder with cheese' (a Royale with cheese). Not coincidentally, in *Boomtown*, the brief exchange between Fearless and Stevens acts as the sequence which ends the story from Fearless's perspective and is repeated (bleached and cut slightly differently) when the narrative shifts to begin the story again from Stevens' point of view. Despite clear stylistic ambitions to create a temporal regime that is defiantly non-conventional, the series is careful not to confuse the audience, and the motif, which necessarily involves abandoning temporal verisimilitude, is clearly signalled by inter-titles, which tell the audience which character's point of view we will be seeing next. In some ways, this locating of the story so securely with one character at a time means that the programme is not so much about repetition as it is a series of stylishly book-ended flashback sequences. Consequently, the series is more akin to *CSI* (which employs mutable, reconstructive 'flashbacks', worked on and developed by the investigators) and even, perhaps, a soap opera such as *Sunset Beach*, which notoriously employed the 'flashback' in an excessive and, ultimately, camp fashion.

In *Sunset Beach*, a relatively short-lived, American daytime soap opera, produced by Aaron Spelling, flashbacks were used to remind and demonstrate to viewers what individual characters were remembering or thinking. In one episode, for example, Antonio, a priest, is talking with another character – Michael – discussing the nature of true love. At each suggestion ('you need to be good friends', 'you need to be able to talk'), there is a cut to a close-up on Antonio's face, and viewers then witness a bleached and fuzzy flashback sequence, which shows Antonio 'being friends' and 'talking' with Gabi – the woman he loves. Unfortunately for Antonio, she is also the wife of his (temporarily) paralysed brother, Ricardo. Although some of the scenes do involve repetition – as regular viewers will recognize sequences shot earlier in the soap's history – others have obviously been shot for this purpose. In this instance, the effect is unlike the previous uses of repetition that I have described. It is not effectively poignant, even though it speaks of loss. Nor is its presence revelatory – as when repetition is used as a device to reveal something the viewer did not see before. Within *Sunset Beach* the excessive and laboured use of the flashback is deliberately outrageous. Four flashbacks in under three minutes of screen-time may only be experienced as silly or playful; equally, their function is not revelatory, as even the infrequent viewer of the show will already know that Antonio is impossibly in love with his brother's wife. In fact, by this point in the episode, we even know that his brother knows and seems to be about to confront his wife with evidence of her infidelity. Here, then, *Sunset Beach* is clearly parodying the use of flashback in other (American) soap operas, which is entirely in keeping with the series' ultimate development as a camp, cult show, which also incorporated fantasy sequences, characters openly talking to themselves and a variety of self-reflexive jokes and narrative homage to a wide range of different films and television programmes (including *The Wizard of Oz*, *Scream* and *The Jerry Springer Show*). Alternatively, if we were to experience the use of flashback as not primarily referring to other texts, but as a narrative strategy integral to the programme, then we could say that the frequent use of the flashback effectively 'stills' the narrative, allowing viewers to 'wallow' with the characters in a suspended state of heightened emotion or suspense.

Chasing time

Successful television narratives have often been those which produce entirely expected, but specifically unknown, outcomes – a characteristic feature of one of the longest-running and consistently most popular genres on television, the game show. In this genre, there are general conventions that the narrative will adhere to (winning or losing), but the specific outcome (who wins or loses) will vary in relation to particular shows and within each episode. Even an extraordinarily rigid format, such as the narrative of the game show, *The Weakest Link*, provides some element of the unknown, since the contestants are different each time and the exact amount of the final prize is not reached until the end of the programme.

So, while Anne Robinson's presentation and questioning, and the organization of the *mise-en-scène* and the game itself remain the same in each episode, who wins and how much they win will differ. In *The Weakest Link*, as in many game shows, the programme makes a feature of the fact that time itself is rigorously monitored – each round of questioning lasts exactly two minutes and contestants have to answer 'against the clock'. Even more obviously, in other game shows, such as Channel 4's *Countdown*, the sound and sight of the studio clock 'ticking down' as contestants rush to provide answers is a key visual motif within the programme.

The notion of time – in intense measured periods or as time running out – is thus explicit and often central to the excitement of the game show narrative, creating a sense of urgency and suspense. In many game shows, time is used as a way of dictating events – the task must be completed within a specific time period. In this sense, then, the game show is a kind of chase narrative, a 'race against time', where time is often broken up into successive, clearly delineated periods. Time may be portioned into 'rounds', and the number of questions asked and answered is dictated both by the contestant's ability and by how much time is allotted. Since time is so valuable on game shows, it may actually feature as something that can be 'won' by individuals as they progress through the game; seconds or minutes may be awarded if contestants succeed at particular tasks or answer questions correctly. Ultimately, they then accumulate 'time' in which to chase the 'big prize' at the end of the game.

Of course, not all game shows implement this kind of 'time economy', but time remains a key formal aspect of the programme in other ways. As Misha Kavka and Amy West have observed, a key feature of reality game shows, such as *Big Brother* and *Survivor*, is the way in which they remove contestants from 'real-world' time and institute instead a time – a temporal regime – that is counted in units (minutes, days, weeks). While some parts of these reality shows do relate to the real time of the outside world – the 'live' eviction episodes in *Big Brother*, for example – the programme is generally concerned to construct its own temporality (often in the form of a countdown to a specific event – an eviction, a challenge or the 'end'). Kavka and West usefully distinguish the time in reality game shows as distinct from 'real-world' time by identifying it as not 'live', but 'present-ist'. Present-ist time, they suggest, is the way in which such a programme 'reorders time, distilling it into socially recognizable units which are reiterable, and hence return as ever new, ever present' (Kavka and West 2004: 150). Present-ist time also serves the purposes of the programme-makers because it is endlessly recyclable and re-presentable. As they (Kavka and West 2004: 151) go on to argue:

> Present-ist time is 'unlocated' because it steps out of the historical continuum, transgressing the laws of linear, infinite time and manifesting a kind of cyclical present which begins and ends whenever and wherever it is transmitted. This present can be read backwards as well as forwards.

Time can be counted down ('three days to go before eviction night') or up ('week seven in the Big Brother house'); events can be seen live (with a short delay) or represented as 'highlights' of the week, or as the contestants' 'best bits'. As in sporting events, certain key incidents, pratfalls, encounters and even the contestants' facial expressions can be slowed down, rewound and repeated, yet, while the game is on, the reordered time is always 'moving on', running out or accumulating. In these reality programmes, contestants are literally detached from the 'real world' and its time. In both *Survivor* and *Big Brother*, contestants are not allowed to bring clocks or watches into the game environment and they do not have access to 'time-telling media'. Thus, as Kavka and West note, in these programmes, temporal disorientation is as important as spatial relocation. While this disorientation may be extreme in these programmes, it is, perhaps, simply an exaggeration of the temporal detachment that is a feature of most conventional game shows. Despite the fact that the programme appears to be a daily event, many shows, such as *Countdown*, for example, record several episodes on one day. In each 'day's' episode, at least one of the contestants will be different, but the presenters may have done little more than change their tie or jacket to suggest the passing of time. The passage of time is also implied through the presenters' address, as they introduce contestants and participants as featuring in 'today's programme', or look forward to 'tomorrow's show'. Interestingly, the duration of *Countdown* as a series (which has now been transmitted for over 20 years on Channel 4) seems to have given the presenters licence to be less discreet about its production practices. In fact, the suggestion that each show is produced on the day for each day is covertly accepted by both audience and participants as an elaborate pretence. As such, it is sometimes gently mocked by the co-presenters, Carol Vorderman and Richard Whiteley, often in banter concerning Whiteley's tie.

In contrast to this, one of the novel features of *Who Wants to be a Millionaire?* in its first run on British television was that it *was* filmed over a series of days and stripped over a week of the schedule. Initially, this framework seemed to encourage a sense of urgency and promoted a feeling that there was potentially a 'real-life' soap opera unfolding. This was exacerbated by the fact that at the end of some episodes contestants might be left in suspended animation, waiting to see if they had selected the right answer, not knowing their fate. As the programme has become more familiar and the 'race' for the first millionaire has now ceased, the intensive stripping of the programme across a week's schedule is sometimes abandoned. In its original form, however, the unconventional scheduling and temporal regime of the show achieved unprecedented ratings and excitement. Yet despite the sense of urgency and participation experienced by the audience, episodes were not screened live; each episode of the programme was recorded the day before transmission. While the fact that it is not actually live is not necessarily peculiar, the enforcement of a specific time limit on each episode might seem harsh on contestants (and provoking rather than exciting for audiences). Presumably, a pragmatic reason for this is that although the programme is committed via scheduling constraints to a specific duration (30 or 60 minutes), the individual attempts to win a million pounds by the different contestants cannot be given a specific or entirely predictable time limit. Some contestants might fail after a few questions, some might be able to answer 10; the time taken to answer questions can also vary. While in the UK the quizmaster – Chris Tarrant – may gently urge contestants to make their 'final answer', the programme does not feature any specific time limit for answering questions once the contestant has reached the 'hot seat'. Yet the programme does not completely exclude time-based constraints as a way of increasing excitement elsewhere in the programme. Two features, the 'phone a friend' option and the hurdle of the 'fastest finger first', are key ingredients in the temporal regime of the programme. The 'phone a friend' option is policed by an on-screen counter, which allows one minute for the question to be asked and the answer given – perhaps one reason why the time is curtailed is to stop any possible 'cheating' off-screen, as phone respondents could, if given more time, look up answers on the internet or in encyclopaedias. The second feature – the 'fastest finger first' – is where contestants have to race against each other to order a list of objects, numbers, dates or personalities in a specified chronology. Once completed, all the contestants' times are displayed (in seconds and tenths of seconds), before the fastest contestant is identified and gets the opportunity to sit in the 'hot seat' and answer questions in exchange for money. In *Who Wants to be a Millionaire?*, therefore, time becomes a framework through which the simple multiple-choice questions gain some kind of resonance and excitement. In many ways, *Who Wants to be a Millionaire?* simply revisits familiar temporal strategies from other game shows; however, since the programme does forsake one time constraint common to other quiz/game shows – that is, how long you have to answer – it gives the audience time to participate, to argue with one another and to shout the answer at the television screen. While this was perfectly possible in *Who Wants to be a Millionaire?*'s antecedent, *Mastermind*, the speed of questioning and the time limit enforced on questions in that programme would give very few audience members time to think or argue about possible answers. In contrast, *Who Wants to be a Millionaire?*, by presenting several potential answers to the audience, not only gives them the opportunity but, just as crucially, also the *time* to participate.

Counting down

Originating on radio, the 'Top 40' countdown on British television is an established programming convention which relates to the popular music charts. Most closely associated with the BBC's long-running pop music programme, *Top of the Pops*, the countdown of hit singles from 40 to 1 was, for several generations of viewers, a familiar and much-anticipated ritual. As the popular music economy has changed, it is, perhaps, less important culturally than it once was; nonetheless, in both *Top of the Pops* and related programmes, such as *CD:UK*, the format basically remains the same. Various pop singles are performed by artists framed within a narrative that uses a chart based on a week's single sales to dictate position. The top-selling single of the week is awarded the 'number 1' spot. New entries or selected artists from a variety of positions are played within the programme and the narrative itself is interspersed with partial countdowns – from 40 to 20, from 20 to 10 and, finally, from 10 to number 1. The number 1 song (with rare exceptions) is either performed in the studio or a music video is played. As most pop songs remain at about three minutes in duration, the programme is a succession of links, brief interviews and performances of the songs themselves.

This accelerated magazine format is one of the key forms of narrative on television and one which demonstrates the close link television has to radio and print media. Programmes as apparently diverse as morning 'lifestyle' shows (*This Morning*), chat shows (*Friday Night with Jonathan Ross*), 'list' programmes (*Britain's Greatest . . ., The World's Worst . . .*), extended charity telethons (*Children in Need, Comic Relief*) and other music shows (*Later . . . with Jools*

Holland) all demonstrate this kind of 'conveyor-belt' structure, in which 'bundles' of time – short pre-recorded items, live links, musical or comedic performances – are presented successively to the audience. While the content of each bundle may be diverse, the overarching feature of the programme is that it will be successive, in that there will be 'something else' along in a minute or two.

Several writers have suggested that this segmented, fragmented narrative is actually characteristic of television itself. John Ellis, in his early book, *Visible Fictions*, was a key originator of this term and suggests: 'The segment is a relatively self-contained scene which conveys an incident, a mood or a particular meaning. Coherence is provided by a continuity of character through the segment, or, more occasionally, a continuity of place' (Ellis 1992: 148). Ellis argues that the 'segment' has an identifiable temporal dimension (not usually longer than about five minutes). Provocatively, he also claims that the 'segment' is actually the building block of nearly all narrative structures on television, arguing that such segments, even in diverse genres such as news or fiction, are effectively interchangeable, and that they differ essentially only through content rather than form. At a very abstract level, Ellis's concept of the segment is seductive – certainly one thing that unites nearly all the programmes I have listed is a continuity of place (a television studio). In programmes such as charity telethons or list programmes, many of the segments might seem to be interchangeable and their actual progression can seem both artificial and arbitrary. Some items might seem longer than others (appalling renditions of pop songs by celebrity chefs) or be more anticipated by the programme itself (as in the return to the rising total of funds raised), but apart from some aspects of content (items may get more risqué as the evening progresses), they feel broadly similar. Yet, in some senses, I think the homogeneity implied by the 'segmented narrative' underplays other important aspects of these and other television narratives.

One of the aspects absent from Ellis's early analysis is the significance of two particular temporal qualities that impact on the meaningfulness of any one segment. First, although a musical performance on *Top of the Pops* is, perhaps, interchangeable with any other, their context is insistently in 'the present tense'; their organization within a narrative of 'the countdown' is one that insists upon the possibility of change or difference (what is its position this week?), and this artificially promotes a sense of urgency. Second, different musical performances inspire different kinds of investment from the audience and this is encouraged by long-term, habitual viewing. Programme events such as *Top of the Pops* are watched by large parts of the audience every week, meaning that the temporal pull the programme has for the audience is not simply generated by the progression and succession within one episode but is drawn out over several episodes over a period of weeks. For *Top of the Pops*, this longer-term progression was a key aspect of the programme: singles would 'climb' to the top of the charts, 'racing' each other for the number 1 position. In recent years, however, the pop music charts have been volatile – marked with a high degree of fluctuation – so that more singles than ever before may enter at number 1 for just a week and then descend rapidly. In addition, very few singles now seem to 'climb' the charts. The loss of a building interest or engagement previously engendered by singles rising to the number 1 position has led to producers seeking a variety of different strategies to restore excitement, including previewing unsigned bands and featuring the album charts (which do retain some element of long-term progression).

Ironically, just as this aspect is fading from the pop charts, it is being reinvented in a slightly different manner for a series of programmes based on telephone votes – shows such as *Restoration* (asking viewers to vote on which landmark British building/architectural site they would like to see renovated) and *Britain's Best Sitcom* (which was one in a series of *Britain's Best . . .* programmes, in this instance, asking viewers to vote for their favourite situation comedy). Both programmes effectively reinterpret the mixed temporal structure of the countdown show. The first aspect is immediacy – elements of all the programmes reproduce an instance of the 'broadcast now' and the final episode is always 'live'. As in reality game shows, such as *Big Brother*, this immediacy is enforced by the way in which the programme sets viewers a time limit within which they may phone in their votes (days, hours and, eventually, minutes). Second, the programmes also relate to time as duration, involving some viewers in extended, committed viewing. Both shows incorporated a series of different, related programmes presented over a period of weeks. In relation to the sitcom, interested viewers could watch programmes devoted to each selected show and watch repeats of their favourite episodes. *Restoration* presents tours of the buildings in question and the people involved in the campaign to 'save' them. It is possible to imagine both programmes in forms that would not involve telephone votes or their 'live' elements. As they stand, these kinds of programmes are clearly part of an initiative to explore the potential for interactivity and for the BBC (which produced both programmes) to meet with its public service requirements by apparently involving the general public in direct decision making. What is interesting, however, is how time-determined this interactivity is.

In some ways both programmes are creating a kind of canon – of sitcoms or of heritage sites. Sitcoms are evaluated for qualities relating to performance, to their story structure and to their popularity, while the heritage sites are evaluated for their architectural interest, their historical value and their importance to their immediate community. 'Timeless' values, perhaps, but by placing these discourses within a narrative frame that emphasizes competition and the need to vote quickly, the 'historic' or eternal values of the objects under discussion are swamped by the demands of the insistent 'present-ness' of their context. It may make for more immediately compelling television, but it undermines the value of the apparent canon that is established. Television has often been criticized as a medium that is 'forgetful', that does not seem to be able to archive popular memory or history (Mellencamp 1990). The insistently present-tense context provided by its continuity announcers and many of the programmes it delivers continually erodes the authority and 'eternal values' of any one version of history and any particular 'canon' that it may try to construct. It would seem that these programmes manifest this problem; however, in the case study for this chapter – on the millennium night presentation by the BBC on 31 December 1999 – I want to think about whether the inability of television to construct or determine a permanent, authoritative version of 'history' is actually a bad thing in itself. It may be that the competing temporalities I have begun to discuss here, which come to the fore in the millennium coverage, could potentially express a more radical and complex version of history, or of the 'times' we live in.

Economy

Ratings

The final way in which I want to examine the organization of time by television is to think of it as an economy. Programme budgets are not calculated in relation to how much individual programmes cost 'by the minute', but airtime either side of a programme on a commercial channel is valued by the second. The value of this airtime is calculated through a process of negotiation between the channel, advertising agencies, marketing managers and organizations which measure the viewing habits of the audience (Nielsen in the USA and BARB in the UK.) Roughly speaking, the larger or more desirable the audience understood to be watching a particular programme, the more expensive the airtime which brackets the programme (immediately before, during and after). The time spent by the audience watching programming (advertisements, sponsored bumpers, trailers, announcements) that is not the programme they specifically wish to view becomes a commodity that channels are able to 'sell' to advertisers. In this sense, the time of the audience becomes a 'commodity' that is bought and sold. The audience does not sell their own 'time'; they give up their time freely (if not always reliably) and seem willing to encounter advertisements as part of the environment which includes the programming they wish to see. While this is also true of other popular media (print media, such as magazines and newspapers, at the beginning of films and on the radio), it is not the case with all popular forms of visual and audio media (such as books or popular music bought on CDs). It is not unique to television, nor is it true for all television systems; the BBC, for example, is funded via a system which requires each household to pay for a license every year to pay for its programming.

The monetary value ascribed to certain minutes and seconds over the broadcast day is based on how many and what kinds of people are believed to be watching. As television technology has developed, in the UK at least, the methods of audience research have also changed, moving from questionnaires in the street, to viewing diaries and, currently, to 'people meters'. People meters are electronic devices hardwired to the television set (and video recorder), which register viewers once a button on a special remote control handset has been pressed. Each individual in the selected household is assigned one handset, and a few sets are made available for visitors. Viewers are required to record when they enter or leave the room, and they are also cued at regular intervals to confirm that they are indeed watching and present. One early glitch related to time was how many minutes of time spent viewing could be presented as a readable rating. Before the expansion of channels and the widespread distribution of the remote control, it might have seemed feasible to argue that people could be faithfully recorded as watching one particular programme in its entirety. Yet the problem is that some individuals clearly watch parts of some programmes and parts of others within the same short time period. The difficulty here, therefore, is which part of the programme is actually being watched and for how long. More specifically for advertisers, the concern is which channel or programme is being watched when the advertisement break is playing. In addition, channels which produce programming that is not necessarily of conventional 'programme length' – such as MTV – might be said to be missing out if ratings are only attached to programmes of a specific duration rather than those of shorter time periods. Thus, while cumulative, approximate ratings for particular television programmes are made publicly available, the actual process of comparing audience data with programming is far more finely tuned. BARB, for instance, claims to provide minute-by-minute viewing data, which it matches to the detailed record of timings of programmes and commercials provided by the television channels. It is, presumably, this information that allows advertisers and channels to estimate the value of particular advertising breaks.

Despite the apparent scientific and statistical grounding for audience measurement, and its increasing technical sophistication, in reality, the 'audience time' as commodity may bear little relation to the 'real time' spent by the audience. Numerous studies have indicated that even if the audience is in the room and apparently watching the television, it may be paying little attention – here, the 'quantity' of time may have been estimated, but the 'quality' of the time spent is not so easily captured. In addition, the attempts to be 'fully representative' of all households can be very difficult to achieve. In fact, a few critics have claimed that television ratings are, in some senses, an elaborate fiction (Ang 1991). One justification for this may be related to the way in which changes to the numbers and selection of panel members or in the method of recording data can apparently cause a radical difference to the way in which the television audience is apparently behaving.

For example, in 2002, BARB changed the make-up of its panel of viewers in an attempt to reflect the changing demographics of the British population. Understandably, the practicalities of the changeover, and the fact that the organization had some difficulty recruiting enough appropriate households, meant that ratings were suspended for a two-week period in January of that year. When the ratings were revealed, however, they recorded apparently dramatic changes in viewing patterns. The three big terrestrial broadcasters, for example, all suffered significant losses in terms of audience (ITV1 demonstrated a loss of 26 per cent). BARB stuck by the figures, claiming that they demonstrated what had been suspected for some time, that other kinds of media use (DVDs, computer games and digital channel viewing) had inevitably affected the main terrestrial channels' audience share. Broadcasters implied that the ratings – past or present – must have been 'wrong'. What it demonstrates, I think, is that the 'time' of the audience, valued within this complicated process of audience measurement, scheduling and the selling of advertising space, is, to a degree, a virtual market where the 'product' – the time of the audience – is only realized through a consensual process of fabrication.

In the United States, audience measurement, conducted by Nielsen, is perhaps surprisingly less technically sophisticated than in the UK, as, until very recently, it continued to rely on written diaries. This process is conducted four times a year, organized via a tradition known as the 'sweeps'. During 'sweeps' months – November, February, May and July – television diaries are collected and processed in a specific order across North America in a 'sweeping process'. (In practice, some of the larger markets are also measured in additional months and this data is used to provide supplementary viewer information.) These 'sweeps' months are important to broadcasters as these will be time periods in which viewers' activities will be registered and, therefore, gain most monetary significance; they are also the points after which low-rating (or underperforming) programmes may be 'pulled' or, at the very least, rescheduled. One regular temporal intervention, in an attempt to bolster ratings during the sweeps, is the practice of 'stunting'. Also known as 'hyping', it can be detected when famous guest stars suddenly appear in long-running sitcoms; when channels schedule cinema blockbusters; or through the incorporation of sensational content into long-running dramatic series or made-for-television movies.

Currently, Nielsen has begun to introduce people meters in different regional markets within the US, just as they have done successfully in other national markets (New Zealand, for example). As in the UK, however, a change in the measurement process has revealed how important and fragile the 'unwritten' consensus is between the audience researchers and television companies. In the US, changes to the demographics of the panels and the method of recording their viewing habits produced an extraordinary alliance between the conservatively oriented Fox television stations (owned by Rupert Murdoch's News Corporation) and the NAACP (the National Association for the Advancement of Colored People), who have been behind a campaign calling itself 'Don't Count Us Out'. The claim was that the new system and the new panel underrepresented Latino and African-American audiences, which might lead to some of their favourite programmes being cancelled. Fox, which produces a relatively high number of programmes aimed at a non-white audience, might justifiably be seen to be concerned. However, some analysts suggested that, in fact, Fox's intervention was solely to do with the way in which the new system had registered falling ratings for their different local stations, and pointed to the fact that other black audience-oriented broadcasters – such as the cable channel, Black Entertainment Television (BET) – had actually recorded a substantial increase in their audience numbers. The debate is ongoing, but, once again, it serves to demonstrate how transforming the time of the audience into a 'commodity' is not an exact or uncontroversial science, despite the fact that its language – of ratings points, statistics and finely nuanced demographics – may make it appear that way.

Conclusion

In this chapter I have argued that television offers, in a variety of contexts, a complex layering of different temporalities and that this is partly supported by the way in which it manages the relationship between sound and image. Briefly introducing the methods through which television records, relays and, in some senses, produces 'time' for its audience, I then went on to discuss several aspects of the way in which time is explicitly ordered or organized by television. First, the television *schedule*, in its most basic form, illustrates how television channels attempt to integrate their programming into the daily lives of their audiences. The expansion of television into the day and night and the increase in the number of channels is, I have suggested, promoting a discernible shift from television being channel-led to programme-based. Time on television has become more regimented, a move characterized by the presence of densely packed, looping mini-schedules and the way in which programmes are increasingly of a fixed duration, appearing on the hour and half-hour. At the same time, seen as a whole, the 'broadcast day' represented by the traditional terrestrial schedule has also been broken up by digital and satellite channels, now making all kinds of programming increasingly available at any time of the day or night. Second, familiar *technologies*, such as the remote control and the

VCR, have fundamentally altered the way in which viewers control and experience time on television and affected the way in which both channel controllers and programme-makers present their programming to the audience. Emergent technologies, such as the DVR, may lead to even more radical interventions in the organization and experience of 'time' via television.

The way in which time is organized within programming has also been discussed; the exciting but often constricting qualities of SNG demonstrate both the value and the limits of what 'liveness' can do for a television audience, which now expects to see the news 'as it happens'. SNG has affected the way in which news is told on television and reveals a surprising mix and slip between different temporalities in the process of 'telling' the news. Following on from this, my discussion of *narrative* looks at three formal properties which relate to time – repetition, the concept of chasing time and conveyor-belt time – to draw out the surprisingly elastic ways in which television narratives manipulate time within a variety of different programmes. Finally, in the section on the *economy* of time, I have suggested that the way in which the 'time of the audience' is made into a commodity, to be bought and sold and fought over by interested parties, is often a very controversial process. In my concluding case study (the coverage of the millennium night celebrations by the BBC, screened on 31 December 1999), I want to return to some of these aspects – most particularly, the qualities of 'liveness' and the importance and limitations of technology in the relaying and recording of time – to describe instances of how different temporalities can be seen to interact with each other within one specific television presentation. I also want to develop some aspects of my argument to explore the complicated relationship between television, history and memory, time as it is remembered, shared and understood.

Case study: millennium night

Light came out of this river since – you say Knights? Yes but it is like a running blaze on a plain, like a flash of lightning in the clouds. We live in the flicker – may it last as long as the old earth keeps rolling! But darkness was here yesterday.

—Joseph Conrad, *Heart of Darkness*, first published 1902

In one revolution, in one day, we bring you the world

—Trailer for BBC's millennium day broadcast

The sun never sets on the British Empire.

—Anonymous

On 31 December 1999, the BBC presented a day of continuous programming, interspersed with short sequences which presented a series of different 'live' midnights from around the world, beginning on islands in the Pacific and concluding with the midnight at Greenwich, London in the United Kingdom. Of this day-long broadcast, I will be looking at the period between 21.20 GMT (Greenwich Mean Time, or Universal Time) and 00.20 GMT. Since even this limited period contains an enormous wealth of material, I will narrow my analysis down to four key events: the lighting of four beacons established to celebrate the millennium at different key cities within the United Kingdom; two 'special' midnights in Bethlehem and South Africa, which occurred at 22.00 GMT; the 'European' midnights at 23.00 GMT; and the 'British' midnight at 00.00 GMT.

As a case study, the millennium night broadcast, with its excessive focus on time as event, is an obvious choice in the context of this chapter. The BBC's claim that it could encompass the global celebrations appeared to be an extraordinarily ambitious project. In fact, this kind of broadcast was, in ambition, if not in scale, similar to other planned public events that national broadcasters often televise – general elections, the solar eclipse on 11 August 1999, Princess Diana's funeral in 1997, as well as the less grandiose celebrations held at the turn of other years. An early predecessor of this kind of broadcast, also produced by the BBC, was the programme *Our World* (1967), which celebrated the launch of the first television satellite – Telstar. This new technology meant that the programme could pick up live pictures around the world. *Our World* was a thus a live programme featuring a succession of 'representative' short scenes from different countries. Notoriously, London was represented by a famously shambolic live performance by The Beatles of their most recent release, 'All you need is love', supported by Mick Jagger (among others). At the time, The Beatles' performance was heavily criticized; now, however, this sequence has become an established favourite in a variety of nostalgic 'clip shows', although its actual origin is not often referred to.

The televising of public events represents a self-conscious attempt by broadcasters to produce 'History' (with a capital 'H'), to mark and in some sense organize public events so that they become meaningful and comprehensible to the audience. The millennium night coverage, therefore, is about time both as chronologically ordered – measured 'clock time' (counting down to midnight with a digital clock generally visible on screen) – and as History – an apparently consensual, public narrative that seeks to establish pictured events as important, spectacular, 'event-full'. Yet, following work by Vivian Sobchack (2002; on New Year's Eve montages produced by American broadcasters) and Stephanie Marriott (2000; who has discussed election nights and the broadcasting of the solar eclipse), I also intend to demonstrate that the relationships between time, television and history, or 'historification', are not as straightforward as they might first appear. I will suggest that the apparently seamless chronological flow of 'scientific' countdown time is frequently disturbed by the accidents of contingency and the impossibility of capturing the truly significant moment 'live'. In addition, in a related but different sense, I will unpick various layers of affective memory and the 'histories' (with a small 'h') that disturb the overdetermined historification of events. In particular, it is the myth, memory and contradictions of the British Empire (which, coincidentally, was approaching its zenith at the beginning of the last century) that is the History behind many of the images and sounds within the broadcast. Yet, surprisingly, the Empire is not a singular History; in fact – at least during these hours – it is not a history which is directly or uncomplicatedly referred to. As a History which speaks to nationhood and to Britishness, it can be seen to underwrite many different aspects of the planned public celebrations and the BBC's coverage, yet it is alluded to only obliquely. The broadcast actually presents a series of conflicting 'histories': the problem of articulating a 'British' nationality, without referring directly to the Empire; the implications of the political but partial devolution of Scotland, Wales and Northern Ireland in the late 1990s to that British identity; and the troubling global legacies of Empire.

The ambivalence that surrounds the memory of the British Empire and its history is tied up in the most frequently repeated image and metaphor in the evening's coverage; the River Thames in London. A key event in the coverage is the much anticipated 'river of fire' – a running flame of light that is set to travel along the Thames from Tower Bridge to Vauxhall Bridge at the same speed at which the earth turns. Rather crudely, therefore, I will draw a parallel between this river of fire and the 'running blaze on the plain' in Joseph Conrad's description of the history of empires. In *Heart of Darkness*, the Thames acts as a significant context from which Marlowe (the protagonist, if not the hero of the book) tells his story about a journey up another river – the Congo. The two rivers are made parallel to one another as Conrad devotes the first few pages to describing how Marlowe and a few friends sit on a boat that is floating on the Thames. The Thames thus serves as an ambivalent metaphor which frames Conrad's story of colonial power in Africa. As the quotation used above demonstrates, the novel uses the Thames to reveal a history which might seem to celebrate the glories of Empire – an Empire of 'Knights' and chivalry, the nobler ambitions of a civilizing Christian mission. Yet, at the same time, the implication is that the Empire itself may be no more than a 'flicker'. Conrad also implies that, despite the triumphant 'flash of lightning', the river simultaneously reveals a darkness – a darkness that supplies the ironies and lessons of history (perhaps the truth that the 'savages' in earlier empires were the Britons themselves, and that empires are also about greed, ambition and fear). I want to argue that the television coverage echoes, however faintly, however absurdly, the myth of Empire presented so ambivalently by Conrad. This can be detected in its almost compulsive return to the Thames; the way it laboriously follows the Queen's 'stately' journey as she travels down by boat; and the way in which the commentary works so hard to anticipate but can only, finally, be disappointed by the set-piece river of fire.

> He broke off. Flames glided in the river, small green flames, red flames, white flames, pursuing, overtaking, joining, crossing each other – then separating slowly or hastily . . . we knew we were fated, before the ebb began to run, to hear about one of Marlowe's inconclusive experiences.

Chronology of events

All the News for 1999

21.18 End of the main national news bulletin presented by Michael Buerk (MB); MB seated at a desk at the side of the specially designed studio. MB, a senior news reporter and anchor, will also be one of the main commentators for the rest of the evening's broadcast.

Stories: Recent stabbing of former 'Beatle' George Harrison. MB concludes with, 'That's nearly all the news for 1999'.

The Four Beacons

21.39 Trailer (voice-over): 'In one revolution in one day we bring you the world.' Images of sun setting with a lion statue in silhouette; folkish female voices singing on soundtrack; images of the world seen from space, superimposed with clock dials showing time passing; different children's faces in close-up, reminiscent of charity advertisements; Asian drummers dressed in red (actions not quite synchronized with but relating to the drum beat on the soundtrack); choreographed figures dancing in a green field.

Exterior shot of the Dome at Greenwich, with digital clock in the top left-hand corner; the presumably inadvertent voice-over from David Dimbleby (DD), initially indistinct, but then clearly stating, 'What are we going to do?'

Cut to interior shot of DD in a studio within the Dome, where he states: 'Things are starting to move; what we are waiting for down here at the Dome is the arrival of the Queen, who is travelling down river from Southwark and, on the way, she is going to light a beacon – one of a thousand beacons being lit all round the country.' As he speaks there is a cut to the Thames and the beacon is already clearly alight. 'There it is, by Tower Bridge . . . beacon that the Queen has just lit.'

Pictures of the Queen looking at beacon; 'BBC Live' ident appears in the top right-hand corner.

21.39 Voice-over continues from DD: 'At the same time, down in Cardiff, where we join Sian Lloyd, another beacon has been lit.'

We see the beacon light up. Indistinct voice-over from Sian Lloyd: '. . . represents the rebirth of the Welsh nation.' In vision, she then hands over to Noel Thompson in Belfast. In vision, he then speaks to two young people who will light the beacon in Northern Ireland. He then hands over to Kirsty Wark (KW) in Edinburgh, Scotland.

21.40 KW in voice-over: 'Well, here in Edinburgh we're about to light the beacon (pictures of student who designed beacon holding flaming torch who then lights fuse) and she's lit it . . . the beacon is alight in Edinburgh.' Pictures of smoke, cut to top of beacon where there is no visible flame. 'There we go, it's going straight up to the top. Well, we're just about to see it lit we hope . . .' Beacon remains unlit.

Cut to exterior shots of Queen's boat as she passes the Tower of London. DD in voice-over describes the itinerary of her journey, commenting at one point that she will pass 'all the famous old docks that are now closed'. High-angle exterior shots of Thames and Tower Bridge; DD mentions that the Queen is now approaching the meridian line on the Thames and describes how this will be signalled by a 21-gun salute from the Royal Navy frigate, HMS Westminster, with the salute set to finish as her boat crosses the line.

21.43 Pictures of beacon being lit in Belfast; subtitle laid over purple margin running across the bottom of the screen confirms 'Belfast live'. Noel Thompson in voice-over describes the scene: '. . . and there she blows'. Close-up shots and sound as beacon flares up.

Return to exterior shots of Tower Bridge and beacon. DD in voice-over: '. . . this is, of course, the centre of the activities. There's been a lot of criticism about London being too much the centre of these events, but this is, after all, the capital city and it is the centre of events tonight . . .'

DD discusses the river of fire and the firework display over the Thames planned for the evening. DD: '. . . meantime the Queen is still on her way.'

Fig 3.2 Millennium Night beacon. Empics/PA

21.44 Shots of all four beacons (all now alight) are pictured in split-screen.
DD: 'There you see all the four beacons of the four countries or provinces of the United Kingdom, the four capital cities or the four big cities of the United Kingdom with their flames burning away there.'

Split-screen then resolves into a close-up shot of the beacon nearest to Tower Bridge in London. DD notes that: 'the lighting of beacons goes back in warfare a long way . . . the warning of the Spanish Armada was given in this way.'

The two 'special midnights'

21.56 Pictures of the boat, *Millennium of Peace* (a tourist cruise boat), carrying the Queen down the Thames. Voice-over from Michael Parkinson (MP), Gaby Roslin (GR) and Michael Buerk (MB) in the studio.

MP: 'We're actually waiting for pictures from Bethlehem, which are coming up shortly. At the moment we're staying with these pictures from the Thames. What I can't wait for is that moment when the Thames is set alight.'

Some discussion between GR and MB as to how fast the flame will go.

21.57 Shots of children – girls – singing in choir. Cut to exterior shot of Big Ben showing the time. MP states: 'Big Ben, four minutes to ten o'clock.' The digital clock on-screen clearly states 21.57.

MB: 'Four minutes to midnight in Bethlehem maybe.'

MP: 'There you are, Manger Square, there you are, the pictures.' Cut back to children singing, which is now identified as Bethlehem.

MP: 'Michael, somewhere you've been to?'

MB confirms this and discusses in a relatively light way territorial arguments over the Square itself. Concludes by saying: 'Let's just hear the noises coming from Bethlehem.' Sounds of children singing. 'Shows the kind of spirit of the millennium, doesn't it, these are Palestinian children who are Muslims, who think that, actually, according to the Muslim calendar, that we are in the year 1420, but they've come together to celebrate it.'

GR: 'I think that it's amazing, in pictures from all over the world, all people of all religions are coming together in this one night and the world is so tiny!'

Palestinian singing ends.

MB: 'BBC's Jeremy Bowen is somewhere in Manger Square, but

I'm not sure we can get in touch with him . . . don't need to, we can see what's going on for ourselves, about 15 seconds to go, in Bethlehem, the birthplace of Jesus Christ, and the starting point for the millennium . . . there are the doves.'

GR: 'There we are.'

MB: 'That is midnight in Bethlehem . . . people there from all over the world there, of course, Michael.'

22.00   MP: 'Do we have any news of Jeremy Bowen yet, is he . . .?'

MB: 'He's in there somewhere.' Bowen appears in shot.

MP: 'There we are, there he is.'

Jeremy Bowen pictured high up, with Square and crowd in background (fades up): '. . . Jerusalem only three miles from here where there are no celebrations at all at the moment because it's the Jewish Sabbath. For the Jews it's the year 5760, for Muslims its 1420, but for here, in Bethlehem, it is, of course, 2000, the third millennium, where they hope they are going to have a very very different time, a much better place for their children in the new year in the new century in the new millennium.' Sound of 'Also Sprach Zarathustra' by Richard Strauss, as used in Kubrick's *2001*, heard in background, which comes to climax.

Cut back to studio to a three-shot of presenters who are seated. MB comments that: 'Bowen never misses a deadline, well, not by more than about 20 seconds. Anyway we're hoping to get some pictures in a short while from South Africa, who have also been celebrating their midnight just about now.'

22.04   MB: 'I think we're getting some pictures, Michael, sorry to interrupt you, from South Africa.'

MP: 'Your old patch.'

MB: 'My old patch.' Pictures of Mandela. 'This is Madiba, President Mandela himself, he's back on Robben Island. You know, he was in prison for 27 years, and for most of that time he was in prison there.'

MB is superseded by a voice-over from Jeremy Vine (remains unseen), who discusses the ceremony, highlighting Mandela's long incarceration (27 years) and the fact that 18 years of this was spent on Robben Island. He provides a context for a ceremony which features a short performance by male African dancers in tribal dress. Vine explains, in voice-over, why Mandela is lighting a candle in his old cell, indicating that it is meant to represent the 'African renaissance' or the 'African millennium' or the 'African century'. Vine notes that there has been a lot of 'scoffing' about this as the continent is riddled with wars and Aids, 'all over Africa', and 'the kinds of chaos we have seen again and again, particularly over this past year.' He does go on to suggest that if there is anybody, 'any one person', who embodies hope for Africa in the coming century, it has to be 'Mr Mandela himself'.

To the sound of an African choir, we see Mandela framed from a very low angle as he lights the candle in 'his' cell. On lighting the candle, Mandela lifts it, momentarily looks out of the cell window and then leaves; as he does so, he necessarily passes the camera and very briefly looks down to gaze directly into the camera lens. Grunts of appreciation and affirmation are audible from MB as he presumably watches the footage, but he does not speak until Mandela has left the cell, when he begins to comment on the symbolism of the candle, suggesting that it is also meant to represent the spirit of reconciliation and the transfer of power. Mandela hands the candle to the new president of South Africa, President Mbeki. Mbeki himself then passes the candle to a young African boy, at which point the camera pulls back and the lights dim to reveal that the candle acts as the tip (the point of the Cape) of an outline of the African continent that is made up of a series of candles, all held by children. All three presenters comment on the poignancy of the ceremony, with MP noting that: 'Mandela is a genius, the simple gesture and he's the master of it.'

22.07 GR: 'That was truly wonderful. Now, clock watching is not the only thing going on down in Greenwich tonight – there's a spectacular pop concert, featuring an incredible line-up of some of the world's greatest big stars, the millennium party in association with British Gas. It all began earlier this evening.'

22.08 Cut to recorded footage of a large choir and a symphony orchestra reaching the climax of Carl Orff's 'Carmina Burana'. Shots of the orchestra, choir and crowd are intercut with exterior shots of the Greenwich Observatory (with its familiar white dome) and the new dome, lit up by different coloured lights.

The prime meridian

22.14 Shots of Thames and Queen's boat approaching naval frigate HMS Westminster. DD (in voice-over): 'The Queen's ship is on its way, very slowly now . . . HMS Westminster the frigate floodlit there . . . It's nice that the Queen is coming down this way by river because this was, during this past millennium, after all, one of the places that was really the heart of British naval power. It's a reminder of the strength of the Royal Navy and the role the Navy played and still plays . . .' Sounds of cannons firing. 'Now the cannons start to fire.' Cut to shots of cannons firing from frigate as Queen approaches meridian line.

'European midnights'

22.50 John Sopel (exterior, background Eiffel Tower) in Paris, discusses French preparations and notes that designer did not want it called a firework display, but a 'ballet of fire'.

He reports that the clock on the side of the Tower, which has been counting down for the last 999 days, had, just before seven o'clock that evening, 'gone on the blink'.

Cut to studio and MB: 'Well, history, er, not the only thing going on the blink.' Audible giggles from GR. 'History has given Europe a cat's cradle of national borders and a lot of really confusing time differences, so here, with a handy guide to where is when across the continent, Peter Snow (PS) and Philippa Forester (PF)' (both known as presenters of the BBC's popular science programme, *Tomorrow's World*).

PS: 'Well, now, the Greenwich meridian is now accepted as all over the world as the official centre of time and space, but my goodness did it take some persuading to get Greenwich accepted. If you reckon that Britain and France have had trouble enough over beef, that's nothing to the decades it took for the French to accept that the prime meridian runs through London.' Explains that it was in 1884, at a world conference, that it was agreed that longitude would start and end at Greenwich. He observes that France and Liberia did not accept this at the time.

PF: 'The French have their own meridian cutting through Paris and they only finally came round to accepting Greenwich in 1911, but even then they couldn't bring themselves to say the G word. The legal time, said the Government, is now Paris mean time retarded by 9 minutes and 21 seconds and, even today, the French are still determined to promote their own meridian.'

Cut to pictures of French villagers planting trees. PF goes on to describe how the French have planted trees along their 'rival' meridian, claiming that it will be visible from space. Points out that GMT is now known as universal time, but concludes that: 'the final irony is that the international body that controls it is based in Paris.'

PS goes on to illustrate, via a map of continental Europe (on large video screen), all the countries that will reach midnight at 23.00 GMT. This clearly illustrates that all European countries (apart from the UK, Ireland and Portugal) will meet midnight at the same time. PF then goes on to preview the 'huge challenge' which is to try to visit 'at least half of them, from the Puerta del Sol in Madrid to the Brandenburg Gate in Berlin'.

22.54 Cut back to MB who comments that: 'our neighbours in Europe are about to start the third millennium.'
Montage of shots of different cities, including Vienna, Paris, Amsterdam, Madrid, Budapest and Berlin. Each brief shot is bridged by a cut to a fixed shot of the earth taken from space, with each city shot 'flying away' over this picture of the earth via a video graphic. MB attempts to identify all cities in voice-over. Vision returns to exterior shot of Eiffel Tower in Paris.

22.58 Exterior shot of Eiffel Tower, fireworks begin to work their way up the tower.
MB: 'What a symbol they've made of the Eiffel Tower . . . This firework display lasts for three minutes before the midnight and then goes on for three minutes afterwards . . . 30 seconds to European midnight . . . 10 seconds to go, live in Paris as Europe meets the third millennium. (Eiffel Tower explodes with light as firework display reaches top of tower.) Wow!'

23.00 Inadvertent cut to two French(?) presenters, but swift cut back to original shot of Eiffel Tower. Intercut with shots of large crowd.
Cut to shot of Pope at lectern in St Peters in Rome.

23.01 Cut back to Eiffel Tower. Voice-over from MB and GR as they discuss Eiffel Tower display.
GR: 'That gets 10 out of 10 in my book, best so far.'
Cut to extended montage of different 'midnights'.
MB: 'Right, let's go back across Europe and see how they greeted the new millennium.' Wenceslas Square, Prague. Digital clock removed. Dam Square in Amsterdam, Holland. Warsaw. Vienna. Copenhagen, Denmark. Geneva. Oslo, Norway. 'This is the moment at which Norway greeted the new millennium.' Shot of large, fairly indistinguishable crowd; a few fireworks explode. Puerto del sol, Madrid. MB: 'With a bit of brio.' Stockholm, Sweden. Swedish royal

family in medium close-up. We can hear clock bell chime out midnight and King Karl Gustaav: 'Skål!'

23.06   Cut back to studio. Digital clock still not visible.
        MP: 'Skål! is right, less than an hour to go, the final countdown has begun and all over the country people are getting ready for the millennium moment. In Edinburgh, Kirsty Wark is hobnobbing with about three hundred thousand close friends.'
        Cut to exterior shots of Edinburgh, shots of crowd with KW voice-over. Digital clock reappears on screen.

All you need is love

23.45   Interior shots of the Dome with music stage seen in long shot.
        DD (voice-over): 'And now the, all the performers and the audience are going to sing the Lennon and McCartney song, "All you need is love", the hit song of The Beatles in 1967, chosen from a long list of other records, and maybe some people will be thinking of George Harrison tonight as they sing this.'
        Close-up shots of stage and performers, intercut with members of audience.

23.48   DD (just audible): 'About another 25 seconds to go.' Song finishes. 'All the performers on stage, all the audience joining in, "All you need is love".'

River of fire

23.58   DD: '23.58 and Edinburgh.' Exterior shots of city, overhead shots of large crowd. 'Everybody (cut back to interior of Dome as – newly knighted – Sir John Taverner's choral work, "Millennium prayer", reaches its climax) counting the minutes, ordinary minutes that are passing just like any other minutes, but leading to an extraordinary moment, we're watching as the last year of the last century of the old millennium slouches off stage to make way for the youthful entry of the new.'

23.59   Close-up on faces of two choristers, who finish singing. Sounds of Big Ben beginning to chime. Cut to shot of Big Ben's face, showing midnight, superimposed on one side of screen, rest of shot filled with high-angle view of Tower Bridge on Thames.

00.00 Fireworks explode as Big Ben begins famous 'bongs', cut to series of wide shots of River Thames, Tower Bridge; ships horns heard, cheers, numerous fireworks explode. Brief cut to Birmingham city centre and large crowd of people. Return to shots of Thames, Tower Bridge and Houses of Parliament.

DD: 'Well, it is now 2000 today, and to mark the birth of the new century the river of fire on the Thames, fireworks all over the country, this great stream of high moving fire going at the speed the earth turns, difficult to distinguish there, I must admit, from the fireworks, turning, in theory at any rate, at the very speed of time, this is BBC One, a Happy New Year.'

Montage of shots of fireworks exploding over the Thames, Tower Bridge, Big Ben and Houses of Parliament.

00.02 DD: 'I have to say, as you've no doubt spotted, there didn't appear to be very much of that river of fire. I don't quite know what happened to it, no doubt we shall discover in time . . . The beacon still burning that the Queen lit earlier.'

Time slips

The broadcast is distinguished by the fact that 'time' not only structures the programme, but is also the event it wishes to describe. The presenters must not only describe the celebrations (the seen events) as they are happening in time, but try to describe time itself *as* an event. The central ambition of the programme is to transmit a series of successive live 'moment(s)', as different countries across the world reach their local midnight and greet the new millennium. Unfortunately, 'time' itself is invisible and, even when represented by the apparently rigorous apparatus of timekeeping – digital clocks, analogue clocks – it frequently reveals the fact that the time kept by the programme is actually an elaborate conceit and may or may not bear any relation to other visible times or to the events-in-time supposedly occurring simultaneously in the 'real world'. One of the ways in which the programme demonstrates this is that, although, in many ways, the broadcast and the presenters are all but hysterical about timekeeping (obsessively telling us the time, showing the time, discussing time passing), elsewhere the programme illustrates a rather cavalier and accident-prone relationship to time. At one point, the 'time' on Big Ben (the most famous clock in the UK) is shown and described by the presenters, just as it is clearly telling a different time to the digital clock also seen on-screen. Certainly, the time difference is small (a minute, perhaps seconds), but in a programme about the importance of one moment in time in relation to another (one second to midnight, one second after), any failure to synchronize effectively the representations of time must be significant. Similarly, the presenters themselves occasionally lapse into 'estimates'. Buerk goes on to suggest, for example, that South Africa is celebrating its midnight 'just about' now.

Again, in another section in the programme, one of the regional presenters, Nick Knowles, who is reporting from a hospital in the hope of capturing a millennium birth, attempts to get the hospital staff to synchronize their watches – not only is it clear that their time is different from the time in the studio (again, the digital clock gives a different time), but Knowles suggests rather vaguely that the time is 'about 10 minutes to'.

Even more problematically, the presenters are frequently betrayed into describing events either as about to take place when they have *already* happened or as happening when they have not *yet* occurred. Here, the planned timetable of events – or the partially scripted, partially improvised narration – snags on the problem of contingency, on the way in which things can be missed for reasons of technological breakdown or because they do not happen when they are supposed to. This is glaringly obvious at two points in the coverage concerning the lighting of the beacons: first, when David Dimbleby suggests that the Queen is about to light the beacon by Tower Bridge. In fact, the beacon is obviously, by the time the viewer actually sees it, already alight, presenting the viewer/listener with a contradiction which Dimbleby does not resolve, except to change the tense of his narration ('going to light . . . has lit'). As the lighting of the beacon is actually seen in some detail later on in the broadcast, presumably there must have been some technical reason for the delay. Second, in Edinburgh, Kirsty Wark proclaims that the 'beacon is alight in Edinburgh', only to backtrack immediately and suggest that, 'well, we're just about to see it lit, we hope'. Here, the beacon simply does not light when it is supposed to. These slips reveal that there are two kinds of time operating on or around the picturing of events. First, the time of the script and the improvised commentary; this is, to use Stephanie Marriott's term, an 'emergent present' that the commentator is 'speaking into' (Marriott 1997). Within this, the presenter is attempting to capture the significant moment either as it is apparently *about to happen* ('the Queen will') or, potentially, *as it happens* ('and the beacon *is* alight'). Unfortunately, this 'constructed' time is undermined by the second kind of time present within the programme – the 'real' time at which events pictured live *have already or have not yet* occurred.

One moment in time?

Ultimately, despite the fact that the programme is apparently designed to celebrate time, like the other 'countdown narratives' I have described, the broadcast is trapped into a narrative that effectively diminishes the significance of what Dimbleby grandly proclaims will be an 'extraordinary' moment. This is because, for the programme to be worthwhile, every midnight it pictures and describes has to be special, each one apparently unique and extraordinary. Obviously, this is impossible and the programme itself demonstrates the invalidity of the concept – no midnight is truly special, since they are all artificially constructed and obviously there is not just 'one' midnight. In its desire to appear inclusive, the programme even undermines the significance of the millennium itself, since its timing is put into question (as a reference to the Muslim and Jewish calendars implies). In a narrative overtly dominated by a linear, sequential temporality (counting down GMT, bouncing from one local midnight to another), the 'New Year's Eve' affect is stretched and exhausted. This becomes particularly clear during the montage of European midnights. First, none of the midnights, with the exception of Paris, is shown 'live', so there is no frisson, no connection between the time of the viewer and the time of the spectacle. Second, despite Michael Buerk's valiant attempts to name all the cities, there is little he can say of interest – if we look at his comments for Norway and then Spain, for example, it is clear that the pictures from Norway are frankly dull (a big civic building/palace in the back of shot and a large but anonymous crowd), while the Spanish images (which include close-up shots of crowd members dancing in silly hats) are only marginally more spectacular. Each midnight that comes and goes becomes like any other.

Another difficulty for the presenters, here and elsewhere, is how to capture definitively the live moment when it does occur. As soon as the presenters' 'speak' the moment when the New Year turns – proclaiming 'Wow!' as Buerk does in relation to Paris – then the moment has already gone and the 'new' year is, precisely, no longer entirely new. As Stephanie Marriott notes, television commentary surrounds, even swamps, the 'significant moment' in talk, but the moment itself remains elusive, even when things go according to plan. Instead, in a broadcast such as this, the presenters are obliged to substitute the running talk of the 'emergent present', which can chase, look back to but never secure the actuality of the 'moments' it describes: 'Events are described in terms of their relation to the present moment: they happen *before* the present moment . . . *at* or *around* it . . . or, potentially *after* it' (Marriott 1997: 190).

As Buerk counts down to midnight ('30 seconds to go . . . 10 seconds to go'), he *anticipates* the moment; he then speaks *at* but not *of* the moment ('Wow!'); later, he and his co-presenter, Gaby Roslin, speak *about* the moment ('best so far'). What this means in relation to time is that the moment's 'meaningfulness', its potential status as an epiphany (where it might be that things, feelings, memories 'come together' in one transcendent instant), slips away. Only the pictures of the 'ballet of fire' exploding up the Eiffel Tower come close; as a single recognizable focus for the television camera, this does, perhaps, just allow the viewer to glimpse an extraordinary moment as it happens, as Buerk's 'Wow!' suggests. Although, of course, we cannot be sure, for, as John Sopel has reported, the clock on the side of the tower has broken down; perhaps, if it had been visible, it, too, might have contradicted the digital clock on-screen, thus destroying the sense of a moment 'shared'. The Eiffel Tower, of course, resonates with other aspects of the broadcast – as mentioned earlier by the presenters, the tower was designed originally as a temporary public structure ('like the Dome') and is therefore a historical antecedent to the temporary and permanent structures constructed (rather controversially) in the UK for the millennium. And although this is not pointed out in the programme, it is also the site from which the first global time signal was sent around the world, at 10 o'clock on 1 July 1913. Therefore, the Tower, aside from being the most familiar and famous visual shorthand for Paris (and for France), foreshadows the day's events. First, its original status was as a celebratory national architectural symbol that has since stood the test of time. Second, in its metal pylon-like structure its employment as the first 'beacon' of electronic time is perceptible as a purely visual symbol, even if its specific historical significance is unknown by the viewer and unacknowledged by the programme.

The lighting of the beacons reveals the problems of contingency, of 'real-world events-in-time' failing to synchronize with the prepared and improvised 'narrative time' of the television broadcast. In the following sections I want to move away from the specifics of 'telling time' –

'liveness' and narrative – to examine how the programme articulates contemporary concerns that were both explicit and implicit in public discourse at the time of the broadcast itself. It is in these sections that I want to explore the relations between History, historification and histories.

A British nation?

For most foreigners Tower Bridge is the centre of London.
— David Dimbleby

Fig 3.3 Millennium Night. Andrew Murray/Rex Features

One of the most significant changes the 'New Labour' government (elected in May 1997) introduced was the 'regional' assembly; Wales, Scotland and, more problematically, Northern Ireland, were granted the right to organize their own regional parliaments, with elected members making real financial decisions, covering aspects such as health, education and cultural policy. Of course, many Scottish and Welsh people identified such parliaments as national rather than regional institutions. Though understandable, this was problematic, since, clearly, the Westminster parliament in London could not be understood as the 'English' parliament, not only because it could act in terms of foreign policy for the whole of the United Kingdom, but also because it still included members from all over the UK. Thus, a tension between a 'British' identity and a regional-national identity necessarily affected the notion of a 'national' celebration for the millennium. The BBC, as a global as well as a

141

national and regional broadcaster, was also implicated. As a public service, the BBC was under pressure to be representative, a pressure which only increased as the process of devolution evolved. In fact, the corporation has had a long history of both denying and trying to prevent a 'metropolitan' bias in its reporting of events and production of programmes. Therefore, in relation to both changes in the wider political culture and the BBC itself, the programme had to encompass the local, the national and the global. Explicitly global in scope, the programme was obliged to identify the London celebrations in the same sweeping terms that it had described other 'national' celebrations, where one city, one square or one 'national symbol' could seemingly represent a whole nation. Yet, at the same time, in relation to its national but also regional audience, the London celebrations had to be reframed as only part of a series of events. Necessarily, this actually demonstrated that there was an increasingly fractured sense of national identity (a situation which was not likely to be unique to the UK). It is this tension that, despite its best efforts, the programme fails to contain.

As I have noted above, at points, David Dimbleby (the voice – as I have argued in the chapter on sound – both of the BBC and, perhaps, of 'Britishness') is determined to assert the right of the capital, London, and its symbol (Tower Bridge over the River Thames) to stand for the United Kingdom. At other points, his commentary almost collapses as he struggles to acknowledge the significance of celebrations taking place in other parts of the country. This is most apparent at the moment at which the image itself 'fractures' in the four-way split-screen, picturing the four beacons from Northern Ireland, Wales, Scotland and England. Just before this sequence, Dimbleby has again defended the right of London to represent the nation ('this is, after all, the capital city'), but when confronted with the split-screen his confidence appears to dissolve momentarily. Initially, he describes the beacons as representing the 'four countries' of the United Kingdom, yet almost immediately – as if he realizes his 'mistake' – the status of the beacons as national symbols is diminished, as he quickly suggests that, in fact, they represent the 'provinces', then the 'capitals' and, finally, four 'big cities'. Ultimately, of course, the problem is resolved visually as the camera returns to concentrate on the beacon at Tower Bridge. While it might seem that Dimbleby (and the broadcast) covers over this fracture (however awkwardly), there are at least two other moments when these 'other' nationalisms 'leak' into the BBC's broadcast. The first of these can be picked up from the commentary by Sian Lloyd, although attention is not drawn to it; her comment that the beacon lit in Cardiff signifies the 'rebirth of the Welsh nation' is clearly heard, nonetheless. Elsewhere in the broadcast, Lloyd is unabashedly, exuberantly nationalist – her first greeting from Cardiff after the New Year is spoken in the Welsh language. In relation to Scotland, Kirsty Wark generally concentrates on the nature of the crowd in Edinburgh and makes no explicit spoken reference to the Scottish nation. Yet she, too, provides a glimmer of the partisan in her presentation when she is pictured at one point happily waving the Scottish flag (rather than the British flag, which, perhaps surprisingly, is not seen anywhere in this part of the broadcast).

Despite these obvious fault lines, the broadcast does articulate or sustain a series of symbols that are fundamental to a sense of Britishness and underscore a 'British History'. The programme continually emphasizes the significance of the zero meridian, the Thames, the Greenwich observatory and longitude. The History that all these symbols represent is the history of British naval power and the belief that (once) Britain 'ruled the waves'. For it was the ability to map the globe, to plan and predict trade routes, to establish train timetables and to bring imported goods 'back home' to 'all those famous old docks' (now closed) on the Thames which was essential to the success of the British Empire. And it is the end of this Empire in the twentieth century and, thus, the 'ghost of empire', which haunts the broadcast. As I have already indicated, the British Empire is never referred to directly, as its history is too problematic and too controversial for a BBC trying to position itself as a national broadcaster on a global stage. However, it is David Dimbleby, as the de facto 'voice of the nation', who, unsurprisingly, calls up this ghost. In one particularly telling aspect of his commentary, we can all but 'fill in the blanks' with 'the Empire'. This is the sequence when he suggests that watching the Queen proceeding down the Thames is 'a reminder of the strength of the Royal Navy and the role the Navy played and still plays . . . (sound of cannons firing) now the cannons start to fire'. It is almost as if he is saved from indiscretion by the intervention of the cannons – the context he leaves unspoken here, of course, might be the two world wars and national defence, but it is, more obviously, the British Empire itself.

The Empire could have provided a solution both to the problem of national identity and to why the UK 'midnight', above all the other midnights, should be so 'extraordinary'. At the turn of the nineteenth century, Britain had recently celebrated Queen Victoria's Diamond Jubilee, in 1897. Queen Victoria was the head of a global empire and Britain (with the specific inclusion and industry of the Scottish and the Welsh people) was, perhaps, *the* world power. Yet by the end of the twentieth century, Britain – under another long-ruling monarch (Elizabeth II) – had experienced the decline of Empire and the rise of other global superpowers. In facing the twenty-first century, the BBC (associated with the Commonwealth, if not strictly the Empire), was, along with the UK itself, struggling to find an identity within this changed global context. For the BBC (as I suggested in the chapter on sound), one way in which it did so was to establish itself as a brand. While remaining a national public service 'at home', it was to become a 'global brand' in relation to the world, promoting commercial enterprise through the sale of different products and programmes via 'BBC Worldwide'. Yet what have to be obscured in the evening's broadcast are the more painful legacies of Empire, which threaten to interrupt the careful orchestration of what Gaby Roslin suggested was a temporally organized, global unity, 'all people of all religions all over the world . . . coming together in this one night.'

Mandela's rebuke

The sequence that perhaps threatens to undermine Gaby Roslin's claim that the world was 'coming together' is the 'midnight' from South Africa. It does so for a variety of reasons. First, of all the midnights seen during the three hours I have highlighted, it is the only one which really focuses on people and, predominantly, on one individual – Nelson Mandela – who is, perhaps, one of the few living icons of the twentieth century. The term 'icon' is often used lightly, but, in this context, it has a very specific meaning. The icon – or, here, the iconic figure of Mandela – is a historical person who not only represents themselves in particular (he is Nelson Mandela), but also represents a series of potential narratives and feelings (the struggle against apartheid, dignity and, perhaps, Africa itself). In this sense, Mandela represents a particular history, but might just as easily be integrated as a meaning-laden 'symbol' into other histories. Mandela is, in some sense, both *of* his time, as a marker of change (the signal that there was to be an end to apartheid in South Africa), and *outside* time – someone whose presence is encrusted with layers of different meanings and emotion that could be used as a kind of shorthand in a variety of contexts. Indeed, the programme itself confirms his status as an icon. There is, for example, Jeremy Vine's observation that if there were 'any one person' who might represent hope for Africa, it would 'have to be Mr Mandela'. Significantly, Gaby Roslin, in commentary I have not transcribed, observes that, for her, seeing Mandela released in 1990 (which she saw on television) was one of the most 'truly incredible moments of my life'. Roslin, the giggling, likeable blonde, who acts as a foil to the two older and more senior male presenters, articulates, perhaps, the views and knowledge of the less well-informed members of the audience (a role made evident by the way in which she spends a lot of time teasing Buerk about how much he knows or has learnt from his script notes). The fact that she knows who Mandela is partly because she saw him on television confirms his status, perhaps, not only as an icon (universally recognized), but also as a *media* icon. In fact, as Michael Parkinson observes, Mandela is also known for his ability to manipulate the media – he is a genius, who is the 'master of the simple gesture'. In other words, Mandela is apparently expert in the production of gestures that will translate or perform well on television.

On one level, the candle lighting ceremony that Mandela takes part in, is clearly a performed, small-scale gesture with which to greet the new millennium. Perhaps it might seem appropriate for a 'developing nation', in comparison to the large-scale celebrations seen and expected from the 'developed' countries – there is an implicit contrast between the small flames of the candles and the proposed river of fire and the thousands of pounds worth of fireworks that were to be part of the celebrations in London. And the ceremony features possible clichés that might diminish the jaded viewer's appreciation – picturesque, small, brown-skinned children, African dancers in 'tribal dress' and the suggestion of a 'light in the darkness'. And while these possible associations exist, at the same time, aspects of the framing, of Mandela's status and performance, suggest to me interruptions, not just to the chain of associations established by the sequence itself, but to the programme as a whole. The most startling moment is when Mandela lights the candle, picks it up, looks briefly out of the window and then passes the camera, briefly gazing into the lens. The low-angle framing of Mandela is important: on the one hand, it presents Mandela as a tall, imposing figure whom the camera 'looks up to'. On the other hand, as Mandela passes by and looks down at the camera (and thus, implicitly, at the television audience), the position of the camera is aligned with Mandela's own previous known position– the prisoner incarcerated in the cell. This potential is increased by the way in which the camera (the prisoner) is 'left behind' as Mandela (now the guard?) exits the cell, since it is a different camera that picks up his journey as he passes down the corridor to the outside. The most destabilizing moments occur, however, when Mandela looks into the camera – here, the television audience is confronted with a spectacle that looks back. While other celebrations do involve 'status' individuals as well as buildings and fireworks (mostly monarchy, including the British Queen), none of these individuals looks back at the television audience, apart from Mandela.

While Mandela does not speak directly to the camera (he does speak to Mbeki, but we cannot hear what he says), he does return the television viewer's gaze in the way that the Queen, for instance, does not. It is a knowing performance. Mandela, as Parkinson suggests, is not innocent of how the media works; he is perfectly well aware of his status. Mandela does not smile, but he does not frown either; rather, his gaze seems to suggest that he understands that he is performing (he does not pretend to be unconscious of the camera), but, by refusing simply to be looked at, he is able to nudge the viewer into questioning their own relationship to that performance. For if Mandela does, as he intends and the commentary confirms, represent not just himself but Africa, too, then he is also asking the BBC's audience to look back to the Empire and to Britain's relationship to that continent. And to think of Africa is to see the poisonous legacy of colonial rule and, in particular, perhaps, the infamous 'scramble for Africa' at the end of the last century. It does not matter for Mandela's purposes that there is no real 'midnight' (the pictures are transmitted some minutes after South African midnight) because the countdown 'time' to the New Year is irrelevant to the sequence. The moment Mandela looks into the camera is significant, not because it has any important synchronic qualities (the movement from one minute to another, from one millennium to the next), but for its diachronic impact (layers of association, of History and histories). It thus interrupts the banal succession of 'moments in time' set up by the programme. Despite the fact that the presenters surround the sequence with talk that tries to make the moment like any other, if perhaps more 'poignant', Mandela's rebuke resists this and stands out as different from the other celebrations aesthetically and for the way in which it relates to time itself.

The river of fire

It is almost too appropriate that the river of fire failed to work. As Dimbleby's comments suggest, it was immediately apparent that the river of fire did not turn out to be the spectacular event that had been so eagerly and frequently anticipated. Once more, real events in time tripped up the part-prepared and part-improvised script of the broadcast. Dimbleby initially describes events as if they are happening as he speaks. He is evidently expecting events pictured to proceed simultaneously with his commentary (by speaking, he hopes to conjure up 'this great stream of high fire going at the speed the earth turns'). Once more, the ambition here is to 'speak into' the moment, so that events will be captured *as they happen*. Unfortunately, for the viewer watching at the same time, the events apparently being described are clearly *not* happening. This means that he is forced to retreat and bury the mistake. At first, he suggests that it must have been difficult to distinguish the 'running flame' from the fireworks (in fact, later in the programme, it is acknowledged that it did not fire at all).

Thus, while the Thames did, of course, present a display of sorts – small reflected lights, criss-crossing one another, refracted by the tides of the river – it did not present a singular triumphant event. This works conveniently for me as a metaphor for the programme itself. On the surface, the broadcast is an attempt by the BBC to make a big statement, to establish a position on a global stage. In reality, however, problems with technology (both televisual and in the 'real world'), as well as the contradictions inherent to identity and History, break up and interfere with the programme's intended chronology or with its prepared 'historification' of events. In fact, as I have demonstrated, the programme found it difficult either to capture 'one moment in time' or to contain the different histories of the people and places it called upon. However, as I hope I have also suggested, this does not mean that the programme was simply inadequate; rather, the confusion and interference manifest in the broadcast reveal a great deal about television's relationship to time and to history.

chapter four

Space

···

Introduction

In this chapter I will be examining the presentation and organization of *space* on television. This will necessarily incorporate an understanding of the construction of *place*. Immediately, therefore, I have expanded the terms of my inquiry and made a distinction between space and place. In this brief introduction, I want to suggest how I will distinguish between space and place, and why the difference and interrelationship between the two is important in the interpretation of television form. Later on in the chapter, I will identify some programmes which emphasize their spatial properties. In contrast to this, I will also explore how one particular television genre, the sitcom, depends on the plausible construction of a 'place' on-screen. Specifically, I will discuss how the BBC series, *The Royle Family*, articulated a very coherent and implicitly sensual place for its characters. One of the main concerns of this chapter, however, is to demonstrate that television routinely integrates space and place: in my discussion of the ITV 'theatre of news', I will describe what this integration can mean in relation to the presentation of news on television. I then go on to address questions of space and place in a slightly different way and explore briefly the development and potential of interactivity for television. Finally, I examine the technique of split-screen in two similar fictional programmes – *24* and *Trial and Retribution* – since this process evidently divides the space on-screen while, at the same time, directly manipulating the representation of place within the narrative. My final case study is of a light-entertainment programme, *Ant and Dec's Saturday Night Takeaway*, which I use not only to draw out the ways in which space and place operate in another programme-context, but also in relation to arguments (first made by Richard Dyer) about the relationship between utopia and entertainment.

Space

Space can be a difficult concept to grasp. One of the reasons for this is that space is not a 'thing' or an object, but can be understood only as a relationship. For example, we might talk about the space *between* words, the space *around* people or the space *in* a cupboard. Space defines the relationship of one object to another – if someone sits too close to you on the bus, you feel that they are invading your 'personal space'. The way in which space is described is usually in terms of quantity: distance (how far?), area (how big?), volume or amount (how much?). Therefore, space is described in terms of quantities that are, in effect, always relationships, and these spatial relations are imbued with the effects of economics, politics and power. For example, the more money you have, the easier it becomes to secure and defend your personal space – with money you could buy a car, so that you do not have to take the bus; you might hire minders to protect your personal space as you walk down the street; or you could simply send someone else out to do your shopping for you. Money, here, allows for the appropriation and definition of space around an individual. On a larger scale, modern technologies, such as the telephone, enable communication to travel across space at a far greater speed than before; the flow of communication across distances is understood spatially, although what the telephone actually does is connect places (where I am to where you are). Because a telephone call can be transmitted across immense distances in a very short amount of time, its effect is seen to be one of time-space *compression*. This is because the space between the caller and the receiver which the telephone call connects is felt to be much closer than it actually is geographically. As I have described in the chapter on time, television is a broadcast medium that can transmit live sound and images across the globe. Television, therefore, also seems to offer the same 'anywhere-at-once' potential of the telephone. In television, the concept of time-space compression is not just imagined but represented, as I will demonstrate in my discussion of news presentation below.

Place

Place is a concept that is much more familiar. This is because, on one level, place refers to things that seem tangible – to houses, cities, beaches, countries and continents. Yet if we examine what we actually mean by place, it is revealed once again to be about relationships. A place is the way in which objects, buildings, people and landscapes are related to one another in space and time. For example, you could think of the places 'my house' or 'my home'. These places might seem, at first, to coincide (the building that I own is the same as where I live), yet, of course, there is no reason why they should. I might own several houses or I might not own the house I call home. And where one place – my house – might seem relatively fixed (my house has an address which has existed for over a hundred years), my 'home' is a much more open concept, located where my family is or relating to the place I feel safe or simply where I come from – whether this was yesterday or 10 years ago. Place, like space, therefore, is imbued with social relationships, although we recognize these as more emphatically personal and emotional. The way in which place is usually described is in relation to its qualitative aspects; that is, we have a sense of or a sensual response to place. In terms of our senses, it might be what we see or hear – 'The hall is too dark', 'That club is too loud'. Equally, we commonly express emotional reactions to particular places – 'This is a really boring town', 'I love my country'. In contrast to our understanding of space, however, places seem to be something we inhabit, that we recognize. Places operate or represent a series of spatial relationships which we make sense of, or become familiar with, over time. This knowledge may be acquired by the way in which we use and occupy these places. For example, on moving to a new town, at first you might rely on a map to find your way to college. At this point, the *space* represented abstractly on the map has yet to become the *place* you are trying to find your way through. Over a period of time, having grown familiar with the town, you will probably abandon the map and find your way about intuitively, by sight and habit, so that, for example, you remember that you need 'the next turning after the bus stop and before the newsagents', rather than the location on the map represented as 'page 32, square D4'. Thus, while you are still working within an almost unconscious set of spatial relationships (you are going left and right on your way, on the pavement, not under it), these relationships do not seem abstract, since they have become intuitive and operate on an intimate and personal scale. For example, you could go a number of different ways to college – at least, according to the map – but perhaps you choose to go one way in particular because it 'feels' quicker, or maybe you know it takes longer, but, conveniently, this way takes you past a friend's house. By choosing particular routes over others, by making judgements that are perverse and personal, the space of a new town, represented abstractly on the map, has become the familiar place you hurry through in the rain.

Places are constructed within audio-visual media (such as television and film) just as they are in the real world, that is, via spatial (and temporal) relationships. On the screen, viewers are directed through the places they see on-screen. As I described briefly in the chapters on image and sound, this is achieved via techniques or practices of composition and editing. Directors and editors can choose to make the places they construct seem easily comprehensible, making them accessible and rapidly familiar to the viewing audience by using an editing practice most viewers know well – such as the techniques of transparent continuity editing, adapted from mainstream Hollywood film-making. Alternatively, they can make places seem difficult and uncomfortable, by using composition and editing practices that audiences are less familiar with – such as jump-cuts and split-screen.

To try to clarify the various ways in which I wish to differentiate space from place, you may find the following table helpful.

SPACE	PLACE
abstract	tangible
[analytical]	[intuitive]
geography	environment
[map]	[journey]
all-at-once-anywhere	here and there
[potential]	[specific]
local-national-global	intimate-familiar-fantastic

What I have tried to suggest here is both how to define space and place and how these concepts are used and experienced in everyday life. The headings in the table can be developed in a number of ways. For example:

• If space is a relatively abstract concept, our approach to it can be understood as largely analytical and intellectual. Place, however, is a more tangible experience and our understanding of and approach to place is most often intuitive. For example, we often use our personal experience of other places to make sense of new places we encounter.

- We understand space through the process and discipline of geography. The tool we use most often here is the map, and we use this abstraction of space (represented via diagrams and text) to plan routes and make estimates about how far away things are and, perhaps, how long it will take us to get from one place to another. In terms of place, we approach it as an environment through which we will use our senses – sight, hearing, touch, even smell and taste – to guide us. When we take a journey through a place, we go round objects, get drawn in, retrace our steps, get lost and, finally, perhaps, find our way about.

- Space has the potential to be understood as all-at-once and anywhere. My finger, for instance, might land anywhere on the map, as I spin a globe or leaf through an atlas. In contrast to this, place is always specific and particular – it can only be 'here' or 'there'.

- In terms of scale, space is understood through public and historic categories – such distinctions are in the order of the local, the national or the global. In terms of place, we relate to it personally and emotionally, knowing and understanding a range of places, whether these are intimate, familiar or even fantastic.

Television can represent or reproduce a sense of either space or place. For instance, in some programming, images and sounds are used to emphasize the potential of television as a broadcast medium – creating an illusion that suggests television can be 'anywhere-at-once'. In other programmes, television presents a version of the world guided by an abstract, analytical approach that I have suggested relates most closely to space. On the other hand, certain television programmes are able to construct a very coherent sense of place – in fact, they can establish environments that become almost as familiar or intuitive to viewers as the real places they inhabit off-screen. However, the representation of space and place does not have to be one or the other – television regularly transmits programming which aims to embrace a sense of both space *and* place. In certain television genres – news, sports and light entertainment, in particular – the communicative and abstract potential of space and the experience and intimacy of place are reproduced, sometimes simultaneously. In my final case study, of ITV's *Ant and Dec's Saturday Night Takeaway*, I want to explore how this kind of programming can, on the one hand, call up the abstract, dynamic potential of spatial representation, yet, on the other hand, be equally concerned to refer to and reproduce a coherent (if fluid) sense of place. And, following work from Richard Dyer, I want to indicate that it is this relationship between space and place that allows this programme to promote an ephemeral, but entertaining, 'utopian sensibility'.

The organization of space and place

If, as I have suggested, television can suggest place and, in some sense, operate spatially, how does it do so? In the following table, I present the distinction between space and place as related to the use of particular audio-visual techniques. Despite the binary layout, what I am presenting works along a continuum. For, as I will explain below in my description of different genres, the distinction between space and place is not absolute. In fact, in relation to some television programmes, there is a deliberate blurring between space and place.

DRAWN	FILMED
(space)	(place)
maps; text; graphs; photos; CGI; animation; video; film	
information	experience
clarification	atmosphere
explanation	illusion
condensation	extension

The two sides of the table relate primarily to space or place. Space and spatial relationships are produced on television predominantly through a variety of 'drawn' techniques. The construction and experience of place, however, are engineered through images which move and which, in different ways, create a sense of depth within the screen.

Maps

This would include weather maps or other maps used in news programmes. In this way, space is identified abstractly through lines and shading – we learn to recognize the strangely big-bottomed shape of the United Kingdom, or the 'boot' of Italy, as a line drawing (or, if not actually a drawing, at least in terms of lines and colour), although very few of us will have actually seen either country in this way for ourselves.

Text

Advertisements routinely employ text, literally, as words (brand names, short slogans) or as numbers (dates, percentages and prices). Text can be used either as the entire final image of the advertisement or laid over the final shot, whether this is the advertised model of a car or a model promoting a particular brand of shampoo. What both these practices do, as John Ellis has suggested, is replace the 'photographic' filmed image with a two-dimensional 'graphic' image, thus disrupting the illusion of a three-dimensional place within the screen (Ellis 2000: 91–102). Often, the final image for a television advertisement for women's skin cream will be almost identical to the same campaign's print advertisement that will appear in a women's 'glossy' monthly magazine. This kind of advertisement includes a still shot of the model's face, incorporates an image of the product (either with or beside the model) and uses text to frame the screen (and/or page). It is not simply that the television image has become 'flat' here, its spatial qualities also relate to the way in which information is being presented in an abstract, heavily coded manner, like the map. The relationships between the model's face, the product and the text do not make any sense in terms of place (where are we?); they can only be understood in terms of space. In other words, we make sense of the image by reading it as a flow between the different elements or we understand the information on the screen as a series of connections: the model looks like this, because of this product, and this product is xyz, which makes the model look like this, and so on.

Graphs

By graphs I mean images which generally present visual representations of statistics, for example, incoming election results or other news items involving numbers or statistics. Most commonly used in economic news, such images are spatial in that they serve to present large quantities of information (gathered over many years or involving large numbers) in a condensed and apparently clear manner. They represent an abstraction of information and they appear scientific and rigorous. Often, their appearance can be redundant – the information is also presented within a voice-over. In many situations, then, the use of graphs is primarily spectacular. In fact, the appearance of graphs employed in different television programmes can vary to quite an extraordinary degree. While conventional pie charts and bar charts may be used, other, less mathematical, graphic illustrations can also be presented. For example, if house prices are seen to be rising, a drawing of a house might be seen to inflate 'proportionally' on-screen; this kind of illustration implies a graph (as prices presented via a bar chart would also be 'seen' to rise or 'inflate'), but in itself the image offers no verifiable or tested information and any authority is really dependent on the veracity of the voice-over. The information given by such illustrations is spatial in nature, not just because they provide an abstraction of information gathered elsewhere, possibly from a variety of sources, but also because they operate via spatial relationships – smaller to bigger, lower to higher – although these relationships may not be given a context from which they can really be judged.

Photographs

It may seem odd to have placed photographs as being closer to space than place, but on television photographs are often used abstractly, to condense visual information; they operate as a reference for the spoken story rather than as a 'way of telling' in themselves. Photographs used in news reports often function in this manner. School photographs or studio portraits of missing or murdered children initially present the viewer with the child as an individual. Over time, such photographs can become less representative of the child and more a reference to the tragic story in which the child took part – a situation perhaps encouraged by the fact that many such photographs are 'professional' portraits, which situate the subject in a 'non-place', with the child posing in front of an indistinguishable backdrop. There are, of course, exceptions, and, indeed, when such a story first emerges, news items focus on the grief of those involved; this framing allows such photographs and other visual representations to 'tell' and to *place* the child as coming from within a specific historical and geographic context. Such image sequences may involve a series of photographs released from family albums and even home video footage, both of which place the child as being from within a family and from a home – a specific place and time. However, as the story moves on and is given less time within news programmes, the story and the child are often referred to visually via a single photograph, which, while remaining specifically representative of the child, increasingly becomes visual shorthand for the story. If the story generates concerns in other areas, this single photograph may reappear in other news contexts that have less to do with the specific representation and situation of the child. For example, the image of the murdered schoolboy, Stephen Lawrence, has reappeared as visual shorthand within stories about racial violence and the response of the police to such attacks. The image no longer locates Stephen himself as the story that is being told.

CGI (computer-generated imaging)

As I described in the chapter on image, CGI has become increasingly common in both factual and fictional forms of television. Its inclusion here relates particularly to its use in news programmes. In these programmes, CGI sometimes does little more than make certain graphic representations more mobile or more spectacular. Such sequences bring together the representation of space *and* place. They are related to space because they condense information and present spatial relationships (as headlines, statistics and maps.) Yet they also relate to place, as they are mobile and, often, apparently substantial, although the seeming three-dimensional status of such images is entirely illusory. Since, in one sense, the two-dimensional images are made into apparently tangible objects, CGI can make the information generated by such illustrations seem more intuitive than analytical. Another common practice is to use CGI to 'dress' the television studio electronically. This creates an environment which is frequently referred to as a 'virtual' space, although we actually identify with it as a particular place. Many television newsrooms (most obviously, in relation to British television, the studios for Sky News) have become increasingly virtual places. News producers employ CGI to generate a flexible, vibrant place for their programme, which can then serve as a familiar, albeit dynamic, environment for viewers. In this new environment, the news narrative is presented increasingly as if it were a journey, where, along with the now mobile anchor, viewers can move around and between different news items.

Animation

While some aspects of television animation may seem flat or two-dimensional, animation as a fictional form of programming often works hard to create a sense of place. Although American series such as *South Park* and *The Simpsons* are resolutely two-dimensional in their construction, it is interesting that both programmes' title sequences involve a journey where the characters and the viewer are taken through the town (South Park or Springfield) that the characters inhabit. In the opening sequence of *The Simpsons*, for example, there is a greater emphasis on producing the illusion of movement along the depth axis (that is, creating the illusion that characters are moving away from or towards the viewer) than is generally the case elsewhere in the programme. The place of Springfield is thereby given a certain amount of illusory depth and substance. Thus, while animation does not necessarily produce places that seem realistic, the drawings of Springfield do express attributes I have associated with place: they offer specific environments that can stage journeys for the viewer; their relationship to the viewer is not abstract, but designed to create atmosphere and a kinetic experience; the viewer is able to imagine the 'off-screen' space of Bart and his family, even if they are perfectly well aware that they are, in fact, entirely fabricated, flat cartoon characters. In this sense, the place of *The Simpsons* extends (in the viewer's imagination) off-screen.

Video and film

As I have already discussed, film and video are able, through the manipulation of space and time, to create believable 'places' on-screen. British soap operas, such as *EastEnders* and *Coronation Street*, may use relatively limited sets in comparison to some fiction feature films, but certain places (the Rovers Return, the Queen Vic, the Fowlers' living room) are returned to again and again, over a period of years, and thus become extraordinarily familiar places to regular viewers. The sitcom – literally, a 'situation' comedy – is nearly always tied to a particular place: *Frasier*'s apartment, *Roseanne*'s kitchen, the 'office' in *The Office* or the pub, The Grapes, in *Early Doors*. The kind and quantity of places in other kinds of fictional drama may be more extensive than in the sitcom, but a sense *of* place and frequent allusions to journeys that can be taken *through* places are often crucial as ways of drawing the viewer into the narrative. *The Sopranos*' opening titles, for example, reproduce a car journey from New York to New Jersey. In this hand-held, intimate sequence, landmarks, signposts and other cars on the freeway flash past in a rhythmic montage of shots, which seemingly situate the viewer – rather uncomfortably – as if driving the car. Yet the ultimate pay-off here comes in the final shots of the sequence. As the viewer/camera reaches the final destination, the camera (and, by implication, the viewer) is left in the car and we watch Tony Soprano (the mafia don) walk up his driveway – thus revealing that he, not the viewer, was in the driving seat.

This preliminary discussion is designed to provide a context for a series of more detailed textual analyses. In the following four sections, I want to explore certain kinds of programming and particular programmes that seem to me to emphasize different relationships to space and place. First, I describe programming that relates, in terms of its form, primarily to space and I will look here at the appearance and operation of a range of channels – shopping and 'sports news' channels, as well as the few 'dating channels' now available via satellite television in the UK. In the second section, I will look at the British sitcom, *The Royle Family*, to discuss how it creates a very strong sense of place, despite the fact that, in some other ways, the programme deliberately sets itself apart from the formal conventions of the television sitcom. Third, I want to address the recent development of ITV news at 10.30 p.m. and suggest how changes to the set, the framing of presenters and reporters and the increased use of CGI play upon the potential of space and the experience of place. Before closing with my final case study of *Saturday Night Takeaway*, I look at two other areas in which we can see the interaction between space and place on television. First, I want to draw attention to the variety of programmes which demonstrate interactivity; this discussion will range from children's programmes, such as the BBC's *Nelly Nut Live*, to sports and news programming provided by Sky. Second, I will comment on the recent emergence, in fiction, of a formal technique normally associated with non-fiction programming on television – the split-screen. My intention will be to discuss briefly how this technique allows for another kind of play between 'space' and 'place'. Split-screen is currently used in a range of different programmes on television, though my analysis will focus on perhaps the two most prominent examples of its use in prime-time live-action drama – in the American spy series, *24*, and in the British police drama, *Trial and Retribution*.

An emphasis on space: text and texting

There is now a wide range of news channels available on satellite television – including sports, business and straight news channels. To a greater or lesser degree, this kind of programming is reliant on text and, thus, on the abstraction of information from many different sources, presented in a two-dimensional manner so that the viewer is presented with an image constructed in a way that privileges spatial relationships. Many channels now employ a continuous 'ticker' of text that scrolls from right to left across the bottom of the screen. They may also frequently divide the screen, presenting the reporter or anchor to one side of graphs, league tables or information from different stock exchanges. Thus, while some part of the image is still filmed, much of the image is taken up by written text – words, numbers or maps and graphs. Equally, shopping channels also involve an almost permanent integration of text (description and price) over the top of filmed images which demonstrate the products on sale. Although the presenter's direct address retains some aspect of place (they speak from the studio to you at home or at work), the real pull of the image is towards space and gestures, towards the much touted concept of a 'data space', potentially available via computers and the internet. The continuous scrolling of the ticker and the insistence on the up-to-date currency of the information apparently being channelled to the watching viewer seems to represent a version of 'data from anywhere-at-once', which, in its intangibility, relates to an idea of space rather than place.

Dating channels demonstrate an even greater emphasis on their ability to abstract information and communication across space and present an image that is almost entirely devoted to text and (at certain times) the static photographic image. On the Dating Channel, for example, the viewer is confronted with a screen divided up into competing blocks of information. The left-hand side of the screen presents a series of text messages – presumably sent in by viewers/users – which scroll continuously down the screen. On the right side of the screen, the top half of the image is occupied by a photograph (generally a head shot) of an individual who is looking for a date (the photograph has often been sent in via camera-phone). This image is provided with a short caption. At the bottom of the left-hand side, another block of the screen is used for advertising, which is usually text: brand names, short slogans or logos. This content, like the other aspects of the image, changes at periodic intervals. This kind of programming does not seem to be like 'television' as it has previously been experienced or presented, and the 'audience' figures or ratings for this channel are likely to be very small indeed. If the channel makes any profits at all, presumably they are not really generated via advertising, but through the costs added to the act of texting the channel. The strongest antecedent for this channel is not really television but the variety of chatlines available via the telephone. It also relates directly to the development of bulletin boards and different fan-sites and websites available via the internet. As I have implied, it is via its association with the telephone (in terms of live communication and time-space compression) that television most often realizes or represents its ability to operate spatially. Yet the connection to space as I have defined it is not just the suggestion of space covered (between different users of the service), but also the way in which the information is being presented on-screen. In this channel and others (Chatbox, Gaydate TV), there is no attempt to represent a sense of place or depth. Instead, the viewer may idly read the text, gaze at the photograph and generally let their eyes roam over the different sections that make up the screen. The channel is clearly designed for users who see their 'advert' or text on-screen and also make contact with other users. In this sense, the channel really is a *channel* for communication. It is one version, perhaps, of a kind of 'no-place', a fantastic context for free interaction between users. The Dating Channel (and others like it) is clearly peripheral – at least for the moment – to the mainstream activities of television, and it is perhaps difficult to see these channels as 'television' at all.

However, as I have already begun to suggest, these channels simply emphasize certain practices that are becoming increasingly common within programming on more mainstream channels. In certain contexts, viewers are now directly encouraged to text in to a variety of channels and programmes. In some programmes – mainstream news bulletins and current affairs programmes such as *Question Time* – this service acts as an alternative to phone calls or email and generally involves presenters reading out messages, so that the texts themselves are not displayed on-screen. On other programmes, however, the texts are displayed and presented in a continuous scroll. At certain times of day, for instance, The Box music channel will display messages from viewers in a continuous ticker, which runs along the bottom of the different music videos selected by viewers. Certain programming offshoots of mainstream reality programmes also display texts; notably, the live stream of programming from *I'm a Celebrity: Get Me Out of Here!*, shown almost continuously on ITV2 for the duration of the show. So, while giving up the entire television screen to spatial representation is a relatively marginal activity, it is clear that many programmes are increasingly incorporating aspects I have associated with space – demonstrating, via texting, the potential of an apparent 'all-at-once-anywhere' and presenting information in an abstract and heavily coded manner. These forms of presentation act to 'flatten' the television image, encouraging viewers to look *over* rather than *into* the screen.

An emphasis on place: the living room and the sitcom

As I suggested earlier, the sitcom reproduces a very strong sense of place. In essence, a great number of sitcoms are dependent on particular places – the bar in *Cheers*, the hotel in *Fawlty Towers*, Gary's flat in *Men Behaving Badly*, the prison in *Porridge*. However, other sitcoms are, perhaps, more dependent on a sense of historical 'period' rather than a specific place – the Second World War in *Dad's Army*, from medieval times to the First World War in the different *Blackadder* series, the 1950s in *Happy Days*. Yet even series like these, which place some importance on a variation of place and, thus, employ a greater number of locations, may still tend, for economic and aesthetic reasons, to limit the number of actual sets they use.

Dad's Army, for example, did incorporate a relatively large number of exterior shooting locations, yet the most used sets were the interior of the church hall and Captain Mainwaring's office, situated immediately off the hall itself.

Perhaps the most common set for the television sitcom is the domestic living room, and a wide variety of sitcoms rely on a 'main room', usually a sitting room, with a couch, chairs and television, where the characters can congregate. In slightly different forms, this can be seen in *Friends, Frasier, Roseanne, My Family, Married . . . with Children, Men Behaving Badly*, and, of course, *The Simpsons*. Usually, as Jeremy Butler describes in his excellent analysis of the conventional set-up for the sitcom, the sitcom sofa is presented either directly facing the watching audience (in the studio or at home) or at a slight angle (Butler 2002: 95–102). In this way, the sitcom set and the characters present themselves to the audience in a manner that is reminiscent of a theatrical staging, and the action is choreographed to move predominantly across the set rather than forwards or back. Other sets are used (often a kitchen and one or more bedrooms), but the outside world rarely appears. Therefore, the sitcom is, characteristically, a closed set and the position of characters within their environment quickly becomes established and remains fixed for the entire series. For example, Martin's (Frasier's father) anachronistic chair in the centre of Frasier's otherwise showroom apartment was a key feature of the series, its final removal indicating the end of the long-running series itself.

In line with the closed set, the shooting style of the sitcom is conventionally close, with the mid-shot and close-up (head shot) being dominant. The camera tends to follow the dialogue, unless the action or reaction of a character is itself the most important comedic element of the scene. In the US, it is still very common for sitcoms to be recorded with a live audience present; this is less common in the UK, although certain series, such as *Men Behaving Badly*, did continue this practice. The presence of the live audience and the need to present them (as well as the cameras) with a view of events has, as Butler suggests, necessarily limited the number of sets and the movement of characters in many series, and determines the continued maintenance of the illusory 'fourth wall' in several American sitcoms. This means that characters tend not to enter from behind the position of the camera or to exit the set by passing the camera, so there is reduced movement in terms of depth. However, in some recent British sitcoms, the creation of naturalistic (if sometimes disturbingly surreal) places has meant that all 'four walls' are in fact realized and given substance; this is particularly true in *The Royle Family*, but also in *Early Doors, The League of Gentlemen* and *The Office*. In fact, as Brett Mills has observed, *The Office* – which sets itself up as a parody of an observational documentary or docu-soap – is not shot like a conventional sitcom at all (Mills 2004). Mills cites this programme as a standard-bearer for an emerging genre he calls 'comedy verité', suggesting a significant move away from the theatrical traditions of previous television sitcom. The movements of characters in such sets are often looser and more mobile than in a conventional sitcom shooting style.

However, even within sitcoms that no longer pursue the tradition of theatrical staging, it is true to say that the same sets reappear week after week, dressed in ways that quickly become important, not just to the housing of the characters, but to the comedy itself. In *The Royle Family*, for example, the *mise-en-scène*, shooting style, sound and writing simultaneously reinforce the closed intimacy of the sitcom 'place', while also providing several sly references to an awareness of the truly artificial nature of the 'sitcom family' and the 'sitcom home'. *The Royle Family*, written by Caroline Aherne, Craig Cash and Henry Normal, was produced by Granada and originally transmitted on BBC Two (the BBC's channel of 'experiment and innovation'). A surprise hit, later series were transferred to BBC One, and Jim Royle's catchphrase, 'My arse!', became well known and much used by the popular press. The series was set entirely in the Royles' small house, and predominantly in their living/dining room. The opening titles were one of the most significant aspects of the show, setting the atmosphere and establishing the 'place' of the series in a very distinctive manner. Starting with a black screen, the image flickers into life, as if the watching audience is inside the Royles' television set; from this position, we first see the legs and lower half of Jim Royle (the father of the family) as he makes his way back from (presumably switching on) the set to his chair, which directly faces the television. From the low angle of the camera, the sofa (arranged at a slight angle from the lower left-hand corner of the screen, leading back into the room) can be seen, with the coffee table in the centre of the screen. Just behind the table is Jim's chair and between the end of the sofa and the chair, an ironing board and a basket of washing can also just be made out. This sequence, and those which follow it, in the titles are tinted in blue-grey shadow, mimicking the effect of the light that might be given off from the television itself. At the bottom right of the screen, the name of the actor who plays Jim – Ricky Tomlinson – appears. There then follows a series of similar sequences introducing the different members of the family, who appear in different positions on the sofa. The sequence ends with the whole family – Dave Best (the fiancé, played by Craig Cash), Denise Royle (the eldest daughter, played by Caroline Aherne) and Barbara Royle (the mother, played by Sue Johnston) – sitting down in what are generally their established positions on the sofa (Barbara nearest to Jim and the kitchen, Denise in the middle, with Dave nearest the television). Anthony Royle (the younger son, played by Ralf Little) sits cross-legged, close to the camera at the bottom of the screen. This is a relatively unusual position for Anthony, as his chair is actually on the same side as the sofa, but cannot be seen in this framing. However, his position within the title sequence is consistent with his 'low' status within the household; as the put-upon younger sibling, he is generally told what to do by everyone else and here, of course, he is sitting on the floor, whereas everyone else – even the fiancé, who is not, at least in the first series, an 'official' member of the family – has a seat. The sequence is particularly distinctive as the camera remains at a low angle throughout, reiterating the point that, in some way, the audience at home is positioned as if they are 'inside' the Royles' television set, when, in fact, of course, it is the Royle family that is on (or in) television.

The shooting style of the series is claustrophobic and similarly self-conscious. The characters are often filmed in very tight close-ups and camera set-ups often involve three faces in one shot (a frequent composition will show Dave, Denise and Barbara caught in a diagonally arranged close-up, gazing blankly at the television). Although close-up shots are relatively common in sitcom, the camera, here, is practically 'one of the family', at times, apparently sitting on the characters' laps or on the coffee table, almost bumping up against their legs. The editing style is deliberately naturalistic, often employing relatively long pauses between cuts, and sometimes simply drifting over characters' faces when they are not speaking, or remaining with one character even when a different character is talking. This creates a deliberately intimate, improvised feel; the humour in the situation is not deliberately signposted for the audience in visual terms, but comes from a gradual understanding of and accumulating empathy for the characters. The camera style, like the humour, is based on observation; accordingly, the series does not have a laugh track. In line with its association with observational film-making, all the sound in the programme, aside from the title music, is diegetic. The use of sound is also important to the crowded 'sense of place'. It includes the almost continuous burble of the television set, the chink of tea mugs, the rattling of pots as they are washed, the exhaling of cigarette smoke and characters stomping up the stairs, as well as, perhaps most unusually, the flush of the toilet, all of which emphasizes a sense of being crowded and a feeling that the characters (mostly happily) are living, audibly, 'on top of one another'.

The intimate, crowded sense of place is further enhanced by the *mise-en-scène*. The living room, kitchen and bedrooms are incredibly cluttered; the characters pass one another overflowing ashtrays, endless cups of tea and fags, sit close to one another, brush past each other in a living room crammed with furniture; and clean washing hangs over radiators and coats over the backs of chairs. At different times, nearly all the characters look at and handle the numerous ornaments, photographs and mirrors that decorate their home. The tactile potential of the *mise-en-scène* is enhanced by the way in which much of the furniture is well-worn and shabby. The characters' dress is also important; over the different series, Jim's clothes become progressively grubby and worn, while Barbara's hair is increasingly dishevelled. One of the charming running gags in the series picks up on this domestic clutter; characters are always looking for things, or losing things, and objects are stashed away in unlikely places (the whiskey in the pot cupboard for example).

This is, therefore, a full house – also filled self-consciously, as the titles indicate, with the sound and light of the television itself. Although characters in other sitcoms will watch the television and we may see *what* they are watching, few series pay such self-conscious or affectionate attention to the relationship between the characters and the television on such a regular basis. For example, an early episode of the first series involves Jim waiting anxiously for the start of *The Antiques Roadshow*, as it begins, he, Dave and Anthony enter the living room, cheerily marching and singing along to the theme tune. The family then proceeds to bet on the likely monetary value of the different antiques shown on the programme. Later in the series, there is a sequence devoted to the quiz show, *Who Wants to be a Millionaire?*, in which the family provide the answers and discuss the appearance of the contestants. The sound of the television clearly permeates and occupies the home; there are frequent admonitions by different characters to get the sound turned up or down, or the channel changed. Thus, while the television can frequently be seen as annoying (Barbara says at one point that nothing ever gets talked about because the television is always on), it is clearly a focal point for the home and the family, a channel through which the characters communicate with each other. The television will be turned on even when Jim insists that the electric fire in the living room should remain off. In episode five from the first series (featuring a late-night row between Dave and Denise) the television is used – slyly – to echo or reinforce the activity taking place in the home. Although the television is, unusually, not switched on right at the beginning of the episode, once the quarrel between Denise and Dave has been resolved Jim turns it back on (despite the fact that he admits that any programmes are likely to be 'shite' at this time of night). As usual in the series, once it is actually on, the camera occasionally settles on the television and it is just possible to make out that it is showing a late-night 'youth' game show, presented by Davina McCall. However, there are moments when the television is used more self-consciously: at one point, Barbara is in the kitchen searching for Rennies to alleviate Jim's graphically described heartburn, the pain from which is causing him to rub his large stomach ostentatiously. As Barbara re-enters the living room, the camera focuses again briefly on the television set and, coincidentally, we witness a close-up shot of a tongue clearly licking something out of someone's belly button. While this quick reference is cheekily sexual in nature (and the row between Dave and Denise was based on sexual jealousy), it also refers incidentally to Jim's stomach problems. At the end of the episode, this relationship between the characters' bodies and the bodies we can see on the television in the living room is repeated when Dave undresses by the light of the television as he prepares to sleep on the sofa. As he does so, his actions are synchronized with the routine of a male stripper, visible on the television set behind him. This implicit doubling of content and action (since we see a male stripper on the Royles' television and on our own) reiterates, once more, the intimacy, closeness and coherence of the Royle family's home as a familiar, naturalistic place. The artificiality of the stripper's performance contrasts and plays against the 'reality' of Dave's behaviour as he gets ready for bed. Seeing the stripper on television reminds viewers that Dave (or Craig Cash as Dave) is giving a 'performance' too. While this might disrupt the naturalistic ambitions of the programme, it actually serves to make the 'place' of the living room seem 'real' in comparison to the artificiality of the stripper we can see on the television. Our intimacy and familiarity with Dave is further emphasized – and played for laughs – as we then see him carefully 'rearrange himself' more comfortably in his boxer shorts before getting into the sleeping bag on the sofa, where, of course, he then farts audibly, evidently releasing quite a smell.

The intimate place of the programme, therefore, is also generated through performance and through the writing. Much of the series' humour is dependent on bodily functions, and Jim, in particular, frequently burps, farts, scratches and picks his nose. Although much of the behaviour is 'disgusting', it is part of the strong atmosphere of sensuality that pervades the household. The characters, within their limited means, are hedonists – they all smoke, drink Pomagne, tea and brandy and eat cake, pork chops, chocolate and polo mints with great relish. The camera's closeness means that we not only *see* what they eat but also *hear* them eat; another running gag involves Denise moaning at her younger brother, Anthony, for crunching or slurping too loudly. The house seems to be thick with the atmosphere of food smells and tastes, cigarette smoke and body odours. Of course, characters in other sitcoms eat and drink, too (Monica in *Friends* is a chef, after all, and her Thanksgiving dinners are a set piece of the series), but the writing in *The Royle Family* continually insists upon the everyday-ness of these sensual pleasures, and the camera consistently closes in on the cups of tea, the overfull ashtrays, the glistening remains of pork chops and gravy, as well as the mouths of the characters as they eat, drink and smoke.

What I have tried to suggest here is that the series revisits certain conventional aspects of the television sitcom (the family home, the sofa and the television), but it does so in a way that intensifies a sense of place. The viewer's relationship with the Royles and their home is intimate and almost overwhelming as a sensual experience. Although the characters may leave the family home (slamming doors as they do so), the viewer never does. Another repeated gag, for example, emphasizes the viewer's entrapment in the home – while the characters frequently look out of the living room window – commenting on the activities of their neighbours, for example – the camera never does so, preferring instead to look at the characters looking, huddled up together, with their backs to the camera and the lace curtain over their heads. Throughout the series, as I have suggested, the shooting style and the performances of the actors are naturalistic, even if their behaviour is occasionally grotesque. And while the journeys we take with the characters through the place may be limited (sometimes just from the kitchen to the living room and not always this far), the movement of the camera through the set, and the way in which the programme is edited, is lingering, immediate and full of detail. Implicitly, therefore, through *mise-en-scène*, through the characters activities and dialogue, the Royle family home is presented as a fully rounded sensual experience – this is a place that is not simply to be looked at, but can be heard and even, seemingly, touched, smelt and tasted.

Space and place: the ITV 'theatre of news'

The ITV news at 10.30 p.m. was relaunched on Monday 2 February 2004. It was a significant day for ITV as it was also the day that the two biggest independent companies within the ITV commercial network – Granada and Carlton – merged, making this new company the largest shareholder in the UK's main terrestrial commercial television channel. The rebranding of ITV had already begun to reflect this anticipated change in ownership, with the emergence of ITV as an explicitly more coherent network. Accordingly, the corporate livery of blue, yellow and white, and the adoption of the three-dimensional CGI 'four blocks logo' became increasingly consistent throughout the network. Only those companies which remained independent after the merger between Granada and Carlton – Scottish Television, Ulster TV, Grampian and Channel TV – retained some autonomy in terms of presentation of news and in some of their ident sequences. The specific relaunch of the ITV news was led by the new editor-in-chief of the ITV News Group, David Mannion. The ITV News Group was a new company that linked the ITN news company (which had previously provided the national news for ITV on ITV1, as well as the fledgling ITV news channel) with the 27 regional news companies that had responsibility for the news presentation from their particular regions. Mannion works jointly for both ITN and ITV; his stated role is to bring the regional news companies and ITN into closer cooperation. His ambition is to institute a more coherent news service within the network as a whole, although he claims that regional news companies will still have some control over the running order and content of news stories for their programmes.

While the revamping of the programme, therefore, had clear links to corporate changes within the ITV network, it was also important as a definite attempt to 'reclaim' the late evening news for ITV, since it had lost ground and audiences to both the BBC and Sky News in recent years. Most commentators agreed that problems had originated in the controversial move of the ITV news from its long established 'News at Ten' slot to 11 p.m. (which proved disastrous in terms of audience ratings). Consequently, although ITV moved relatively quickly to reclaim the time slot, they were usurped by the BBC, which, in the interim, launched its own 'Ten O'clock News' (moving its programme from the previously established time of 9 p.m.). This then led to a period when the ITV programme was known derisively as the 'news at when?', as it appeared for only three days at its old time slot of 10 p.m. and at later times on other days of the week. The new establishment of a specific time – 10.30 p.m. – which was not in direct competition with BBC One, was therefore significant. One of the clear ambitions for the programme would be to re-establish a secure place within the schedule.

In some sense, the programme redesign was important because the late evening news bulletin was one of the few distinctively corporate 'places' that would be seen throughout the country every weekday. For national broadcasters, and especially those, like ITV, who are bound by some public service requirements, the newsroom, by default, exists as a kind of 'home' for the channel. This is partly because the news is on every day of the week and at specific times in the day; news presenters may therefore become the most familiar faces from a particular channel. This relationship is made all the more intimate as, by speaking directly to the camera, news anchors are set up in an intimate relationship with viewers. They work hard to establish trust, authority and empathy for themselves, for the programme and, ultimately, for the channel (and corporation) itself. The title sequence and setting for the news, therefore, provide one of the most familiar 'places' on any channel. The new ITV news set is particularly intriguing because, while it remains an important 'place', its operation and appearance is dominated by the realization of 'space'.

The 'hard set' design of the studio is relatively simple: an oval, silver desk is positioned at the centre of the studio. Leading directly back from the centre of the desk is a raised runway (under-lit with white light, integrating it with the silver desk), which links to a further curved runway (also under-lit) that forms a large semicircle at some distance, curving behind the desk. The anchor usually begins their presentation at the meeting point between the straight runway and the semicircle and continues to present the first half of the bulletin standing up, only retreating to the desk for the second part of the bulletin, generally after the commercial break. The dominant feature of the set, however, is the huge video wall (20 metres wide and 3 metres high), which follows the curved runway and thus serves as the entire backdrop to the studio itself. The wall can play film, integrate graphics and photographs and facilitate a live two-way between the news anchor in the studio and the reporter in the field. The aim, apparently, is to allow the news anchor to 'tell a story by walking from one side of the semi-circular studio to the other' (Deans 2004). The programme is filmed using five different cameras – one fixed, three mobile and one 'jib' (mobile crane) camera. Editing between these five cameras enables the movement within the set to be very fluid, moving back to reframe the anchor at key moments, swooping in and out at the beginning or end of the programme itself. Although sparse, the three-dimensional aspect of the actual hard set of the studio is continually emphasized as the editor switches between the different cameras and the framing itself often includes the other cameras in shot.

This means that, in some sense, the studio is clearly a 'real' place. Viewers may therefore respond to the kinetic energy of the camera movement, to the editing and to the increased mobility of the news anchor, in a way that I have suggested may be connected to a sense of 'place' on television – since it presents a number of different 'journeys' and creates a particular atmosphere or experience through performance and visual style.

At the same time, however, the increased capability for the integration of graphics (maps, graphs, symbolic images, photographs) onto the one plane of the news wall would seem to relate more closely to the qualities of space that I previously identified in relation to dating and shopping channels. Indeed, a typical sequence might involve the news anchor standing in front of the wall, which incorporates several images laid on top of one another: the American flag, almost transparent, but perceptibly waving in a breeze, over which we can see the photographs of the two presidential candidates; another photographic image of the White House between them; and then, perhaps, written text appearing, as if in a PowerPoint presentation, providing information on the key election issues. The anchor stands in front of these images, but there is no longer a clear sense of place, as any depth is clearly illusory and we understand the images in terms of how they relate to one another as ideas (of America, of the presidency, of the relationship between the pictured candidates). The relationship between the images is of a conceptual and abstract order rather than tangible or material. However, elsewhere in the bulletin, similar images may be used, but this time there is a move away from the representation of space to the creation of a 'virtual place'.

Fig 4.1 The ITV 'theatre of news' © ITN Archive.

In 'The Briefing', a short report filmed in a virtual-reality studio, a particular issue of the day is given further analysis. In this sequence, the reporter does not simply stand in front of the different layered images, but may actually walk over some images – usually a map of some sort – and apparently directs other three-dimensional graphic sequences, which occupy and even move through the space around them. For example, in a report on the build-up to the presidential elections in the United States, the reporter, James Mates, stands on what appears to be a circular stage, moving around the stage during the course of the item to incorporate, or make room for, the different elements within the report. Behind him are a series of floating (two-dimensional) screen images: the furthest away shows an extended stars and stripes flag, again, gracefully blowing in the wind; in front of this image are two separate photographic portraits of the two candidates; closer and more central is yet another image of the White House. At one point, in synchronization with Mates' narration, a three-dimensional simulation of a 'poll of polls' unfolds. This graphic is placed at a slight angle to the camera and to Mates. There is a red line suspended in mid-air for President Bush, and a blue one for John Kerry; as Mates talks, the lines rise, fall and cross over one another as we track the fluctuations in the support for each candidate over the past year. At another point, Mates moves to one side of the stage and directs the viewer's attention to a 'screen' which also appears at a slight angle, suspended in mid-air. This screen is then used to integrate a short filmed report, the initial image dissolving to focus on the filmed insert. Once this filmed insert ends, we return to Mates, who is standing on a graphic representation of a map of the United States; at this point, individual states – Pennsylvania, Ohio, Missouri – are identified through text and colour in response to Mates' narration. Throughout the report, Mates uses his hands, eyes and position to direct the viewer's attention to the different elements as if he were in control of events and therefore able to manipulate the space around him. Therefore, the viewer is presented with a virtual-reality environment, in which the reporter participates on our behalf. Since, in this instance, the presenter is seemingly *in* the space and not standing *in front of* the images, the illusion of depth is maintained.

This creates, I would suggest, a 'virtual place/space' that is of a different order to the depthless space engineered by the video wall. Despite its overwhelming presence, the video wall remains distinct from the 'real place' of the news anchor, who is always in front of, not 'inside' the screen. Although a live two-way may begin with the anchor talking to the two-dimensional image of a reporter (who is, therefore, briefly apparently 'flattened' over the wall and even, seemingly, 'inside' the wall-as-screen), this 'image bridge' is rapidly superseded by a full-screen image of the reporter, transferring the 'location' from the news studio to the scene of the news event. Therefore, while a little more dramatic or spectacular than conventional news framing, the sense of the news studio as a real place, which connects to other real places, is preserved. In 'The Briefing', however, the filmed insert does not transfer the viewer to a simultaneous elsewhere in the sense of going to another place 'live', but refers the viewer to a series of densely edited recorded images that are referential to particular events or persons, rather than being predominantly representative of a particular place (as in the live reporter's presence within the 'news scene'). In such sequences, therefore, the viewer is presented with a potentially rather disorientating hybrid of space and place. While there may be realistic representations of objects and places (the reporter, the filmed insert), they interact and occupy the same context as the abstract graphic representations which I have aligned with space (the map, graphs, still photographs and flag). In 'The Briefing', place and space are made equivalent, 'glued together', interacting with one another in 'real time'. There may be something a little absurd about these sequences, and they are perilously close to the parodic graphic simulations used in the spoof current affairs programmes, *The Day Today* and *Brass Eye*. However, they are clearly successful; audiences for the news programme are increasing and both the set and the use of graphics have recently won awards. For my purposes here, however, this hybrid space/place demonstrates something specific about the way in which television can operate and orchestrate a sense of space and place together. Evidently, the construction of place, here, allows for the creation of atmosphere and seems designed to inspire an intuitive response from the audience through the use of colour, movement and 'realistic' spectacle. At the same time, the use of 'scientific' models of illustration would seem to encourage a more analytical engagement, as their appearance requires a different kind of comprehension from the viewer.

If the situation is disorientating, it is because, as viewers, we are constantly asked to fluctuate between these two perspectives or ways of interpreting the information presented on-screen. While, as I have suggested, both perspectives appear in many different contexts on television, the distinction, here, is that they occupy the screen simultaneously, with neither perspective dominating nor giving way to the other. The closest analogy to this experience is the computer game, for in many games there are frequently instances where a 'spatial' overview of the game (seeing the territory as if on a map from above, having your progress recorded via on-screen statistics) is integrated with a more intimate perspective, which is intent on creating the illusion of your being 'in' the environment of the game itself. Yet there are two important qualifications here: first, the viewer is not 'playing' the virtual simulation in 'The Briefing' and, therefore, is not in control of how the different elements interact with each other (learning in the computer game environment is about self-navigation rather than being directed through someone else's narration); second, any computer game, however fully realized, is always determined by the dimensions and potential of its original programming (its rules, its information), and this aspect of the game (its origin and limitations) is usually hidden from the player/viewer. In other words, however objective and expansive any individual news item appears, it is always 'authored'; but the incorporation of scientific illustration in 'The Briefing' may award it an apparently rigorous, neutral 'gloss' that may make it seem less subjective than other filmed reports. What becomes further obscured in this process is the long-running problem of television news. Who is the author of the news? Who are the authorities that establish what stories, images and statistics can be seen and heard? Or, more significantly in this context, who designates *how* such stories are seen and heard? The question of 'how' – as I hope I have demonstrated – is equally important to the understanding and perception of the news on television.

Interactivity: nothing more than a 'Winky Dink' kit?

In the following analysis, interactive television refers to the way in which the viewer's activity (using a tool such as remote control, computer or telephone) can interact with a television programme so as to make a difference to the appearance and progress of the programme itself, as it is seen on-screen. However, before I develop my argument, I need to make two important points. First, although I will be talking about the activity of the viewer, I am not able to provide any definite evidence as to how and when viewers interact with television; my aim, here, is simply to provide a brief description of what interactivity does to the appearance and potential experience of television. Second, in this section, I am confining my discussion to interactivity that is the result of something that the viewer physically *does* in order to participate or engage with different television programmes. All viewers, to a greater or lesser degree, engage with television at the level of some kind of mental response – they understand what is going on, laugh or moan or cry, for example – and, thereby, they are, on one level, interacting with different programmes. Such interaction at a mental or cognitive level is not what I am discussing here. Instead, I am more interested in exploring how the touch of the viewer (pen to paper, feet on the studio floor, finger to telephone dial, fingers to keyboard, finger to remote control) can affect what is seen on-screen.

From this perspective, interactivity has always been a part of television. Viewers writing in to respond or complain, have, from the earliest days of broadcasting, had their views read out on-air by different presenters. Increasingly, with the use of telephones, and, now, via email and texting, viewers' comments continue to feature in a variety of programmes, now increasingly transferred on to the screen as written text. A relatively small number of viewers also participate in television directly, as they appear on game shows as contestants, in studio audiences, as members of crowds, in documentaries, docu-soaps and other 'reality' programmes. In a very general sense, this activity means that the place of television is infiltrated or occupied in some way by the viewer, although their presence and activity may be very carefully regulated by the programme's producers. In these circumstances, it is rare for the behaviour of the viewer to run counter to the expectations generated by the programme's format, and, although important to the running of the programme, such activity rarely disrupts the narrative or preordained appearance of the programme. In a way, the viewer's appearance or activity here is subsumed into television itself. One extraordinary version of this is in the BBC's children's programme, *Nelly Nut Live*.

This is an animated programme, featuring a little girl called 'Nelly' and her teddy bear, 'Miss Bunny' (voiced in a supremely camp manner by a male actor), in which Nelly discusses her day and interacts with the audience via email and phone calls. Obviously the animated drawings themselves are pre-recorded and edited, but the characters' voices appear to be live and are dubbed over the action of the characters. Overall, the programme's central conceit – in which the live voice animates the recorded drawings – does seem to work relatively well, although the lip-synching is very approximate. In one regular feature of the show, children are encouraged to ring in to talk directly with Nelly; if successful, they are then instructed to randomly select an animated figure through which they can speak (animals or characters such as 'Jude the biker dude'). Once selected, the responses and questions from the child are approximately synched with the pre-recorded movements of the lips and gestures of the animated character; in this way, the child's voice is effectively subsumed by the animation (although, of course, part of the joke of the programme is the extreme mismatch between the children's voices and their apparent 'on-screen' presence). In effect, the child's presence is little more than a ventriloquist's act; the programme provides the dummy for the child to speak through and, like ventriloquism, the effect is unnerving, awkward and sometimes very funny. Yet what is also revealed is how contained the presence and voice of the child is and, for my purposes here, this stands as an extraordinary instance of how many viewers' activities within programmes are similarly controlled and contained. Like the contestant in the game show, who must stand on their mark and speak only when spoken to, or the abusive caller whose phone call is cut short, the viewer's interaction with the programme is generally carefully regulated and, to a certain extent, homogenized by each programme's established operations, which remain consistent throughout.

A different kind of interactivity keeps the viewer outside the 'text' of the programme, but allows individual viewers to open out the place of the programme via their remote control or through access to a related website. Through the use of digital technology or via the internet, certain programmes are now made available to some viewers as places that can be 'unpacked' or re-ordered by viewers, so that the appearance and progress of the programme can be altered for each viewer with access to their own screen and remote control. Perhaps surprisingly, there are instances of this kind of interactivity taking place before the advent of digital television and the remote control. In an article on early children's television in the United States, Lynn Spigel (1998: 125) describes the CBS show, *Winky Dink and You* (1953–57):

> *Winky Dink* offered children the possibility of drawing on the television set through the purchase of a special *Winky Dink* kit, complete with rub-off crayons, and erasing cloth, and the all-important 'magic window', a piece of tinted plastic that, when sufficiently rubbed by the child's hands, stuck to the television screen. With this apparatus in place, the child could draw along to the animation on the screen, perhaps filling in features on cartoon characters' faces or completing story narratives by drawing in the necessary scenery and props.

Here, the child was offered the opportunity to individually determine and alter the image they saw on their television screen. In the current versions of digital interactivity, the 'Winky Dink' kit is no longer rub-off crayons and tinted plastic, but a television with digital access and a remote control.

In Sky News Interactive, for example, the viewer can now arrange the news stories for themselves. Using their remote control, viewers can choose between different news stories – headlines, top stories, showbiz and sports. Stories are accessed once the viewer selects a particular 'screen' within the screen menu (literally highlighting a particular mini-screen from a series of eight mini-screens laid 'face up' on a menus screen as if they were playing cards). Even the content of the continuous ticker running along the bottom of the image can be selected. In this way, what is seen on-screen, as well as *when* it is seen, is, to a degree, organized by the viewer. Of course, the content, appearance and duration of the stories is still determined by the news reporters, producers and editors. However, the spatial ambitions of news programming – and here I mean those qualities I have associated with space, such as condensation, abstraction, a sense of news from 'anywhere-at-once-now' – seems to have been realized in relation to individual viewers. Ironically, this is possible, or plausible, because the original site or place for the news is already well established – the news may come from 'anywhere', but it comes to one place – the Sky News room/centre itself.

Other successful interactive sites – such as Sky Sports Interactive and the *Big Brother* series – also rely, paradoxically perhaps, on a strong sense of place to anchor their spatial activities and the activity of the viewer. In the coverage of some Premier League football games in the UK, Sky Sports offers viewers with digital television a range of different perspectives for selected games. In relation to these games, viewers are offered an interactive menu, which shows a series of eight screens: one 'master' screen, which refers to the conventional framing and editing mix, with commentary by professional broadcasters; three different screens each showing a limited camera angle from different places within the stadium (one at either goal end and one placed on the halfway line); the master screen in image, but with fan commentary; 'player-cam', where a camera focuses on one individual player (and will change to a new player at different points during the game); 'highlights' (edited highlights of the game in an accumulating but continuous loop); and a statistics page (where the league tables and game statistics about ball possession and goals scored are displayed). The viewer can select any one of these screens at any time they choose. Certain screens (such as player-cam and the statistics screen) incorporate a smaller screen displaying the 'master' version of the game. Other activities are also encouraged, such as email or texting questions and comments. There is also the opportunity to bet on different outcomes (who will score the first goal, how many corners will be awarded) and to play a daily football quiz, although these activities temporarily remove the viewer from an audio or visual relationship to the game in progress. In many ways, football, like the news, might seem to be an ideal programme to be 'unpacked' through interactive technology. As a very partisan spectator sport, it is expected that different viewers will support different teams and might want to occupy different 'points of view' in relation to a particular game. Equally, when attending in person, spectators will be used to having radically different views of the game itself, depending on their position at the ground, and it is possible they might want to replicate this experience at home. The increasing importance of 'star' players, or the intense interest in players' personalities within contemporary football, would also seem to suggest that some viewers would be keen to focus on individual players, especially if what the players do, say or experience 'off the ball' can become important in the ongoing discussion of the team's progress. Thus, the fixed place of the football match (in terms of duration, number of players and physical location) allows for an extended 'unpacking' of different versions and viewing opportunities.

The importance of the actual place of a programme and the potential for interactivity as a process of unpacking is echoed in the reality game show, *Big Brother*. In this programme, there is, once again, a fixed environment (here, a house rather than a football pitch), a fixed (if more extended) duration and a similarly limited number of players (contestants), who are both competing and interacting with one another. In the UK, the interactive potential of the show not only includes my first kind of interactivity (phone votes and texting), but also offers viewers with digital television the opportunity to focus exclusively on edited highlights, or to opt, at certain times, for their own version of activities in the house, through cameras focused on individual contestants, as well as other camera viewpoints, fixed around the house and garden.

Equally, in large sporting events, such as Wimbledon and the Olympics, broadcasters are increasingly allowing viewers to select which particular games and sports they wish to view, although not always what points of view they will be offered once they have selected the specific game or sport they wish to watch. Some aspects of these new opportunities seem to have proved successful with viewers, particularly the element of choice of games or sports and the extended opportunity for discussion on forums around the 'game' – whether this is a specific football match or a particular season of *Big Brother*. Yet the opportunity to view in a way that disrupts the expected or anticipated narrative of the programme-event (watching a player off the ball on player-cam or an empty room in the 'Big Brother' house) still seems idiosyncratic and perverse. For me, watching a player on player-cam was fascinating, as it revealed a different tempo to the game – I could watch the player hesitate, pause for breath and run fruitlessly after the ball. For a football fan, player-cam might be immensely frustrating, as the narrative of the game (which follows the ball) could easily happen elsewhere and is only just visible on the small master screen within the top right-hand corner of the frame. Equally, I found something charming, but ultimately uncomfortable, about choosing to watch a contestant on *Big Brother* sleeping for 25 minutes, before I gave up and went to my own bed.

On the one hand, these chosen perspectives might be seen to offer a new intimacy with players and contestants as we focus on their 'private' activities, both within and beside the main narrative of the programme-event. On the other hand, the position is also a detached, purposeless one, and puts the viewer in an indifferent, mechanical relationship to what is being seen on-screen (it is difficult to think of a good reason for watching someone you don't know sleeping for 25 minutes, other than that 'you can'). Despite the fact that this kind of interactivity seems to offer an opportunity for a closer experience that relates to the construction of place within certain programme-events (in terms of intimacy, personalized experience and atmosphere), at the same time, it aligns the viewer more directly with the indifferent, abstract space of surveillance, which can be an uncomfortable position to occupy. Commonly, the position of surveillance is associated with control and mastery, which, presumably, should be attractive to the viewer; certainly, this is how interactivity is generally promoted to the television audience. Alternatively, I think it has been underestimated how the opportunities and organization of 'surveillance' also place the viewer in an implicit position of responsibility, not just for choosing what they are seeing (with the possibility that they might 'miss something' important happening elsewhere), but also in the sense of being a witness, of being responsible for what they see, however impossible it might be for them actually to change what they see happening on-screen. It is often argued that the viewer of reality programmes enjoys their position since this means they can act as a witness without responsibilities (the individuals arguing, crying or injured have agreed to be seen on-screen and the programme's producers have decided how we should perceive them). However, once the producer's role has been reduced and it is the viewer's choice as to what they see on-screen (whether this is someone sleeping or crying), then either they must adopt a position of complete indifference (as if they were as mechanical as the camera itself) or acknowledge – however inadequately – that they have some responsibility for what is taking place, even if it is something as unproblematic, though suggestive of vulnerability, as watching someone sleep.

Split-screen: push and pull in split-screen narratives

Split-screen is not a new device in television programming and it has been used frequently in a variety of programmes since the 1970s. It can serve both as a source of spectacle and as a way of providing information about characters quickly, and is thus often used in title sequences – most notably in American shows, such as *Charlie's Angels* and *Dallas*. The use of split-screen to promote spectacle and to provide a framing device for action is also found in animation – for example, in *Totally Spies* (which clearly pays visual homage both to *Charlie's Angels* and to Japanese anime), as well as in the more self-consciously artful *Samurai Jack* (which refers directly both to Chinese illustrative techniques and to comic-strip layouts). It is also used in news, sports programming and light-entertainment shows. One instance of this can be found in a regular item from *Noel's House Party* – a hugely popular, live, light-entertainment show produced by the BBC in the 1990s. In the 'NTV' segment, the home viewer would be filmed secretly from a hidden camera (usually on the top of the viewer's own television set). They would then be surprised by Noel Edmonds (the show's host) talking directly 'to them' via their television, as he would then reveal (relatively) intimate details of their lifestyle and personal habits. Once the 'jig was up', Edmonds and the surprised viewer would talk to one another via a split-screen: a full-screen image of the viewer at home would be overlaid with an image of Edmonds in the studio via a small screen in one corner of the frame. In this way, the real space between Edmonds and the viewer could be imaginatively 'collapsed' into one image. As a device to cross space between individuals in different places, it remains common in many other light-entertainment shows. The distance crossed does not need to be that great – split-screen is also used in chat shows, such as *Trisha* and *Ricki Lake*, where participants only a short distance away, behind the stage, are shown, via split-screen, to be in the same image as their spouses, lovers, parents, friends or enemies on stage. It is also employed in this way in *Who Wants to be a Millionaire?* On some occasions, via split-screen, the short distance between the contestant in the hot seat and their anxious partner seated within the studio audience is collapsed to add to the dramatic effect. As we shall see, it is also used on several different occasions in *Saturday Night Takeaway*.

However, in this section I want to look at the current employment of split-screen in live-action drama, specifically in the American series, *24*, and in one particular series of the British crime drama, *Trial and Retribution*. The origin for split-screen in television drama has been more explicitly connected, not to its common use elsewhere on television, but to its use in feature film. In an article for Salon.com on the mainstream re-emergence of split-screen in *24*, Julie Talen (2002) outlines some of the ways in which split-screen has been used in feature film-making. Talen identifies Abel Gance's *Napoleon* (1927), which used three distinct screens, as one of the earliest and most famous film experiments producing a split-screen effect, and then goes on to chart its appearance in later avant-garde practices, such as Andy Warhol's *Chelsea Girls* (1965). She then describes how split-screen briefly became synonymous with a 'modern' look in more mainstream film-making, famously in *The Thomas Crown Affair* (1968). As she notes, however, this innovation quickly became dated and did not emerge as a consistent practice in mainstream film, although Brian de Palma did employ some split-screen in several successful features, including *Carrie* (1976), *Dressed to Kill* (1980) and *Snake Eyes*

(1998). However, more recently, the high-quality and cheaper split-screen techniques made available through digital video editing have encouraged video artists and certain film-makers to reintroduce it into their work. The most high profile of the experiments on which Talen focuses is Mike Figgis' *Timecode* (1999), which splits the screen into four different sections for the entire duration of the film. Talen makes two important observations about the use of split-screen on which I want to elaborate and which I will then relate to my own arguments concerning space and place.

First, she notes that, in many instances, split-screen acts to cross space – and thus, as I have suggested, to collapse space – but *not* to cross time. *24*, in particular, is careful (mostly) not to elide time through its division of space. This is because its narrative premise is dependent on a sense of time passing as simultaneity. For *24*, then, it is important for the dramatic pull of the narrative that the two or more screens that we see within the one frame actually refer to the same moment in time. In effect, the split-screen is a substitute or condensation of the common film practice of parallel editing – where there is a cut from one scene to another (apparently happening at the same time), so as to build suspense or dramatic contrast. In *24*, this dynamic tension can be organized within a single frame, making it both an economic and intense narrative. There are, however, occasional, exceptional moments that disrupt this. At the climax of the first series, as Jack Bauer (the hero) holds his dead wife in his arms, we see (in split-screen) sepia images, replaying moments of his domestic life as we saw them in the very first episode. Perhaps only here, at the moment of complete trauma and resolution, is the temporal simultaneity of the images overturned, so that the main character can be awarded a fuller subjectivity through the use of split-screen as a personalized flashback.

In contrast, *Trial and Retribution* is not tied to temporal simultaneity in the same way, and characters' subjective memories and fears are frequently replayed in split-screen. For example, in the recent series, 'Blue Eiderdown', the murderer confesses her crime; as she does so, we see a brief replay of the murderous events – not from her perspective, but as they were originally presented in the opening sequence. Even before her confession, some aspects of this same sequence (which shows the body of the murdered woman floating down, in slow motion, from a tower block) have already been replayed when the most senior of the detectives – Michael Walker – visited the crime scene. Their use, here, is not entirely adequate, nor can it be properly explained either as an attempt to present the subjective feelings of Walker or as a reconstructive flashback; the detective does not 'own' or author these images in any way, since they are identical to the images we see in the opening sequence and again at the end. Thus, their reappearance ultimately becomes a rather empty stylistic flourish, detached from the integrity of the imagined space within the screen (where the images might relate to one another in a more than superficial sense) or to the dynamic of the narrative or characters (where the images serve to push the narrative along or add depth to the emotional portrayal of the characters).

Talen's second observation relates to the use of split-screen, not simply to cross space, but to offer us different views and, often, closer views of the same individual or event (which, of course, still implies space being crossed, just much less space). Frequently, in *24*, for example, the same event – often someone speaking on the telephone – will be shown simultaneously via split-screen from several different angles, or even from the same angle, but at different focal positions, so that in one image we are apparently closer to the event and individual pictured than we are in the other. Talen suggests we might call this technique 'close and closer'; certainly, the effect can create a strange sense of being 'pushed away from' or 'pulled into' the narrative, as attention flickers from screen to screen. The same practice occurs in *Trial and Retribution*, although it is more sparingly used and, generally, at moments of specific tension or excitement (during the sexual activities of the main characters, for example). The effect in *24* is to intensify the pace of events and it is, perhaps, used more frequently, as feelings of confusion, speed and anxiety remain consistently high throughout each episode of the series. By reproducing one place over and over again within the same image (hovering or hanging around the event, as it were) the use of split-screen here (perhaps surprisingly) emphasizes stasis over movement. Visually reinforcing the temporary stasis of the narrative provokes tension in the audience, since we are always aware that time is passing and that this time is still passing while we are visually (if not actually) 'hanging about'. In *Trial and Retribution* this 'close and closer' effect is used to create temporal stasis in a more spectacular and often blatantly pornographic manner. Here, split-screen seems to slow down or unpack the action, so that characters' bodies and gestures are 'cut up' between different screens, allowing the audience to glimpse (simultaneously) brief, fetishized fragments of the characters' sexual activity – as our eyes flick between different screens, showing wider shots, alternating with close-ups of breasts, tongues and mouths.

Split-screen is quite an aggressive technique. It indicates that the visual style is unambiguously self-conscious and it is similarly demanding, since the viewer may frequently feel they are struggling to follow what is going on. In *24*, the potentially aggressive impact of split-screen is mitigated by the use of sound. In a split-screen sequence involving a phone call, it is just possible to hear some ambient sound from one image at the same time as we hear dialogue and sound effects located in the other image. However, it is generally the case that dialogue does not overlap between the two scenes and that the sound volumes are moderated in relation to who is speaking (if we are with Jack, his voice and sound dominate; if we are with his wife, Terri, her voice and sound will dominate). In sequences featuring more than two screens and for those not involving a telephone call – often seen as the programme 'begins again' after a commercial break – music will be used to bridge between all four scenes. In *24*, then, sound is used to direct attention and avoid confusion. Interestingly, this does not hold true for *Trial and Retribution*. In several sequences, at the beginning of a transition to split-screen, it is common for the sound levels between the two scenes to remain the same and for the dialogue between the scenes to overlap. There may even be a sound wipe (sound from one scene fades down) as there is a visual wipe (as one split-screen enlarges to take up the entire frame). This polyphony of sounds and voices adds to the confusion, but also implicitly suggests that there are competing stories, competing points of view. In 'Blue Eiderdown', this is played out in the antagonistic relationship between the detectives, Roisin Connor and Michael Walker. In *24*, while there are conspiracies at work and, therefore, different amounts of knowledge held by different characters, the final story or world-view is Jack Bauer's. It is *his* position the audience is encouraged to identify with, and, while things happen to other people, they tend to happen because Jack has, or has not, acted. In *Trial and Retribution*, the main characters not only experience different events (though they are loosely related to the same crime), but it is made clear that they see events (in fact, they see 'the world') in different and often conflicting ways. For example, at the beginning of the first episode of 'Blue Eiderdown', there is a split-screen: one screen pictures Walker and Sergeant Satchel (who are at the victim's apartment), while the other shows Connor (who is at the police records department). As we see and hear Satchel explain to Walker that Connor 'has a bee in her bonnet about the victim's mother' (who, it emerges, was also a murder victim), we also hear and see the police file of evidence relating to the mother's murder being clumsily handed to Connor, who says, 'Careful'. Here, therefore, the split-screen explicitly presents two competing world-views (as regards the investigation – and, perhaps, the best way to investigate), as well as an 'expanded' view of the same story.

How does split-screen relate to my discussion of space and place on television? Obviously, there are two primary connections – one to space, the other, perhaps more surprisingly, to place. On the one hand, it is a device that is spatial in that it relates to the 'crossing' of space and, in some instances, it clearly produces images that can be read analytically rather than as straightforwardly representational. It also presents a world that seems to be available 'anywhere-now', although this is tempered by the need to create suspense and, thus, keep some events hidden. The use of split-screen confirms that the images presented by the television screen are two-dimensional and encourages the viewer to 'look over' rather than necessarily 'look into' the screen. On the other hand, the practice of using split-screen to create an effect that suggests we can be 'close and closer' works in a way that is perhaps more akin to the creation of place. In this sense, split-screen seems to gesture towards experience, towards intimacy, and to promote a viewpoint that is suggestive of uncertainty and which is dynamic and kinetic. As I have suggested, it can serve to pull or push the viewer in and out of the image – creating an illusion of depth and thus suggesting that there is a tangible place within the screen.

Generally, however, the use of split-screen is still disorientating and its presence wilfully interrupts the coherence or integrity of the places represented on-screen and, potentially, disturbs the viewer's identification with the characters and events portrayed. Split-screen makes clear that the image is a constructed image, 'flattened' and malleable – thus making it harder for viewers to unambiguously invest in the characters and the places they inhabit. Unsurprisingly, therefore, *24* and *Trial and Retribution* embed the use of split-screen in a visual style that is otherwise excessively intimate and atmospheric. Both series are dominated by the use of close-up, not in the static, melodramatic manner of a daytime soap opera, but in a style developed from American series such as *NYPD Blue* and *Homicide: Life on the Streets*. In these series, as other writers have noted, the camera is almost continuously in motion, mimicking the hand-held 'shaky' style associated with observational documentaries – hesitant, intimate, almost intrusive close-up, and all but tripping over the action that takes place. In *24* and *Trial and Retribution*, the already exaggerated documentary style is recalled, but certain practices (the hesitant but intrusive close-up, the shaky camera movement) are, perhaps, even more extreme. By (over)compensating in terms of atmosphere and proximity, it seems to me that both series clearly encourage viewers to experience that sense of immediacy and intimacy more usually associated with the creation of place on television. Indeed, on closer examination, it is evident that the split-screen is not just compensated for, but actively incorporated into the visual style of the programme.

Both series employ a wide range of different framing devices (windows, doors, architecture), which are used to divide the space 'naturally', thus creating a split-screen effect within the *mise-en-scène*. For example, in the early hospital scenes in *Trial and Retribution*, the characters are placed within a series of divided metal and glass doors, which inevitably 'cut up' the space presented on-screen. Later in the programme, the sex club at which the victim worked (rather conveniently) uses a multi-camera surveillance system, which therefore allows for split-screen to occur 'inevitably' at certain points within the representational place being constructed. In *24*, the screens and blinds used to organize and make private the office space in CTU's home base also divide the *mise-en-scène* within individual screens and, thus, 'naturally' provide for the creation of frames within the frame of the image. Another image – often used to promote the series itself – shows Bauer driving while looking into his car's rear-view mirror. This allows for a 'natural' split-screen: while we can see the back of his head in shadow, the mirror reveals – simultaneously – his eyes and worried expression as they are apparently lit up by passing traffic. This 'naturalized' split-screen effect is further enhanced as he often makes use of a monitor which can rise up from the dashboard of the car, thus incorporating yet another screen within a screen (here we have the television screen, the windscreen and the monitor screen). These integral split-screen compositions allow the 'artificial' split-screen device used to seem less absurd or alienating than it might do in other less busy visual narratives.

While self-consciously artful, the use of split-screen in drama is carefully managed so as not to disrupt entirely the expected dramatic narrative. In *24* it seems clear that the use of split-screen fits with the notion of spying, surveillance and 'integrated' technology. Within the necessary restrictions of the time of the programme, it also acts as an economic dramatic device by collapsing the suspense of parallel editing into one frame. In *Trial and Retribution*, the theme of surveillance is less acute, although the series does focus on criminal investigation. Instead, as I have suggested, its use may be linked to the concept of competing narratives and to a deliberate stylistic flourish that engages directly with the content of pornography and exploitation.

Conclusion

In this chapter I have defined particular ways of understanding space and place as they might relate to television. My argument has been that the organization or operation of space and place are characterized by different television images. Generally, I have suggested that space can be identified through processes and image techniques that tend towards abstraction, which are conceptual rather than concrete and offer the viewer the illusory potential of 'anywhere-at-once-now'. I have provided examples of primarily written and 'drawn' (or two-dimensional) images that seemingly realize the spatial ambitions of different television programmes. In contrast to this, I have identified the operations of place as more closely related to representational images that work hard to create the illusion of tangible, atmospheric environments that can be read in a seemingly intuitive manner by the television audience. I have suggested that aspects of the *mise-en-scène*, camera work and writing can encourage viewers to embrace or invest in these places in ways that are directed by their senses and emotions. Perhaps the most important aspect of my discussion, however, is the fact that space and place do not have to be distinct on television. Indeed, I have argued that many programmes (both factual and fictional) often employ aspects of both space and place in their attempts to engage viewers. In my discussion of some developments within 'interactive television', and of the current use of split-screen in dramatic fiction, I have tried to suggest how the dynamic tension between space and place can be played out in a variety of different programmes. In my final case study, of both the chapter and the book, I want to explore these distinctions again, relating them to arguments first made by Richard Dyer concerning light entertainment and entertainment more generally. In a series of papers on 'Light entertainment' and 'Entertainment and utopia', Dyer addressed issues to do with the formal aspects of television and their possible meaning and emotional impact. It should become clear that my development of his arguments not only relates specifically to the concerns of this chapter, but, more broadly, to the ambition of the book as a whole.

Case study: *Ant and Dec's Saturday Night Takeaway*

People want to feel special . . . During the week if you watch a bad drama or a disappointing documentary, there's always the next day. But Saturday, that's your special night. Michael Jackson [ex-chief executive of Channel 4] always used to say that Saturday night was Christmas Day every week.
—Rosemary Newell, Channel 4 head of programming and strategy, quoted in the *Observer*

It's snowing in the studio!
—Declan Donnelly, *Saturday Night Takeaway*, 7 November 2004

Ant and Dec's Saturday Night Takeaway is produced by its stars, Anthony McPartlin and Declan Donnelly, and made through Granada for ITV1. It is a mid-evening, light-entertainment show, transmitted periodically, usually for series running for six weeks. There have been three series thus far and the show has been heralded as the 'saviour' of Saturday night television, winning several awards and proving to be a ratings success. In its most recent transmission period it formed part of a 'spectacular' Saturday night line-up on ITV1, sandwiched between a 'reality' talent show – *The X-Factor* (featuring Sharon Osbourne, Simon Cowell and Louis Walsh as judges and talent spotters) – and the popular game show, *Who Wants to be a Millionaire?*

Ant and Dec have had a long career on television and in entertainment: beginning as actors, as the characters PJ and Duncan in the BBC's children's series, *Byker Grove*, they went on to have brief success as pop stars (initially as PJ and Duncan and then as Ant and Dec) before moving on to present the extremely popular Saturday morning children's magazine show, *SM:TV Live*. Their initial attempt at prime-time light entertainment, *Slap Bang!*, did not take off, but their activities as co-presenters for two popular 'reality' shows, *Pop Idol* and *I'm a Celebrity: Get Me Out of Here!*, were deemed to be a key part of both programmes' success. Their next foray into light entertainment, *Ant and Dec's Saturday Night Takeaway* – an affectionate pastiche of a wide range of past light-entertainment programmes, including *Noel's House Party*, *The Generation Game*, *The Muppet Show* and *Beadle's About* – established Ant and Dec as, currently, Britain's most popular 'entertainment presenters'. Still relatively young, the key characteristics of Ant and Dec's personae are their strong regional identity (both come from Newcastle and retain their distinctive Geordie accents and a notional 'working-class' association) and their genuine friendship. While both are attractive, neither has matinée idol looks. Ant, taller and darker, adopts a slightly more aggressive, occasionally 'grumpy' persona, while Dec, shorter and 'cuter', performs a role that is slightly more conciliatory and eager to please. Both performers, however, play up to their image as 'lads' or 'cheeky' boys. Perfectly well aware of their indebtedness to past programmes and performers, they still present themselves as innovators and, while knowing and fond of the double entendre, they are never cynical or intentionally salacious.

The programme is transmitted live, but several elements – 'Ant and Dec Undercover' (where the duo are disguised and trap unwary celebrities into potentially embarrassing situations) and 'Little Ant and Dec' (where two young boys from Newcastle pretend to be 'little' versions of the presenters and interview celebrities in their place) – are obviously pre-recorded. While the content and running order of the programme will vary slightly from week to week, it will nearly always involve: two versions of the integrated game show, 'Grab the Ads' (one for the studio audience and one for the audience at home); one or more 'live' performances from current chart acts; an 'Undercover'; a 'Little Ant and Dec' interview (sometimes framed by an appearance from the 'little' boys in the studio itself, where they may pass comment on this week's celebrity); a stunt involving a member of the audience; and 'What's Next?', a segment of the show where Ant and Dec are unhooked from both autocue and their earpieces and take part in an unrehearsed activity, ranging from 'bottom slapping' with male Bavarian dancers to taking part in a mini-version of the game show *Countdown* or, quite frequently, an impromptu musical performance.

What is surprising about this programme is how little, in its essentials, it differs from past light-entertainment shows. It offers similar pleasures to those discussed by Richard Dyer over 30 years ago – the promise of escapism, 'harmless' entertainment, slightly bawdy but not malevolent humour, a little bit of glitter and excitement, community and participation. The programme is not 'about' anything – its function is to be entertaining. Numerous people and places can be represented, addressed and incorporated, but their inclusion is based on their potential to make the audience at home and in the studio *feel* – to make them laugh, cry, cringe or be surprised. As Dyer (1992: 12, 13) suggests, then, 'entertainment is not so much a category of things as an attitude towards things'. More specifically, the form and practice of the kind of television entertainment he describes has not fundamentally altered in the last 30 years – a form which, in itself, drew on previously established popular entertainment traditions:

> Leisure and entertainment are separate from and in opposition to work and domestic cares . . . It derives its characteristic form – the string of short items, with or without link-man, the popularity and vulgar reference, the implicit sexuality and open sentimentality – from the development of entertainment in the pubs and clubs patronized by the urban working class.

Certain aspects of this heritage may have been diluted (Ant and Dec did not have experience in 'working-class' pubs and clubs and almost all the other performers now featured in their show originate within popular music or from television and film), but the associations remain the same. Ant and Dec have 'worked hard' to gain their position; they have good but not 'showy' skills as actors, comedians and singers and are, therefore, in the tradition of working-class performers as 'all-rounders'. More importantly, however, they are attractive personalities, characterized by their popular touch, energetic vulgarity and good humour.

Within the context of this chapter, however, the most significant aspect of Dyer's analysis is his reference to the concept of utopia. Utopia, which has its origins in a play on Greek words meaning, alternatively, 'no place' or 'good place', provides, for Dyer (1992: 18), a way of defining the ambitions, or the stuff of entertainment itself:

> Two of the taken-for-granted descriptions of entertainment, as 'escape' and as 'wish-fulfilment', point to its central thrust, namely, utopianism. Entertainment offers the image of 'something better' to escape into, or something we want deeply that our day-to-day lives don't provide. Alternatives, hopes, wishes – these are the stuff of utopia, the sense that things could be better, that something other than what is can be imagined and maybe realized.

Utopia, therefore, in Dyer's use of the term, is a possible, imagined place, where things are possible and may be 'better'. At the same time, as he later notes, the notion of utopia in entertainment is not, finally, about the realization of an actual place, but about the way in which utopia might 'feel'. In that sense, it may be characterized equally as a direction, a process that is performed – a utopian sensibility that is achieved through reaching for utopia rather than in its concrete realization. For me, therefore, utopia offers an intriguing combination of both space and place: it is, at once, a 'no-place' (never reached, it exists as a never-ending journey, a continually reworked and imagined fantasy) and a 'good place' (a representation of a temporary environment where good things can and do happen). As Dec says at one point, 'It just doesn't get better than that . . . but it does'.

Dyer lists a series of key characteristics, which he suggests relate this notion of utopia to certain recurring traits present in entertainment: abundance, energy, intensity, transparency and community. Significantly, however, he is keen to stress that these characteristics are reproduced via an 'affective code' that is articulated by both representational and non-representational images and sounds (Dyer 1992: 18):

> This code uses both representational and, importantly, non-representational signs. There is a tendency to concentrate on the former, and clearly it would be wrong to overlook them – stars are nicer than we are, characters more straightforward than people we know, situations more soluble than those we encounter. All this we recognize through representational signs. But we also recognize qualities in non-representational signs – colour, texture, movement, rhythm, melody, camerawork – although we are much less used to talking about them.

I have quoted Dyer at length here, since what he is arguing for relates not just to my discussion in this chapter, but also, perhaps, to my ambitions for the book as a whole. First, he is clearly determined to address the way in which television entertainment engages its audience in a directly emotional manner, and he is not simply concerned to uncover or describe these traits as opportunities for identification or representation. Instead, he addresses the importance of affect, sensibility and the transient, vivid experiences this particular genre offers the audience. Second, he is insistent about the importance of the non-representational quality of the images and sounds that produce this sensibility. He highlights the importance of 'colour, texture, movement, melody, camerawork' in a way that is not just relevant to my analysis of *Ant and Dec's Saturday Night Takeaway*, but which also relates more generally to the approach to television taken throughout this book.

If we examine Dyer's list of characteristics, then, conveniently, they can be (loosely) associated with my discussion of space and place. Abundance, energy and intensity might be related to the possibilities suggested by space: 'anything from anywhere', flows, travel (both literal and as escapism), distances crossed quickly or immediately and images that are abstract, spectacular and intense. Transparency and community are suggestive of the tangible, atmospheric, known or knowable environments I have associated with place. In addition, in his discussion concerning the dynamics of the utopian sensibility engineered by entertainment, Dyer provides an argument which coincides neatly with my previous observations concerning the relationship between space and place – that is, that they need not necessarily usurp each other, but can interact with one another to create an audio-visual narrative which blatantly combines both the unreal and impossible with a version of the familiar and known world of the everyday (Dyer 1992: 25):

> In Variety the essential contradiction is between comedy and musical turns; in musicals, it is between the narrative and the numbers. Both these contradictions can be rendered as one between the heavily representational and verisimilitudinous (pointing to the way the world is, drawing on the audience's concrete experience of the world) and the heavily non-representational and 'unreal' (pointing to how things could be better).

How, then, is this utopian sensibility glimpsed or orchestrated in *Ant and Dec's Saturday Night Takeaway*? We can begin, obviously, with the title sequence. In fact, the programme does not begin with the titles, but always with a preliminary sketch, ostensibly taking place 'behind the scenes', in Ant and Dec's dressing room. It provides the opportunity for the appearance of one or more guests (and is, therefore, a preview of the show's offerings) and is structured as a rather lame gag, generally involving the gentle humiliation of either one of the guests or Ant and Dec themselves. It ends with either Ant or Dec demanding that the titles should be rolled. Right at the start, therefore, the essential contradiction that Dyer highlights is brought to the fore: there is the supposedly ordinary backstage, where Ant and Dec mingle with their willing celebrity chums; at the same time, however, there is a show, a title sequence to set in motion that is outside this 'ordinary' backstage, which designates the 'other world' – the fantastic world – of television entertainment. The actual title sequence itself plays yet again on the dynamic between 'real' environments and the imagined potential of 'light entertainment' to 'explode' these places and, ultimately, to connect them to the fantastic possibilities of television.

The title sequence starts as we see Ant in 'his' apartment opening the door to Dec. Both boys are smartly dressed in black shirts and trousers (although they wear finely tailored lounge suits to present the show). Pointing at his watch, Dec indicates to Ant that they are late; they nod in agreement and then proceed to charge through the wall and onwards, through a series of rooms and walls (passing through a domestic living room, a girl's bedroom and, finally, the backstage of a television studio). While all the rooms are recognizable, they are not in any sense realistic – clearly, what is important is the imaginary possibility of having Ant and Dec in your living room, not the reality that somebody else already has. The sequence ends with the boys jumping away from the camera into a 'white space' (as they leap into the studio or the television screen itself?), which generates the text of the programme title, spinning towards the camera. It is this final move which seems to me to provide a specific example of the interaction between space and place. On the one hand, the boys' final 'leap into oblivion' is about space, about potential, about going 'no-place', and here, Ant and Dec (very briefly) flirt with oblivion and 'unreality'. At the same time, as the three-dimensional graphic that makes up the actual programme title comes apparently tumbling towards the audience, this 'no-place' is awarded an illusory tangibility. The relationship between space and place is thus briefly reversed: the abstraction of the titles, of the text, is made tangible, just as the 'real' people – Ant and Dec – have seemingly been lost in the two-dimensional no-place of the screen. But of course, if we are regular viewers, we know that this oblivion is purely temporary, for immediately there the boys are, at the top of the steps, in the midst of the studio audience, waiting to take their place on the stage below.

While it may seem a little ridiculous to have focused on such a transitory image from the title sequence, it is important because it instigates a move that is repeated at several points within the show. One of the key aspects of the programme is the management of the contradictory impulses within the show itself. Part of the show's operation is to produce the illusion of a specific place, to suggest that the programme offers a 'great night out', a place that is more accessible and more genuine than the alternatives organized by other programmes on other channels, running at the same time. The organization and *mise-en-scène* of the studio, therefore, is key to the creation of a plausible, inhabitable and hospitable place. As a live show, one of the most important aspects of both the *mise-en-scène* and the sound environment is the presence of the studio audience, who are directed to stand up and dance, cheer, clap and sing along on cue. Ant and Dec stand among the audience at the beginning of the show, not just to reassure us that they are there in person, but also to emphasize the presence of an excited and excitable audience. I do not think the studio audience acts primarily to represent the viewers at home, but rather to perform as genuine participants or guests in their own right (although, of course, their real access to the show itself is limited). The set is relatively sparse, with two small circular stages set up in different ways over the course of the show (for musical performances, brief chats with celebrities and Ant and Dec's final 'What's Next Behind-the-Curtain?' challenge). Some of the mechanics of the production – the cameras, autocue, earpieces and final written cue cards – are made evident. The 'Takeaway' studio is, then, a realized place, a work environment for some and a place of play

Fig 4.2 *Ant and Dec's Saturday Night Takeaway.* Ken McKay/Rex Features

for others; it is both where the programme is made and where the programme apparently 'is', as if it had some existence outside of transmission.

In contrast to this, the narrative pull of the show is to create a sense of excitement and abundant possibilities – that you might win a prize, be tricked, meet your favourite celebrity, be humiliated and then redeemed. Therefore, the show needs to represent the apparent potential of television to take 'us anywhere' or to make anything possible. One common way in which the programme demonstrates this is through a stunt involving a member of the audience. In the last show in 2004, Donna was pulled from the studio audience. Donna is apparently 'known' to Ant and Dec and they reveal her obsession with Kylie Minogue (the diminutive Australian pop singer), detailing facts about her long history as a fan and, finally, dangling a pair of sparkly pink hot pants, which Donna allegedly wears to Kylie's concerts. (In her most recent success, Kylie's performances in high-cut hot pants became tabloid fodder.) Donna is surprised but clearly hopeful as to what might happen next. She is, of course, not disappointed; asked to direct her attention to a huge playback screen in the studio, she is greeted by Kylie, who apparently 'can't be with her', but who promises two VIP tickets to her upcoming concert in London. Donna is pleased, but, as Dec suggests, of course, it '*can* get better than that', and behind another screen in the studio, lying on a couch and fanned by male 'slaves', Kylie is revealed to be in the studio, after all. Donna is taken over to meet her in person. Kylie then promises to perform for Donna later in the show. There is one further twist to the tale – it appears that Donna has a best friend, Omah, who is also a huge fan; what

Fig 4.3 Ant and Dec with guests. Ken McKay/Rex Features

a shame he will be missing this performance! For it emerges that Omah is not in the studio, but at another television recording taking place that evening – for *The X-Factor* – where the studio audience, having seen that programme transmitted earlier in the evening, are now waiting for the results of a telephone poll. Through the 'magic' of television, the two friends are quickly put in touch and Omah is offered the opportunity to come and see Kylie's performance via a ride on the 'Takeaway' delivery motorbike, through a 'busy Saturday night' in London.

There are several aspects that articulate the tension between space and place here. First, why does the programme bother to show Kylie on-screen when they have her in the studio? I would suggest that aside from providing a useful back-up if Kylie had fallen ill, it also reminds the audience and viewers at home that Kylie is 'special' – that she is from the 'somewhere else' of celebrity. Her appearance, literally larger than life, on a screen reinforces her status as an image. In some senses, therefore, in order for the stunt to seem exciting, we need to be reassured that Kylie has a spatial, two-dimensional quality, a status above the ordinary and that she is something other than tangible (we could say that there is the idea of 'Kylie' and Kylie herself). Second, it repeats the apparent generosity of the gesture, the bountiful good nature or the essential characteristics of both star and hosts: what cheeky chaps Ant and Dec are to tease Donna and the audience; what a good sport Kylie is to take part in such a ruse. The spatial characteristics of the item are most explicit, unsurprisingly, in the link between the two studios. Initially, Dec appears to *The X-Factor* audience on the large display screen in that studio. He greets *The X-Factor* presenter, Kate Thornton, and they then indulge in some light banter concerning her show. A surprised Omah is quickly identified and then linked to Donna. In order to manage this link, the image incorporates two screens (one showing Omah and the other, Donna) angled slightly towards one another, floating over a 'Takeaway background', one screen subtitled as the 'X-Factor studio', the other as the 'Takeaway studio'. This background is a black space, through which loops and streaks of luminous colour chase over the screen. It is nowhere, an unreal space, but is clearly in tune with the colour and design of the 'hard set' of the actual Takeaway studio. The image itself collapses the distance between the two real places, establishing a fantastic space – a 'we can do that' space.

This might seem to be an unremarkable aspect of the show, but its presence is key to the programme's management of space and place. There is no real place here – the image is entirely fabricated. What it offers is an illusory space – identifiably a space that is *Ant and Dec's Saturday Night Takeaway* – but one which serves as a visual context for the 'contradictory impulses' that Dyer identifies and which I have elaborated. This non-place appears at different bridging moments in the show: as a background to the titles; between items; in the 'bumpers' as we come back to the show from the commercial breaks; and also as the background to images of the prizes to be won and the names of people who ring in, in the hope of winning those prizes. It is non-representational space, but its appearance – a depthless blackness with a continuous loop of colourful light trails – is explicitly dynamic. As a light display, or as muted electronic fireworks, it does not represent anything in particular, but is an effect generated to underscore affect – suggestive of excitement, hope and possibilities. It is, however, not really a 'special' effect in either sense of the word: it is neither particularly spectacular nor doing anything unexpected. One of the ironies of light entertainment is that, despite its need to present itself as special, it is fundamentally routine – the same things happen week after week; the fantasy is precisely *not* fantastic, but anticipated.

The programme reproduces forms and practices that can be associated with carnivals and public festivals. The disguises worn by Ant and Dec in their 'Undercover' item, as well as the joke disguises often forced on celebrities by Little Ant and Dec, suggest a carnival spirit of masks and pretence. Even the presence of Little Ant and Dec works to call up the surreal and playful world of the carnival. They are mini-doppelgangers – 'dwarf' versions of the hosts dressed up in suits. They relate in contemporary terms to the 'mini-me' character played by a real dwarf in Mike Myers' 'Austin Powers' films. While using actual dwarfs might have proved to be too controversial, with their risqué questions and their cute but nonetheless disruptive behaviour, the boys do perform a similar function to that of the mini-me character. There is straightforward dressing up, too – the audience are often encouraged to dress up in hats and funny glasses, and Ant and Dec frequently have to dress up in their 'What's Next?' challenge. The world is not turned upside down by these practices, but they do allow certain boundaries to be crossed. Little Ant and Dec, for instance, are children, and this gives them licence to say and do things adults could not. Aside from the scripted 'rudeness', the disruptive quality of the child emerges when they encourage their star interviewees to wear the joke disguises they have brought; this both subtly undermines the glamour of the celebrity and also means that the boys are often allowed to touch the celebrities in ways that an adult interviewer would rarely attempt. In 'Undercover', Ant and Dec often play the 'unfortunate' (bedridden, slow or desperate characters) in a way that forces celebrities to reveal the extent of their tolerance for the public and their fans. By dressing up for 'What's Next?', Ant and Dec submit – as the audience in the studio already has – to the demands of this carnival. By detaching themselves from the guide or control of the autocue and producer's voice, they are, in one sense, out of control, but swiftly tied into a predetermined routine (whether this is chasing trained dogs round an obstacle course or singing with Kermit the Frog).

It is interesting to compare the final 'What's next?' item with the other musical performances in the show. As Dyer suggests in his arguments, musical performances in entertainment often serve to 'obliterate' or 'contrast' with the representational place of the studio or programme-context and thus, implicitly, with everyday reality. In *Ant and Dec's Saturday Night Takeaway*, the musical performances by current chart acts, while apparently 'live' in the studio, are made distinct from the rest of the programme. As Dyer describes it, this move is often characterized by 'a marked shift from the real to the non-real and from the largely representational to the largely non-representational (sometimes to the point of almost complete abstraction)' (Dyer 1992: 26). So, for example, singers will often perform on one of the circular stages, but this will be backlit with strobing, abstract light patterns, thus obliterating the substance and tangibility of the hard set. In addition, the image itself may be slightly slowed down and the rhythm of the editing roughly synchronized with the beat of the music; the point of view will be unstable and jump between wide shots and close-ups. In my terms, therefore, the representational place of the studio has been abandoned for the more abstract, energetic space of performance. It might be expected that this would happen in relation to Ant and Dec's performances, but this is rarely the case. Instead, the ambition here appears to be to emphasize the concept of participation (by the boys, the audience and, perhaps, the viewers at home), and thus there is a focus on the amateurish aspect of their performances in this context.

In the final episode of the most recent series, Ant and Dec were 'surprised' by Kylie, who appeared from behind the curtain to give them a Christmas present. Inside were microphones and silly Christmas hats. The boys went on to sing a Christmas 'standard', well known in the British context – 'I wish it could be Christmas everyday' (originally by Wizzard). Good-naturedly, the boys stumble through a couple of verses, backed by dancers and singers in Christmas costumes. They then run in to the audience, persuading audience members to sing along with the aid of handwritten cue cards. Finally, they are joined on stage by their different 'star' guests (Kylie, once more in a white fluffy hat; Geri Halliwell, ex-Spice Girl, decked out in tinsel; and Lee, from the boy band Blue, in another silly hat). Little Ant and Dec also appear, wearing angel wings and halos. Numerous balloons have cascaded down on to the audience, but now it begins to 'snow', thus emphasizing the tactile, sensual depth of the place on-screen. What is significant here is that the performance is not separate from the studio or the audience; it is a transparent, communal celebration which includes everyone and bends the universe to its will, to the extent that, apparently, it is even 'snowing in the studio'. It is, of course, meant to fulfil the promise that it could be like 'Christmas every day', just as Michael Jackson apparently suggested every Saturday night on television should be (although, in reality, Christmas is seven weeks away). As Ant and Dec run into the audience, as snow, balloons and glitter fall, the Takeaway studio becomes – temporarily – a utopia, a 'good place' to be.

At the same time, of course, it is also rubbish. The boys barely sing in tune, their hats do not stay on, the costumes look cheap and we know it is not real snow. In terms of production values, it rates much lower than many regional theatres' annual pantomimes. Why is this? One reason is presumably pragmatic; that budgets do not allow for better costumes and real snow. Second, the point of the item is that the boys are not rehearsed – they should stumble, corpse and perform, apparently, as *themselves* and not as skilled professional performers. Their natural behaviour is part of the transparency within the utopian sensibility – proving that they are what they seem to be. Another possible reason relates to an aspect of the utopian project I have not explored as yet, which is the fear of utopia. Utopias have been described in many different ways, but what they imply is the fulfilment of human desires and an escape from the dreariness of the everyday. If we think about what this actually means, there is some cause for anxiety. If we get everything we wish for, what more could we possibly desire? In other words, what is there to look forward to? Does utopia also suggest that if everyone is made equal and gets what they need, they will be the same? If we leave and escape our everyday, do we not also leave behind those we love (and, perhaps, why we love them, since we love them precisely because they fulfil some aspect of what we 'need')? Are we not, possibly, in some hidden way, defined by our unfulfilled desires – desires which would no longer exist if we really had everything we wanted? Does entry into utopia, therefore, imply that we become not like ourselves, that we must leave behind the imperfections that make us who we are, as individuals? Utopia, therefore, is a source of potential anxiety. Another way of putting it might be to suggest that most people come to feel that Christmas Eve is better than Christmas Day itself: the excitement and pleasure is in *nearly* being there, in *nearly* getting what you want, rather than the potential disappointments or overwhelming stimulation of the day itself. Light entertainment works on television despite the fact that it can be amateurish, almost *because* this means that it does not *quite* give us what we want; instead, it provides glimpses and plays with fantasy, but does so in a way that is controlled and limited quite carefully. Dyer (1973: 36) suggests that this is the result of an 'imaginative thinness', which is often stretched most tautly in the celebration of Christmas, since Christmas is both a real public festival and, at the same time, an empty spectacle of meaningless consumption:

> This puts television entertainment in an impossible position. It has nothing to sell viewers and only the increasingly empty symbols of Christmas with which to entertain them. At the same time Christmas is a festival and it is its business to register this, to promote the good times.

While I can sympathize with this point, and have myself pointed to the 'thinness' or inadequacy of the utopian sensibility engineered by *Ant and Dec's Saturday Night Takeaway*, I still enjoy the programme – an enjoyment that Dyer, to his credit, never denies (at least in relation to some shows). I watch *Ant and Dec's Saturday Night Takeaway* with my daughters in the same way I watched *The Generation Game* (the hit light-entertainment show in the UK during the 1970s) with my family when I was a child. I am uplifted temporarily by the twinkle in the boys' eyes, by the communal singalong; entranced, just a little bit, by the snow falling and the glitter in the air. My eldest daughter is excited by the prospect of Christmas, recognizes the song from The Tweenies' rendition and wants to stay up to hear the result of

The X-Factor poll. None of this is important, but television is acting as a specific kind of place here. For me, it links to the past – to my memories of my family life – and to the future of my family life now (there is Christmas to prepare for). Artificially, perhaps, it transmits energy, laughter and excitement. It is a place which acts as a transitory embrace, a fantasy of community, where the sensual abundance, the tactile qualities articulated on-screen are echoed briefly at home – another daughter rolls off the sofa in giggles, the youngest slaps the television screen in excitement.

This brings me, perhaps, to my final problem, and one I have tried to avoid up until now. In providing a detailed textual analysis of a programme such as *Ant and Dec's Saturday Night Takeaway*, am I simply attempting to justify my own viewing pleasure and thus, perhaps, the pleasures of television? Well, yes, of course I am. Equally, I am not trying to suggest that these pleasures work against the grain of the producers' intentions; indeed, I am sure they would be delighted that I see so much and enjoy so much of a show they work so hard to make entertaining. Nor am I claiming that everyone should enjoy it, or could enjoy it, if only they could see it in the way I do, or employ the models I have offered for interpretation it is, after all, a question of taste. I have been coy on the question of taste, but my tastes and viewing pleasures will no doubt be evident to any reader who has read the book thus far. I am fascinated by the forms of television, but I am not in a position to make great claims as to what interpreting these forms might do. Perhaps some readers will go on to make better television shows; others may simply see television in a different light; I hope, too, that some readers will use some of the information here to feed analyses that do challenge poisonous representations and the false impressions generated by different programmes. My enjoyment of television is not an unguarded or unqualified pleasure and, once more, I find myself in agreement with this observation from Richard Dyer (1992: 7), which may serve to close both this case study and the book:

> Entertainment offers certain pleasures, not others, proposes that we find such-and-such delightful, teaches us enjoyment – including the enjoyment of unruly delight. It works with the desires that circulate in a given society at a given time, neither wholly constructing those desires nor merely reflecting desires produced elsewhere; it plays a major role in the social construction of happiness. We have to understand it itself, neither take it as given nor assume that behind it lies something more important.

Bibliography

ALLEN, Robert C. 1992. *Channels Of Discourse, Reassembled.* London and New York: Routledge.

ALLEN, Robert C. and HILL, Annette (eds). 2003. *The Television Studies Reader.* London and New York: Routledge.

ALTMAN, Rick. 1987. Television sound. In Newcomb, Horace (ed.), *Television: The Critical View.* Oxford: Oxford University Press, 566–85.

ALTMAN, Rick (ed.). 1992. *Sound Theory, Sound Practice.* London and New York: Routledge.

ANG, Ien. 1991. *Desperately Seeking The Audience.* London and New York: Routledge.

BANKSTON, Douglas. May 2001. Searching for clues. In *American Cinematographer,* 58–65.

BAZALGETTE, Cary and BUCKINGHAM, David (eds). 1995. *In Front Of The Children: Screen Entertainment and Young Audiences.* London: BFI.

BIGNELL, Jonathan. 2003. *An Introduction To Television Studies.* London and New York: Routledge.

BJARKMAN, Kim. August 2004. To have and to hold. In *TV And New Media,* vol. 5, no. 3, 217–46.

BODDY, William. 2004. *New Media And Popular Imagination.* Oxford: Oxford University Press.

BONNER, Frances. 2002. *Ordinary Television.* London: Sage.

BOYLE, Raymond and HAYNES, Richard. 2004. *Football In The New Media Age.* London and New York: Routledge.

BRITON, Piers D. and BARKER, Simon J. 2003. *Reading Between Designs: Visual Imagery And The Generation Of Meaning In* The Avengers, The Prisoner *and* Dr. Who. Austin: University of Texas.

BROWNRIGG, Mark and MEECH, Peter. 2002. From fanfare to funfair: the changing sound world of UK television idents. In *Popular Music*, vol. 21, no. 3, 345–57.

BUCKINGHAM, David. 2002. Child-centred television?: *Teletubbies* and the educational imperative. In Buckingham, David (ed.), *Small Screens: Television For Children*. London and New York: Leicester University Press, 38–61.

BUTLER, Jeremy G. 2002. *Television: Critical Methods And Applications* (2nd edn). Mahwah, NJ: Lawrence Erlbaum Associates.

CALDWELL, John T. 1995. *Televisuality: Style, Crisis And Authority In American Television*. New Brunswick, NJ: Rutgers University Press.

CALHOUN, John. 1 April 1999. Time for *Teletubbies*. In *Lighting Dimensions*, at http://lightingdimensions.com/mag/lighting_time_teletubbies/index.html (accessed January 2005).

CHION, Michel. 1994. *Audio-Vision: Sound On Screen*. New York: Columbia University Press.

CHION, Michel. 1999. *The Voice In The Cinema*. Gorbman, Claudia (trans.). New York: Columbia University Press.

CONNOR, Steven. 2000. *Dumbstruck: A Cultural History Of Ventriloquism*. Oxford: Oxford University Press.

COOK, Nicholas. 1998. *Analysing Musical Multimedia*. Oxford: Oxford University Press.

CORNER, John. 1999. *Critical Ideas In Television Studies*. Oxford: Oxford University Press.

CORNER, John. 2003. Television, documentary and the category of the aesthetic. In *Screen*, vol. 44, no. 1, 92–101.

CREEBER, Glen (ed.). 2004. *Fifty Key Television Programmes*. London: Arnold.

DEANS, Jason. 26 January 2004. ITV news goes upmarket. In *The Guardian*, at http://media.guardian.co.uk/broadcast/story/ (accessed January 2005).

DOANE, Mary Ann. 2000. *The Emergence Of Cinematic Time: Modernity, Contingency And The Archive*. Cambridge, MA and London: Harvard University Press.

DYER, Richard. 1973. *Light Entertainment*. London: BFI Monograph.

DYER, Richard. 1992. *Only Entertainment*. London: Routledge.

ELLIS, John. 1992. *Visible Fictions: Cinema, Television, Video* (2nd edn). London: Routledge.

ELLIS, John. 2000. *Seeing Things: Television In The Age Of Uncertainty*. London and New York: I.B. Tauris.

FEENY, Catherine. 19 September 2003. Stargate Digital: the best kept secret in TV. In Creative Planet Communities newsletter, at http://www.uemedia.net/CPC/vfxpro/article_4684.shtml (accessed January 2005).

FRITH, Simon, GOODWIN, Andrew and GROSSBERG, Lawrence. 1993. *Sound & Vision: The Music Video Reader*. London and New York: Routledge.

FRITH, Simon. 2002. Look! Hear! The uneasy relationship of music and television. In Negus, Keith and Street, John (eds), Music and television (special issue), *Popular Music*, vol. 21, no. 3, 291–305.

GERAGHTY, Christine. 2003. Aesthetics and quality in popular television drama. In *International Journal Of Cultural Studies*, vol. 6, no. 1, 25–45.

GLEICK, James. 2000. *Faster: The Acceleration Of Just About Everything*. London: Abacus.

GOLDMAN, Michael. 1 May 2002. Speaking of film. In *Millimeter*, at http://millimeter.com/ (accessed January 2005).

GREENHALGH, Peter. April 2001. Beautiful lighting and vibrant colours underpin gritty urban drama. In *In Camera*, 22.

GRIFFITHS, John. June 2002. Hold that fiber. In *Emmy*, vol. 24, no. 3, 94–101.

GRIPSRUD, Jostein. 1999. *Television And Common Knowledge*. London and New York: Routledge.

HANSEN, Christian, NEEDHAM, Catherine and NICHOLS, Bill. 1991. Pornography, ethnography and the discourses of power. In Nichols, Bill (ed.), *Representing Reality*. Bloomington: Indiana University Press, 201–28.

HARRIES, Dan (ed.). 2002. *The New Media Book*. London: BFI.

JACOBS, Jason. 2000. *The Intimate Screen: Early British Television Drama*. Oxford: Oxford University Press.

JACOBS, Jason. 2001. Issues of judgement and value in television studies. In *International Journal Of Cultural Studies*, vol. 4, no. 4, 427–47.

KAHN, Douglas. 1999. *Noise, Water, Meat: A History Of Sound In The Arts*. Cambridge, MA: MIT Press.

KAVKA, Misha and WEST, Amy. 2004. Temporalities of the real: conceptualizing time on reality TV. In Homes, Su and Jermyn, Deborah (eds), *Understanding Reality Television*. London and New York: Routledge, 136–54.

KERN, Stephen. 1983. *The Culture Of Time And Space: 1880–1918*. Cambridge, MA and London: Harvard University Press.

LANG, Kurt and LANG, Gladys. 1993. The unique perspective of television and its effect: a pilot study. In *American Sociological Review*, vol. 18, no. 1, 3–12. Reprinted in Corner, John and Hawthorn, Jeremy (eds), *Communication Studies: An Introductory Reader* (4th edn). London: Edward Arnold.

LASTRA, James. 2000. *Sound Technology And The American Cinema*. New York: Columbia University Press.

LEEUWEN, Theo van. 1999. *Speech, Music, Sound.* London: Macmillan Press Ltd.

LATEMPA, Susan. October 2002. The women of *CSI.* In *Written By: The Magazine Of The Writers Guild Of America,* at http://www.wga.org/WrittenBy/1002/csi.html (accessed January 2005).

LONDON-ROWELL, Tracie. August 2003. Interview. In *Word,* no. 6, 26.

LURY, Karen. 2002. A time and a place for everything: children's channels. In Buckingham, David (ed.), *Small Screens: Television For Children.* London and New York: Leicester University Press, 15–38.

LURY, Karen. 2002. Chewing gum for the ears: children's television and popular music. In Negus, Keith and Street, John (eds), Music and television (special issue), *Popular Music,* vol. 21, no. 3, 291–305.

MAASO, Arnt. 2002. This goes to eleven: 'high' and 'low' sound in television. In Ericson, Staffan and Ytreberg, Espen (eds), *Fjernsyn mellom hoy og lav kultur.* Kristiansand: Hogskoleforlaget.

MACGREGOR, Brent. 1997. *Live, Direct and Biased?: Making Television News In The Satellite Age.* London: Arnold.

MAGID, Ron. November 2002. Family plots. In *American Cinematographer,* 70–79.

MANOVICH, Lev. 2001. *The Language Of New Media.* Cambridge, MA and London: MIT Press.

MARRIOTT, Stephanie. 1996. Time and time again: 'live' television commentary and the construction of replay talk. In *Media, Culture And Society,* vol. 18, no. 1, 69–86.

MARRIOTT, Stephanie. 1997. The emergence of live television talk. In *Text: Interdisciplinary Journal For The Study Of Discourse,* vol. 17, no. 2, 181–99.

MARRIOTT, Stephanie. 2000. Election night. In *Media, Culture And Society,* vol. 22, no. 2, 131–48.

MARRIOTT, Stephanie. 2001. In pursuit of the ineffable: how television found the eclipse but lost the plot. In *Media, Culture And Society,* vol. 23, no. 6, 725–42.

MCCARTHY, Anna. 2001. *Ambient Television.* Durham, NC and London: Duke University Press.

MELLENCAMP, Patricia. 1990. TV time and catastrophe, or beyond the pleasure principle of television. In Mellencamp, Patricia (ed.), *Logics Of Television: Essays In Cultural Criticism.* Bloomington: Indiana University Press, 240–67.

MILLS, Brett. 2004. Comedy verité: contemporary sit-com form. In *Screen,* vol. 45, no. 1, 63–78.

MILNE, Mike. Interview, at www.bbc.co.uk/dinosaurs/tv_series/graphics.shtml (accessed January 2005).

MOORE, Frazier. 16 June 2004. Will new-show flood ever end? at http://www.myrtlebeachonline.com/ (accessed January 2005).

MORSE, Margaret. 1983. Sport on television: replay and display. In Kaplan, E. Ann (ed.), *Regarding Television: Critical Approaches*. Los Angeles: American Film Institute, 44–67.

MORSE, Margaret. 1998. *Virtualities: Television, Media, Art And Cyberculture*. Bloomington: Indiana University Press.

NEGUS, Keith and STREET, John (eds). 2002. Music and television (special issue), *Popular Music*, vol. 21, no. 3.

OPPENHEIMER, Jean. June 1999. Young blood. In *American Cinematographer*, 90–101.

OPPENHEIMER, Jean. October 2000. The halls of power. In *American Cinematographer*, 74–83.

OPPENHEIMER, Jean. November 2002. Espionage 101. In *American Cinematographer*, 80–9.

PROBST, Chris. June 1995. Darkness descends on *The X-Files*. In *American Cinematographer*, 28–32.

ROWE, David. 2004. *Sport, Culture and the Media* (2nd edn). Berkshire: Open University Press.

SCANNELL, Paddy. 1988. *Radio Times*: the temporal arrangements of broadcasting in the modern world. In Drummond, Philip and Paterson, Richard (eds), *Television And Its Audience*. London: British Film Institute.

SCANNELL, Paddy. 1996. *Radio, Television And Modern Life*. Oxford: Blackwell.

SCANNELL, Paddy. August 2002. *Big Brother* as a television event. In *Television And New Media*, vol. 3, no. 3, 271–82.

SCANNELL, Paddy. 2004. What reality has misfortune? In *Media, Culture and Society*, vol. 26, no. 4, 573–84.

SIDER, Larry, FREEMAN, Diane and SIDER, Jerry (eds). 2003. *Soundscape: The School Of Sound Lectures 1998–2001*. London and New York: Wallflower Press.

SOBCHACK, Vivian. 2002. Happy New Year and Auld Langs Syne: on televisual montage and historical consciousness. In Friedman, James (ed.), *Reality Squared: Televisual Discourse On The Real*. New Brunswick, NJ: Rutgers University Press, 92–116.

SORLIN, Pierre. 1998. Television and the close-up: interference or correspondence? In Elsaesser, Thomas and Hoffman, Kay (eds), *Cinema Futures: Cain, Abel Or Cable?* Amsterdam: Amsterdam University Press, 119–26.

SPIGEL, Lynn. 1992. *Make Room For TV: Television And The Family Ideal In Post-War America*. Chicago: University of Chicago Press.

SPIGEL, Lynn. 1998. Seducing the innocent: childhood and television in post-war America. In Jenkins, Henry (ed.), *The Children's Culture Reader*. New York and London: New York University Press, 110–36.

STOUT, Andy. February 2002. *Broadcast* (pullout section), 16.

TAGG, Philip. 2000. *Kojak: 50 Seconds Of Television Music* (available via Mass Media Music Scholars' Press Inc.).

TALEN, Julie. 14 May 2002. *24*: split-screen's big comeback. At http://Salon.com/.

THOMPSON, Kristin. 2003. *Storytelling In Film And Television*. Cambridge, MA: Harvard University Press.

WEISS, Elisabeth and BELTON, John (eds). 1985. *Film Sound: Theory And Practice*. New York: Columbia University Press.

WELLS, Paul. 1998. *Understanding Animation*. London and New York: Routledge.

WELLS, Paul. 2002. *Animation And America*. Edinburgh: Edinburgh University Press.

WHANNEL, Garry. 1992. *Fields In Vision: Television Sport And Cultural Transformation*. London and New York: Routledge.

WIENER, David. March 2002. Hot on the trail. In *American Cinematographer*, 62–71.

WOLLASTON, Sam. 2 August 2004. A flipping nightmare. In *The Guardian*, G2 supplement, 18.

WOOD, Anne. August 1998. In *PBS Online*, at http://pbskids.org/teletubbies/parentsteachers/progphilo.html (accessed January 2005).

WOOD, Anne and DAVENPORT, Andrew. Frequently asked questions. In *BBC Online*, at http://www.bbc.co.uk/cbeebies/teletubbies/grownups/faq.shtml (accessed January 2005).

WURTZLER, Steve. 1992. She sang live, but the microphone was turned off: the 'live', the recorded and the *subject* of representation. In Altman, Rick (ed.), *Sound Theory, Sound Practice*. London and New York: Routledge, 87–104.

ZETTL, Herbert. 1990. *Sight, Sound, Motion: Applied Media Aesthetics* (2nd edn). Belmont, CA: Wadsworth Publishing Company.

Index